De Gratia

Christianity and Judaism in Antiquity

CHARLES KANNENGIESSER, SERIES EDITOR

Volume 4

DE GRATIA

*Faustus of Riez's Treatise on Grace
and Its Place in the History of
Theology*

By

Thomas A. Smith

UNIVERSITY OF NOTRE DAME PRESS
NOTRE DAME, INDIANA

Copyright © 1990 by

University of Notre Dame Press

Notre Dame, Indiana 46556

Library of Congress Cataloging-in-Publication Data

Smith, Thomas A., 1956-
  De gratia : Faustus of Riez's Treatise on grace and its place in
the history of theology / by Thomas A. Smith.
      p.   cm. -- (Christianity and Judaism in antiquity ; v. 4)
  Includes bibliographical references and indexes.
  ISBN 0-268-00866-3 : $26.95
  1. Faustus, Bishop of Riez, 5th cent. De gratia. 2. Grace
(Theology)--History of doctrines--Early church, ca. 30-600. 3. Semi
-Pelagianism.   I. Title.   II. Series.
BR65.F35D4 1990   89-40747
  234--dc20   CIP

To my father, Kenneth Roche Smith.

"Quid autem habes quod non accepisti?"

CONTENTS

ACKNOWLEDGMENTS

The present study began its life as my doctoral dissertation at the University of Notre Dame, "The *De Gratia* of Faustus of Riez: A Study in the Reception of Augustinianism in Fifth-Century Gaul." I again thank those who helped that project along: Robert Wilken, who first encouraged my pursuit of the topic; Frederick Crosson and Daniel Sheerin, who provided kind and expert criticism; and Thomas O'Meara, O.P., whose friendship and erudition have been great helps. I was greatly privileged to work under Charles Kannengiesser, S.J., whose scholarly gifts were matched by his generosity and patience in directing my research.

My colleagues in the Department of Religious Studies at Loyola University, New Orleans, have provided an atmosphere of encouragement and good cheer for this endeavor. Jeannette Morgenroth Sheerin of Notre Dame Press has shown exemplary care and intelligence in editing the manuscript.

My children, Kelly, Natalie, and Alexander, have endured my work with understanding. Finally, and most of all, I owe a great debt to my wife Colleen, my most encouraging coworker, gentlest critic, and closest friend, whose many labors of love have included, but are not limited to, the typing of this study. The merits of this work owe entirely to these people; its defects are my own.

Thomas A. Smith
New Orleans
March 1990

INTRODUCTION

The treatise *De gratia* was written in 474 by Faustus, bishop of Riez in southern Gaul, against the predestinarian doctrine of Lucidus, a Gallic priest. It was composed at the request of an episcopal synod at Arles. The present study reexamines that treatise. The need for such a reexamination becomes clear as one reads the many and varied, and often polemical, estimates of Faustus's doctrinal orthodoxy. Such evaluations, in all their variety, can be found from the fifth century into the modern period among both theologians and historians of Christian doctrine. Invariably doctrine of grace as expressed in, or extrapolated from, the *De gratia* has been primarily responsible for his reputation. The task before us here will be to disengage ourselves from later polemical concerns and to understand the text of this treatise on its own terms. It is hoped that in the course of such study—historical, theological, and literary in its scope—we will be better equipped to evaluate the many interpretations of Faustus. Perhaps, too, we will be able to shed some helpful new light on the ways in which Augustinian teachings on grace were received in Gaul between St. Augustine's death in 430 and the so-called second council of Orange in 529. In these introductory remarks we will survey in brief scope the reception accorded the *De gratia* in the history of Christian thought.

The first evaluation of Faustus's theological legacy comes to us in the compendium *De viris illustribus* of Gennadius of Marseilles, written at the end of the fifth century. Gennadius expresses a very positive judgment on Faustus as a man devoted to the study of the Scriptures, among whose works is an "opus egregium" whose title is given as *De gratia Dei, qua salvamur, et libero humanae mentis arbitrio, in quo salvamur.* Faustus teaches in this work, says Gennadius, that "God's grace always invites, precedes, and assists our will, and whatever reward the freedom of the will might gain for holy labor is not one's own desert, but God's gift."[1] Gennadius hails Faustus as a champion of orthodoxy against various errors.

Some, at least, did not entirely share Gennadius's approving attitude toward Faustus. A document known as the *Decretum Gelasianum*, purporting to have come from a Roman council of seventy-two bishops under Gelasius I, whose papacy extended from 492 to 496, places Faustus's work on a list of "apocryphal" books, along with the works of John Cassian, Arnobius the Younger, and scores of others.[2] This decree is not attested elsewhere in its own time; many scholars now regard it as a compilation of documents from various periods, assembled either in southern Gaul or in northern Italy in the early years of the sixth century.[3] Whatever its authorship or provenance, the Gelasian decree gives evidence that Faustus's work on grace was regarded by some as a work of the second rank: not

---

[1]*Gennadius liber de viris inlustribus,* ed. E.C. Richardson, LXXXVI, p. 91. Throughout this study, shortened references are given to works cited in full in the bibliography.

[2]Mansi 8: 165-70.

[3]*Das Decretum gelasianum de libris recipiendis et non recipiendis,* ed. E. von Dobschütz, 8.4; G. Bardy, "Gélase (Décret de)," *Dictionnaire de la Bible,* Supplément 3: 279-90.

heretical, to be sure, but also not established as an authoritative doctrinal treatise.

Faustus's teaching on divine grace first became more widely suspect as the result of some rather strange machinations early in the sixth century.[4] The impetus was provided by a group known as the "Scythian monks," led by John Maxentius and Peter the Deacon. These were in correspondence with a group of African bishops exiled on Sardinia. The spokesman for the exiled African bishops, Fulgentius of Ruspe, was to be put forward as a critic of Faustus of Riez.

The Scythian monks began to attract attention around 519 in Constantinople. Of an extreme cast of mind, they had adopted a theopaschite formula in their zeal against Nestorianism. In a show of anti-Pelagian fervor, perhaps to establish a reputation for orthodoxy in the West, they sought the condemnation of the teaching of Faustus of Riez, now long dead. John Maxentius appealed formally to the papal legates in Constantinople,[5] but without success. The Scythians next took their case to a North African bishop, Possessor. He was apparently not of a mind to dispute over grace and free will and so referred the case to the bishop of Rome, Hormisdas. The pope replied that St. Paul, the Fathers, the councils, and Augustine taught what the Church teaches; Faustus was not of the same authority. He added some harsh words against the contentiousness of the Scythian monks.[6] Maxentius in turn responded with some warmth to Hormisdas, sending along

---

[4] A general account of this episode is given by Tibiletti, "Fausto di Riez," 56-87. The same author gives more detailed attention to the role played by Fulgentius of Ruspe in "Polemiche in Africa," 499-517.

[5] *Ep. ad legatos sedis apostolicae* (PG 86, I: 75-86).

[6] *Ep. Papae Hormisdae* (CCL 85A: 115-21).

for good measure a selection of short phrases culled from Faustus's *De gratia*, juxtaposed against long sections from Augustine's anti-Pelagian works.[7] Maxentius's summary of Faustus's doctrinal failings portrays him as a crypto-Pelagian, exalting human nature and only adjoining (*adiungit*) grace to human labor.[8] Worse, in a sense, than Pelagius, Faustus seems to refute Pelagius' teaching, but does so cleverly or deceptively (*callide*) while in fact denying divine grace.[9] Maxentius rails against those who go so far as to defend Faustus's books as catholic, chief among whom is the African bishop Possessor.[10]

Thoroughly dissatisfied in their dealings with Possessor and Hormisdas, the Scythians appealed to the exiled North African bishops on Sardinia. Peter the Deacon wrote a letter to these bishops containing a long recital of the orthodoxy of himself and his cohorts. At the end of this letter he anathematizes "Pelagius and Caelestius, as well as Julian of Eclanum and those who believe things similar to them, especially the books of Faustus, a bishop of Gaul, who came from the monastery of Lérins."[11] This letter contains the same estimate of Faustus's doctrine as that found in Maxentius's response to Hormisdas;[12] Faustus, in writing against predestination, has de-

---

[7]*Resp. adv. ep. Hormisdae* II. 15 (CCL 85A: 142-53).

[8]Ibid. (143-44).

[9]Ibid.

[10]Ibid. (143).

[11]*Ep. scytharum monachorum ad episcopos* VIII. 28 (CCL 85A: 172). The same epistle is found under the title *Epistula XVI* of Peter the Deacon in CCL 91A: 551ff.

[12]At this point I take issue with Tibiletti's reconstruction, which suggests that Maxentius is dependent upon Peter the Deacon ("Fausto di Riez," 573). If true, this would make the Scythians' appeal to the exiled bishops prior to the correspondence with Hormisdas. Such a chronology is difficult to maintain.

parted from the tradition of Paul and the Fathers. He has emptied the grace of Christ, merely subjoining it (*subiungit*) to human labor.[13]

The exiled bishops responded with a long synodal letter in 523, setting forth a rigorously predestinarian view of divine grace and of fallen human nature.[14] Further, they informed the Scythians that one of their number, Fulgentius of Ruspe, would write "seven books against the two books of Faustus of Gaul."[15] The promised treatise, if it was written, is not extant. One that did come from the pen of Fulgentius, *De veritate praedestinationis et gratiae Dei*,[16] was a pessimistic portrayal, grounded in texts of Scripture and in excerpts from Augustine, of the capabilities of sinful human nature. This work nowhere alludes to Faustus of Riez's writings. Fulgentius's treatise would come to enjoy the favor of Caesarius, the influential metropolitan of Arles who was to summon the so-called second council of Orange in 529. The proceedings of this assemblage never make mention of Faustus; they simply renew the Augustinian condemnation of Pelagianism.

Despite his never having been formally condemned—again, there is no evidence of knowledge of the Gelasian decree—Faustus continued to gain a reputation as a deceptive Pelagian. There is reason to doubt whether those who persisted in pronouncing Faustus heterodox had ever read the *De gratia*. At the beginning of the seventh century, Isidore of Seville is content simply

---

[13]*Ep. scyth. monach. ad episcopes* VIII. 28 (CCL 85A: 172). Cf. John Maxentius, *Resp. adv. ep. Hormisdae* II. 15 (CCL 85A: 144).

[14]*Ep. XVII Episcoporum* (CCL 91A: 563-615).

[15]*Ep. XV episcoporum*, 19 (CCL 91A: 456).

[16]CCL 91A: 458-548.

to repeat the old charge of the Scythians: Faustus was a Pelagian and was deceptively clever in hiding his sympathies.[17] So, too, the anonymous author of the *Vita Fulgentii* accuses Faustus of deception in appearing orthodox while being a Pelagian.[18]

Traces of the Pelagian taint accompanied Faustus's reputation into the Carolingian period. The extreme predestinarian Gottschalk of Orbais (c. 804-c. 869), opponent of Rabanus Maurus on the issue of grace and free will, seems to have known of Faustus's reputation by way of the *Vita Fulgentii*. He praises Fulgentius for writing against Faustus.[19] Gottschalk's like-minded contemporary, Servatus Lupus (c. 805-62), abbot of Ferrières, mentions Faustus in a letter to an abbot Odo, referring to "infaustum Faustum,"[20] and distinguishing this Faustus, the one mentioned by Gelasius, from the Manichean opponent of Augustine of the same name.[21] In another letter, to Charles the Bald, he specifically warns of the dangers of reading Faustus, since his works had been stripped of authority by Gelasius and seventy learned bishops.[22] Lupus's references are the first conclusive indication that anyone employed the Gelasian decree in judging Faustus's orthodoxy.

---

[17]Isidore of Seville, *De viris illustribus* 27, 35 (PL 83: 1097). The reference comes in connection with his discussion of Fulgentius.

[18]PL 65: 145.

[19]*Gotteschalchi Orbac. monachi confessio prolixior* (PL 121: 357).

[20]*Servati Lupi epistulae, Ep.* 111. 7.

[21]Ibid., *Ep.* 112. 6: "Faustum dirigi postulavi, non quem refellit Augustinus, sed quem notat in decretis Gelasius."

[22]Ibid., *Ep.* 131. 12: ". . . memorati Fausti scripta his verbis exauctoravit: opuscula Fausti Regensis Galli apocrifa."

Faustus finds mention also in the ninth-century *Chronicon* of Ado, bishop of Vienne. Ado's account is badly flawed; he refers to Maxentius as a learned priest of Antioch and asserts that Alcimus Avitus of Vienne had confuted Faustus.[23] He too reproduces Maxentius's criticism of Faustus but gives no evidence of any direct knowledge of the *De gratia*.

It would seem that interest in Faustus waned during the remainder of the Middle Ages. Sixteenth-century controversies over grace mark the re-emergence of such interest; in the work of Desiderius Erasmus it took on for the first time the dimensions of authentic scholarship. In Basel in 1528 the *editio princeps* of the *De gratia* appeared, complete with a preface written by Erasmus.[24] Erasmus seems to have served as a kind of patron to the work, and it attracted his lively interest. He bemoans that fact that the *De gratia* did not come into his hands before he wrote against Luther on the free will.[25] He portrays Faustus's work as essentially an anti-Pelagian, Augustinian tract that cautiously affirms free will while warning against attributing anything to our own merits.[26] At the same time, citing the Gelasian decree, he acknowledges that there are those who regard Faustus as having had Pelagian sympathies ("Faustum aliquando cum Pelagio sentisse").[27] Erasmus makes several favorable comments on the Latin style of the *De gratia*, noting similarities of vocabulary with Eucherius of Lyons and Sulpicius Severus.

---

[23]*Chronicon, aetas sexta* (PL 123: 107A-B).

[24]*Fausti episcopi de gratia Dei et humanae mentis libero arbitrio, cum D. Erasmi Roterodami praefatione* (Basel, 1528).

[25]Ibid., Preface, 3: "Utinam mississet antequam de libero arbitrio scriberemus adversus Lutherum."

[26]Ibid., 3A.

[27]Ibid.

Faustus's style is "most apt for teaching, clear, distinct, concise, and not unpleasant."[28] Two features of Erasmus's treatment are noteworthy. First, he gives the first evidence later than the sixth century of direct reading of the *De gratia*. Second, apart from a brief mention of the decree of Gelasius, he is silent about the suspicions cast on Faustus's doctrine in earlier centuries. Erasmus, taking the treatise more or less at face value, regards Faustus as a circumspect defender of Augustine against Pelagius.

The reformational context within which Erasmus wrote was, of course, a great time of battles about the doctrine of divine grace. Then followed various intra-Catholic controversies over grace. Among the first and most important of these took place between the Jesuit Molina and the Dominican Bañez. It found its climax in the *Congregationes de auxiliis*, summoned at Rome from 1590-1607 to consider charges of Pelagianism leveled at the theology of the Jesuits as found in Molina's *Concordia*. The conferences ended with no definitive pronouncement, but in the course of their discussions theologians coined an entirely new term in the history of doctrine: *semipelagian*. The term was applied to Gallic writers like Cassian whose influence could be detected in the *Concordia*.[29] The taint of suspicion applied to these writers seems to have affected the manner in which Faustus of Riez was treated.

Two historians of this period, both involved in the discussions surrounding the *Congregationes*, provide us with portrayals of Faustus. Robert Bellarmine, S.J., in his patristic work *De scriptoribus ecclesiasticis*

---

[28]Ibid.: ". . . ad docendum aptissimum, perspicuum, distinctum, brevem nec insuavem tamen."

[29]The standard account of the origin of the term "semipelagian" in the *De auxiliis* controversy is Jacquin, "A quelle date apparaît le term 'Semipélagien'?" 506-8.

(1613), says that Faustus believed "illuminatio, virtus, et salus non a Christo, sed a natura."[30] This phrase, and the viewpoint it represents, are taken up entirely from Maxentius, though they were repeated by Ado of Vienne.[31] The judgment is made with no reference to the text of the *De gratia*. Bellarmine's contemporary and fellow cardinal, Caesar Baronius, was even more hostile to Faustus; he marvels that Gennadius could have approved a work in which heresy lies, as a thorn among many flowers.[32] Again, we find no indication of firsthand familiarity with Faustus's work.

One voice had been raised earlier, in 1571, in defense of Faustus: that of a theologian of the Academy of Louvain, Ioannes Driedo. He had read the *De gratia* and thought that the accusations of Pelagian sympathies leveled at Faustus were inaccurate. For Driedo, the *De gratia* represented an essentially Augustinian position which Faustus took up against predestinarian excesses.[33]

Though he was a leading Jesuit theologian and independent of the position of the Dominicans, Francisco Suarez's work on divine grace, published posthumously in 1620, contains a hostile judgment on Faustus. He employs the label semipelagian to describe the writers of Provence and says that Faustus thought like a semipelagian even as he employed

---

[30]*De script. eccl.* (Rome, 1613), 129.

[31]Maxentius, *Resp. adv. ep. Hormisdae* II. 15 (CCL 85A: 143-44); *Chronicon, aetas sexta* (PL 123: 107B).

[32]Baronius, *Annales Ecclesiastici* (Rome, 1603) VI, 444.

[33]Ioannis Driedonis, *De captivitate et redemptione humani generis liber unus* (Louvain, 1571); *De concordia liberi arbitrii et praedestinationis divinae liber unus* (Louvain, 1566). The Dominican H. Serry, writing several years later a history of the *Congregationes de auxiliis*, wrote of Driedo and his Louvain colleague Ruardo Tapper as being infected with semipelagianism in making such a judgment on Faustus; cf. *Opera omnia* II (Lyons, 1770), col. 763.

expressions that had a catholic meaning.[34] Faustus's works had always been suspect in the Church and had been condemned by orthodox Fathers.[35] Again, old charges from Peter the Deacon and John Maxentius resurface: Faustus conceals his erroneous meaning with ambiguous and equivocal language; he attributes salvation to human free will and merely subjoins grace to it.[36]

Jacques Sirmond, S.J. (1559-1651), a younger contemporary of Bellarmine, Baronius, and Suarez and one of the most learned men of his day,[37] produced a brief history of the doctrine of predestination. In this history he gives extended treatment to Faustus of Riez. After arguing from various sources for the existence of a predestinarian heresy in fifth-century Gaul, he gives a fairly detailed account of events surrounding the writing of the *De gratia*.[38] Sirmond is quite favorably disposed toward Faustus. Like Driedo, he draws attention to the antiheretical intent of the *De gratia*; he remarks upon the suspect character and false statements of Maxentius and the

---

[34]Suarez, *Operis de divina gratia tripartiti* (Lyons, 1620), 168B, 169D.

[35]Ibid.

[36]Ibid., 169D: "licet ambiguis et aequivocis locutionibus studeat Faustus occultare sensum suum erroneum [. . .] manifeste se prodit: quod initium fidei, vel salutis tribuat libero arbitrio, et illi veram gratiam subiungat."

[37]Sirmond edited scores of texts, especially those pertaining to the early history of France, e.g., Geoffrey of Vendome, Sidonius Apollinaris, Paschasius Radbertus, Avitus of Vienne, Hincmar of Reims, et al., as well as noteworthy editions of Eusebius of Caesarea, Theodoret of Cyrus, and Fulgentius of Ruspe. Several of his editions were later adopted by the great collections of Labbe, Mansi, and Migne. He conclusively disproved the popular identification of Dionysius the Areopagite with the author of the Pseudo-Dionysian corpus—a major step in patristic scholarship.

[38]Sirmond, *Historia praedestinatiana* VII (PL 53: 682f).

Scythian monks.[39] While acknowledging that some elements of Faustus's treatise should be treated with caution, he stresses that the only two popes who pronounced a verdict on Faustus's books—Hormisdas and Gelasius—did not condemn them: "it was enough to say that they were not of the highest authority, that is, apocryphal, not heretical."[40] Sirmond's treatment, while it may contain a Molinist bias, is nonetheless noteworthy for its historical erudition and its familiarity with the relevant texts.

Despite the efforts of Sirmond, a continuation of negative evaluations of Faustus perdures in works of the latter half of the seventeenth century. The Augustinian theologian and historian, H. de Noris, shows himself in his *Historia Pelagiana* to be an opponent of Faustus's thought. To his credit, unlike many other critics of Faustus, Noris seems to have read the text of the *De gratia*. For him, Faustus is essentially anti-Augustinian, attributing the beginning of faith (*initium fidei*) to the human free will and conceiving of grace as a purely external phenomenon. The alleged predestinarian heresy against which Faustus did battle was to Noris a fiction created by the "Massilians," that is, the writers of southern Gaul, in order to veil their attacks upon Augustine.[41] A somewhat more extreme attitude toward Faustus is expressed by Gilbert Mauguin, who published his works on predestination and grace in 1650. For Mauguin, the existence of a predestinarian heresy, and of the synod of Arles that commissioned the *De*

---

[39]Ibid. VIII (685D-686A). He also mentions the favorable judgment of the two Louvain theologians Driedo and Tapper (cf. 686D).

[40]Ibid. (686D): ". . . satis fuit non primae illos auctoritatis, hoc est apocryphos dicere, non haereticos."

[41]Noris, *Historia Pelagiana* (Petavii, 1708) II, 15, p. 141.

gratia, and of documents attesting this synod were all malicious fictions meant to give an appearance of orthodoxy to Faustus's *De gratia*.[42]

With the entry of Protestants into the discussion, Faustus's treatise finds another enemy in the Calvinist theologian and historian Jacques Basange (1653-1723), whose *Animadversiones criticae de S. Fausto Rhegiensi* became the prolegomena to Faustus's works in the Migne edition.[43] Basange purports to follow a middle road. Sirmond, he says, has erred in praising Faustus's patrons Hilary of Arles and Gennadius, who are semipelagians; further, Sirmond tries to avoid the objections of Fulgentius and Avitus "with frivolous argument."[44] Mauguin, on the other hand, errs in attributing many forgeries to Faustus.[45] All the same, Basange marvels that Faustus should be numbered among catholics and saints, as has been the custom of some more recent writers; he employs words like *versipellem*, "one who changes skin," and *velpeculam*, "a little fox," to describe Faustus's duplicity. He refers to previous judgments like that of Gelasius and mentions Baronius's metaphor of a thorn concealed among flowers.[46]

The *Mémoires* of the great French Roman Catholic church historian Louis Sébastian Le Nain de Tillemont, published at the very end of the seventeenth century, may have depended upon Noris for their judgment of Faustus. Faustus's *De gratia* opposes Augustine; he refutes the most obvious features of Pelagianism only in order to make his own doctrine more

---

[42]Mauguin, *Veterum auctorum qui IX saeculo de praedestinatione et gratia scripserunt* II, 546ff.

[43]PL 58: 777-84.

[44]Ibid. (780A-B).

[45]Ibid.

[46]Ibid.

palatable through subtlety.[47] Tillemont cites Baronius and repeats some of the judgments of Suarez.[48]

The Jesuit Johann Stilting emerged as the great defender of Faustus's doctrine of grace in the eighteenth century. In a rather long treatment of Faustus, he shows his familiarity with the *De gratia*, using excerpts from it to refute some of the old charges derived from Maxentius and the *Vita Fulgentii*. He points out that Maxentius's charge that Faustus teaches the sufficiency of nature is unfounded, and that Ado of Vienne had no knowledge of the works of Faustus.[49] According to Stilting, Faustus never wrote against Augustine. Quite the contrary, Faustus was a defender of Augustine. Against Suarez, Stilting denies that grace is for Faustus a purely external phenomenon.[50] Thus Stilting's apology for Faustus moves in two directions: it refutes the obvious and superficial accusations of earlier writers and attempts to interpret Faustus's expressions in an Augustinian sense.[51]

The nineteenth century, surely a golden age for the writing of the history of Christian doctrine, was a fruitful and rather less bellicose time for the study of Faustus's *De gratia*. The treatise continued to be of some interest for issues in dogmatic theology. A typical example is the use made of the *De gratia* by Johannes von Kuhn, a leading figure of the Catholic

---

[47]Tillemont, *Mémoires pour servir à l'histoire ecclésiastique des six premiers siècles* (Brussels, Fricx, 1694-1709) XVI, 7.

[48]Ibid.

[49]"De S. Fausto Regiensi," in *Acta Sanctorum septembris* (Antwerp, 1760) VII, 674-76.

[50]Ibid., 683-84. His stance vis-à-vis Suarez is clear from this paragraph heading: "Reliquae Suarezii obiectiones diluuntur," p. 683.

[51]Tibiletti, "Fausto di Riez," 585.

Tübingen school in the middle of the century. In his *Katholische Dogmatik*, he uses a brief citation from the *De gratia* as an illustration of the semipelagian distinction between divine foreknowledge and predestination.[52]

By far the most important scholarly advance in the study of Faustus of Riez came from August Engelbrecht at the end of the nineteenth century. His critical studies of Faustus's writings culminated in the publication in 1891 of the *Fausti opera* in the Vienna corpus.[53] The volume included the *De gratia*, the small treatise *De spiritu sancto*, several letters, and the so-called pseudo-Eusebian sermons, attributed en masse by Engelbrecht and others to Faustus. In his prologomena to Faustus's works, Engelbrecht adopts a noncommital posture regarding Faustus's orthodoxy and his relation to Augustine. Acknowledging both the critics and the defenders of Faustus in the history of doctrine, the editor notes that some of the earliest criticism was unwarranted. At the same time, he regards Stilting as being too benevolent toward Faustus, as passing too easily over the difficulties of reconciling Faustus's thought with that of Augustine.[54]

The most detailed study of Faustus to emerge from the nineteenth century was the 1895 monograph of Anton Koch of Tübingen, *Der heilige Faustus, Bishof von Riez*.[55] Like Engelbrecht, Koch treats Faustus in a moderate fashion. He has some concern about rehabilitating Faustus's reputation, and bemoans the fact that while John Cassian is regarded as the

---

[52]*Katholische Dogmatik* (Tübingen, 1859) I, 862.

[53]*Fausti Reiensis praeter sermones pseudo-Eusebianos opera*, CSEL 21 (Vienna, 1891). Engelbrecht's related studies of Faustus are listed in the bibliography of the present study.

[54]Ibid., xvi-xviii.

[55]Stuttgart, 1895.

great theoretician of asceticism, Faustus is commonly known as a teacher of semipelagianism.[56] While Koch acknowledges Faustus's doctrine to be "formally and materially semipelagian," he claims that it is of broader significance in the development of the Church's doctrine of grace. If, he says, one does not assert Augustine's authority onesidedly with blind passion and a stockpile of school theories, but rather takes into account the historical setting of Augustine's anti-Pelagian writings, mindful of the continuity of development in Christian doctrine, then perhaps a scientific answer to the apparent difficulty is possible.[57] One of the distinguishing features of Koch's study, therefore, is his pointing out that Augustine's authority on the doctrine of grace was neither as complete nor as obvious in the late fifth century, especially regarding predestination, as many of Faustus's earlier critics assumed; a substantial portion of the monograph is devoted to a discussion of the question of Augustine's authority.[58] In the course of this discussion he indicates that the essential point of difference between the semipelagian, i.e., Faustian, position and Augustinian teaching is precisely the latter's doctrine of predestination, which the Church itself did not entirely receive as its own.[59] The important and commendable role played by Faustus and other semipelagians was to serve as a kind of counterpoint or antithesis to the more radical tendencies within Augustine's doctrine of grace.[60] Koch's treatment, with its Hegelian emphasis on the dialectical

---

[56]Ibid., i.

[57]Ibid., i-ii.

[58]Ibid., 129-91.

[59]Ibid., 186, 191. Cf. also the discussion of the second council of Orange (195-205).

[60]Ibid., 205.

development of doctrine, marks an important step away from the entrenched
polemical attitudes that previously hindered an accurate understanding of
Faustus.

The bulk of Koch's important work was devoted to matters of
historical context and theological reception. A substantial portion, however,
explicated the doctrine of the *De gratia*, illustrating it with examples from the
text. This is the first such study in the long history of the *De gratia*. A
primary concern in the course of this doctrinal study is to locate Faustus in
relation to Augustine and the so-called semipelagians, among whom John
Cassian is the most prominent. Koch concludes that Faustus's *De gratia* is a
semipelagian work and in fact "die beste Apologie des Semipelagianismus."[61]

No other studies in the nineteenth century were specifically devoted
to the *De gratia*. Friedrich Wörter's history of semipelagianism makes
mention of Faustus, but he does not draw conclusions markedly different
from those of Koch.[62] The broader histories of dogma written in the late
nineteenth and early twentieth centuries do little to shed additional light on
Faustus. Harnack, Loofs, Seeberg, and Tixeront treat Faustus as the main
exponent of fully developed semipelagianism.[63] All point to his external
notion of the work of divine grace as against Augustine's internal conception.

---

[61]Ibid., 122.

[62]*Zur Dogmengeschichte des Semipelagianismus* (Münster, 1899.) One
may say that Wörter seems less willing than Koch to admit affinities between
Faustus and Augustine. Cf. the discussion of concupiscence in chapter 4 of the
present study.

[63]A. von Harnack, *Lehrbuch der Dogmengeschichte*, III (Freiburg,
1890), 225-27; F. Loofs, *Leitfaden zum Studium der Dogmengeschichte* (Halle,
1893), 241-42; R. Seeberg, *Lehrbuch der Dogmengeschichte*, II (Leipzig, 1910),
515ff; J. Tixeront, *Histoire des Dogmes*, III (Paris, 1912), 295ff. ; While Seeberg,
515, sees Faustus as essentially opposed to Augustine, Harnack notes, 226, n. 4,
that Faustus takes care not to struggle against Augustine, but to battle only

While some work has been done since the nineteenth century on Faustus's letters and the thorny question of his sermons,[64] little attention was paid to the De gratia until the 1938 study of Gustave Weigel, S.J., *Faustus of Riez, An Historical Introduction*.[65] A somewhat less detailed version of Koch's earlier treatment, this study is similarly sympathetic to Faustus. Weigel discusses the historical circumstances of the writing of the *De gratia*, but does not attempt a doctrinal analysis of the text.[66] Weigel's monograph remains quite useful, especially for its reconstruction of the dates and chronology of Faustus's life, though its discussion of the *De gratia* is only cursory.

The 1970s—forty years after Weigel's monograph—brought a small renewal of interest in Faustus as a figure in the history of doctrine, and therefore in the *De gratia*. The eminent Italian patrologist Manlio Simonetti produced an important study in 1977 that focused on the use of Scripture in the *De gratia* and seriously questioned the traditional categories Pelagian and semipelagian as applied to Faustus.[67] For Simonetti, Faustus's main

---

Augustinianism. He cannot resist adding: "So ist es bis heute in der katholischen Kirche."

[64]The present study will avoid almost entirely the massive critical problem of the "pseudo-Eusebian" sermon collection, some of which is from Faustus's hand. The most recent attempt at a resolution of the authorship question may be found in the edition of these sermons, *Collectio Gallicana*, published in 1971 by Fr. Glorie in CCL 101-101B.

[65](Philadelphia: Dolphin, 1938).

[66]Weigel mentions in his preface, 3, that a doctrinal analysis was planned for the future. It never saw publication but part of it may be reflected in his article "El concepto de la fe, según los Semipelagianos. Un analisis de la doctrina de Fausto de Riez," *Revista Universitaria* 25 (1940): 35-53. In the article Weigel puzzles without resolution over whether faith is somehow "natural" for Faustus or a divine gift.

[67]"Il *De gratia* di Fausto di Riez," *Studi Storico-Religiosi* 1 (1977): 125-45.

burden was to achieve a balanced scriptural account of the rapport between grace and free will in the face of predestinarian excesses. In the following year Salvatore Pricoco published a complete study of the monastery of Lérins, placing Faustus as a figure within this monastic context.[68] By far the most important figure in the renewed study of Faustus is another Italian scholar, Carlo Tibiletti. In two studies focusing on the *De gratia*, Tibiletti has shown Faustus to be more compatible with Augustine than has been commonly thought.[69] By comparative study of a number of passages from the *De gratia* and from Augustine, he has documented the considerable presence of Augustine in Faustus's treatise. A third study surveys some of the major figures in the history of the reception of Faustus and argues also that non-Augustinian elements in the *De gratia* can be explained without recourse to Pelagius.[70] Tibiletti's most recent study focuses on the North African polemic against the Gallic writers, especially that of Fulgentius.[71]

Certainly the continued study of Faustus of Riez and the *De Gratia* has advanced the discussion beyond the doctrinaire standpoint of the earliest critics. One can no longer regard Faustus as a Pelagian, that is, as one who denies the need of divine grace for human salvation. The alternative, which has held virtually unanimous sway since the seventeenth century, has been to identify him as a semipelagian, a term whose inadequacy is universally recognized even as it is used. Even Faustus's defenders, like Koch, do not

---

[68]*L'isola dei santi: Il cenobio di Lerino e le origini del monachesimo gallico* (Rome: Ateneo e Bizzarri, 1978).

[69]"Libero arbitrio e grazia in Fausto di Riez," *Augustinianum* 19 (1979): 259-85; "La salvezza umana in Fausto di Riez," *Orpheus* 1 (1980): 371-90.

[70]"Fausto di Riez."

[71]"Polemiche in Africa."

hesitate to identify him as perhaps the chief exponent of semipelagianism, by which they mean the monastic theology in Gaul which proved resistant to Augustinianism and occasioned the writing of Augustine's late treatises *De dono perseverantiae* and *De praedestinatione sanctorum.* The recent studies of Simonetti, Pricoco, and Tibiletti, however, suggest that locating Faustus theologically may require more precise categories that give attention to a broader array of factors historical, exegetical, and theological. A useful first step may be to prescind from a priori categories such as Augustinian, Pelagian, and semipelagian, and simply attempt to understand the *De gratia* as nearly as possible on its own terms.

At the end of his study of the history of criticism of Faustus, Tibiletti alludes briefly to the important revision that has taken place in modern scholarship on Pelagius.[72] If moderns are now able to regard Pelagius with some equanimity, even if not with full approbation, there is all the more reason to undertake a profound historical and philological re-examination of Faustus of Riez.[73] In this way his authentic voice can be heard, apart from the accretions of later accusations. The following study does not pretend to be the profound historical and philological reexamination called for, but I hope that it will begin to clarify the direction of such inquiry. It will be the first work devoted entirely to an understanding of the *De gratia* in its historical, literary, and theological contexts. Having undertaken this

---

[72]"Fausto di Riez," 587. This body of scholarship, while not directly concerned with Faustus, is an important backdrop for the present study. The pioneering studies of A. Souter, Georges de Plinval, Torgny Bohlin, R. Evans, and Peter Brown (see Bibliography) have allowed modern scholars to see Pelagius on his own terms as a theologian and exegete, and as a partaker of a tradition of theological discourse much older than Augustine.

[73]"Fausto di Riez," 587.

task, we will be rewarded with a more precise understanding of the reception of Augustinianism in fifth-century Gaul.

The study proceeds in five chapters. The first locates Faustus and his treatise in the historical and theological environment, both broad and more proximate, of his time; special attention is paid to Pricoco's work on Lérins and its relevance for the study of the *De gratia*. More literary in its interest, chapter 2 considers the *De gratia* as a systematic and persuasive work emerging from Faustus's circumstances. Chapter 3 attempts to identify Faustus's own theological culture by uncovering the principal sources that lie behind the treatise. Explicating the doctrinal assertions of the treatise, chapter 4 demonstrates how the author adapted his sources in the light of his own theological concerns. Finally, we shall be equipped by chapter 5 to conclude with some suggestions regarding the place of the *De gratia* in the history of Christian theology.

CHAPTER ONE
THE HISTORICAL AND THEOLOGICAL
SETTING OF THE *DE GRATIA*

Faustus of Riez's treatise *De gratia* must be understood within four distinct but closely related contexts: (1) ecclesial life, and especially the role of the bishop, in Southern Gaul during the last decades of the western empire, (2) the monastic theological culture of Lérins, where Faustus was monk and abbot before his accession to the see of Riez in 462, (3) the broader reception of Augustinian thought in Gaul, and (4) the proximate circumstances in which Faustus wrote the treatise in 474. The present chapter, by way of introducing later discussions of the text proper and of its place in the history of doctrine, examines each of these four contexts. By locating the work in relation to the concerns of its own time, one may avoid some of the anachronisms and dogmatic preoccupations that have impaired our understanding of Faustus and of so-called semipelagianism.

Christian Gaul at the End of the Imperial Age

Although an emperor was in place at Rome until 476, when Odoacer deposed Romulus Augustus, officially ending the western empire, imperial political control and social organization had in fact been declining precipitously since the first decade of the century. Invasions across the Rhine

by Vandals, Visigoths, Burgundians, and others, and Alaric's notorious sack
of Rome in 410 were but counterparts to an internal erosion which had begun
even earlier as indigenous peoples and their aristocracies took on increasing
local authority. Even the rise of "Romance" languages, which in Gaul and
Spain displaced Celtic, owed nothing to centralized Roman control but was
the product of the influence of provincial Latin-speaking landowners, tax col-
lectors, and bishops, who considered themselves Romans.[1] Still, the
permanent breaching of the Rhine frontier at the outset of the fifth century
meant the beginning of a decidedly sub-Roman world. As the peoples
migrated and settled through the Germanic and Belgic provinces and moved—
not without violence—into Aquitania, central Imperial authority came to be
much more *de iure* than *de facto*.

Christian writers of the fifth century in Gaul had now to grapple
with the entirely new, and often frightening, situation of life under siege.
Despite occasional respites—in 418 officials of the diocese of Vienne were
able to gather at Arles—it was clear, at least to perspicacious observers, that
the world in which the Church could depend upon the majesty of the Roman
Empire was coming to an end. Gaul in the wake of the "barbarians" was in
immense distress, and Rome, which had all but sacrificed Gaul early on in its
struggle to defend Italy, was virtually impotent. The poet Orientius,
probably to be identified with the Gallo-Roman bishop of the same name,
paints a stark picture in his *Commonitorium*:

> Neither the difficulties of dense woods and high mountains, nor the
> strong currents of roiling rapids, nor the shelter of the setting of
> fortresses or the ramparts of cities, nor the places made inaccessible

---

[1]Brown, *World of Late Antiquity*, 40.

by the sea, nor the dreary solitude of the desert, nor canyons, nor
even the caves overhung with boulders, are able to avoid the hands
of the barbarians. . . . A mother dies pitifully with her children and
husband; a master is put into servitude with his servants; some are
thrown out into the fields like dogs; many have lost their lives in
their burning houses, which became their funeral pyres . . . all along
their path is death, suffering, destruction, fire, and mourning. All of
Gaul is but one smoking pyre.[2]

Nor were such Christian writers given to facile answers. Salvian of
Marseilles, writing c. 440, could ask rhetorically yet plaintively: "Why
should the situation of the barbarians be so much better than ours?"[3] The
blows that struck Roman Gaul also struck the consciousness of the Church,
many of whose members had long been unable to dissociate membership in
the Roman Empire from membership in the Church, and the problem of
God's having allowed an Arian, non-Roman people to overrun a stronghold of
catholic faith occasioned a number of Christian responses.

From the anonymous *Carmen de Providentia*, dating from the
second decade of the century, we are familiar with one common and
understandable reaction: a simple lament over one's losses. "One laments
over his stolen talents of silver and gold; another suffers over his furniture
being carried off and because the daughters of the Goths have taken his
jewels; yet another is tormented because his herds have been led away, his
houses burned, his wine drunk."[4]

---

[2]CSEL 16: 234. Unless otherwise indicated, all translations are my
own.

[3]*De gub. Dei* III. 1. 2 (CSEL 8: 41-42).

[4]PL 51: 637, lines 903-6.

What strikes the author of the *Carmen de Providentia* as particularly tragic, however, is the loss, occasioned by events and encouraged by the impious, of confidence in divine Providence :

> While the image of our smoldering homeland lies in our soul and things that have perished stand everywhere before our eyes, we are broken, we are given over to wailing and are drenched with tears. While we may act pious, we are turned to pleading. Nor do certain of those around us cease to assail our troubled mind. With the darts of their tongues they attack our wounded hearts: "Tell us the reasons, you who believe that the labors of human affairs stand by the will and rule of God! For what crime did this city perish? Or that place? Or this people? Why did they deserve such evils?"[5]

One should not suppose that apostasy was especially common within the Gallic church or that a recrudescence of paganism lay in store; no real evidence exists for this.[6] Nevertheless, one can hardly overstate the pastoral crisis of the newly disrupted social and political setting, and the consequent need for renewed confidence in the divine plan.

This need found a theological answer in such literary works as the *Commonitorium* of Orientius and the *Carmen de Providentia*, both products of the second decade of the century, and the treatise *De gubernatione Dei* of Salvian of Marseilles, dating from around 445. Despite the differences among these works, they share the twofold message of, on the one hand, the

---

[5]Ibid., 617, lines 17-26.

[6]Élie Griffe, *La Gaule chrétienne*, vol. 2: *L'église des Gaules au Ve siècle*, 24, n. 23.

sure purpose of God's will, despite the current losses, and on the other a kind of resignation in the face of the inevitable. "For the same" blows

> strike all the faithful, but with twofold reason. While sinners are tortured by something, saints are ennobled by it, and while it sentences the one as punishment for a crime, it crowns the other as a reward for virtue. . . . But the wise servant of Christ has lost none of those things which he has scorned, having already placed his hope in heavenly things. And if something amid the tempest of worldly labors befalls him, he suffers it intrepidly, certain of the honor promised him and desiring to be found a victor in the struggle. And you who cry over your squalid fields and deserted houses, the destroyed terraces of burned villas: Should you not rather shed tears over your own ruins, when you look upon the devastated inward parts of your heart? Upon the great filth which has covered its beauty? Upon the enemies established in the citadel of your captive mind?[7]

To this sort of message Salvian in particular adds a tone of moral chastisement: the reason for the fall of ostensible Christian Roman hegemony was the sad moral state of the Romans themselves. Declaring with astonishing insight that "the Roman republic is either already dead or certainly drawing its last breath,"[8] he depicts this death as the result of a

---

[7]*Carm. de Prov.* (PL 51: 637, lines 897-900, 908-18. Cf. Orientius, *Commonitorium* II, lines 185-88 (CSEL 16: 234).

[8]*De gub. Dei* IV. 6 (PL 53: 77B).

divine judgment upon the vices of Gallo-Roman Christians, whose moral purity compares unfavorably with that of the barbarians.[9]

Although the tone of fifth-century Christian authors in Gaul suggests a lapse into a sort of introspective resignation, this did not issue in a passive or quietistic Christianity. On the contrary, Gaul during the difficult years from 407 to 476, and especially after 453, witnessed social and political activism on a remarkably large scale on the part of Gallo-Roman bishops. The vital involvement of these men—among them the bishop of Riez from 462, Faustus—in social and political leadership constitutes one of the most immediate consequences of the upheavals in Gaul. As examples one may cite Sidonius Apollinaris, bishop of Clermont/Auvergne, and Patiens, bishop of Lyon.

The thoroughly Romanized area of Gaul known as Provincia Romana, or simply Provincia—present-day Provence—had been largely spared as the Germanic tribes gained control of the Belgic and Germanic provinces and established themselves in Aquitania. A semblance at least of Roman culture continued in great cities such as Arles and Marseilles. The Visigoths, however, who had established their court in Toulouse in 418 and had attacked both Arles and Narbonne, remained a pressing danger. Theodoric II ascended the throne in Toulouse in 453. Abetted by a power vacuum in Rome, he moved eastward: he laid unsuccessful siege to Arles in 458 and occupied Narbonne in 462. Sidonius Apollinaris, not yet a bishop, at this point seems not to have been overly concerned about Theodoric, despite a manifest dislike for barbarians and a high esteem for Roman culture.[10]

---

[9]Ibid., VII. 11. 49; V. 3. 14 (PL 53: 139A, 97A).

[10]Sidonius's disdain for the barbarians, even as he cooperated with their efforts, is amply documented. He complains of the smell of Burgundians (*Ep.* II. 1. 2, VII. 14. 10; *Carm.* XII. 1-22), and sneers at their lack of culture (*Ep.* IV. 8. 5).

Sidonius was of aristocratic birth and well-connected enough to have access to the court of Toulouse. One wonders whether something of the court theologian shows itself when, on a visit to Narbonne shortly after its occupation, Sidonius calls Theodoric "the glory of the Goths, pillar and savior of the Roman people."[11] At first, then, Sidonius, aristocrat and *soi-disant* man of letters, seems to have adopted the strategy of cultivating his ties with the new regime. To such a man, the Visigoths, who were after all officially federates of the empire, would have represented less a threat than a potentially useful connection.

The sudden disappearance of Theodoric in 466 and his succesion by his brother Euric quickly forced a new way of thinking upon Sidonius and others. Euric was more militarily adventuresome than Theodoric, and envisioned an Arian Visigothic kingdom extending from the Loire through Spain. In 471, perhaps provoked by a feeble military gesture by the Roman emperor Anthemius, Euric crossed the Rhône and penetrated well to the east; in the countryside along his path "omnia vastavit."[12] At this very time, 470 or 471, Sidonius was proclaimed bishop of Clermont/Auvergne. In the face of Euric's new threat, Sidonius became the leader of patriotic resistance in his home city. Given his social status and his cultivated sense of *Romanitas,* one might ask whether he resisted actively in the name of Roman civilization or of the faith. In fact, however, the two were inextricably linked for Sidonius, as for many. In any case, the episcopal role for him became that of a political, even military, leader, and his efforts were repaid with a brief exile at

---

[11]*Carm.* XXIII, 70-71 (PL 58: 732B): ". . . decus Getarum, Romanae columen salusque gentis, Theodoricus . . ."

[12]*Chronica gallica* anni 511 (MGH, AA IX, 664).

Euric's behest after the city fell to those whom the bishop had called "public enemies," the "pact-breaking race."[13]

Patiens, bishop of Lyon, provides another example of the important role played by bishops as the empire crumbled. When after their 471 raid of Provence the Visigoths under Euric returned to their bases, they left behind them the threat of famine, having burned crops as they went. Patiens responded by sending bargeloads of grain down the Saone and Rhône to be distributed free of charge to the needy cities of Arles, Riez, Avignon, Orange, Alba, Valence, and Trois-Châteaux.[14] Thus relief efforts of the kind that might in other times have fallen to civil magistrates became the tasks of bishops, many of whom, being of landed aristocratic background, had the necessary resources available to them.

A further aspect of the role of the bishop in Church life had to do with the ransoming of prisoners. Negotiating for, and ransoming, captives had become almost entirely a Christian pursuit, one particularly incumbent upon bishops. Sidonius, writing of the ordination of a certain Simplicius as bishop of Bourges, mentions that the candidate had often negotiated with barbarian kings on behalf of his own city and had known at firsthand what it was to be a prisoner of the barbarians.[15]   Faustus of Riez in the *De gratia* cannot avoid comparing the action of divine redemption to the work of a legate or priest interceding on behalf of a captive populace.[16]

---

[13]Sidonius Apollinaris, *Ep.* VII. 7. 2; VI. 6. 1. (PL 58: 573, 555A). See the account in Griffe, *La Gaule chrétienne* 2: 71-92.

[14]Sidonius Apollinaris, *Ep.* VI. 6 and 12 (PL 58: 555C-557A, 560A-564A).

[15] Ibid. VII. 9 (PL 58: 581): ". . . non ille semel pro hac civitate stetit vel ante pellitos reges vel ante principes purpuratos . . . Postremo, iste est ille, carissimi, cui in tenebris ergastularibus constituto multipliciter . . ."

[16]Faustus, *De grat.* I. 16 (CSEL 21: 50, lines 19ff.).

Even in the very last years before 476, Gallo-Roman bishops played a prominent role in what amounted to the formal ending of Roman hegemony in Gaul. By 474 the new emperor Julius Nepos, who was virtually a puppet of the Goths, could only hope to save the little that was left to the *Res publica* by means of negotiations with Euric. These last peace negotiations involved several of the leading bishops of the besieged provinces, among them Leontius of Arles, Graecus of Marseilles, Basil of Aix, and Faustus of Riez. The talks concluded in 475 with a treaty that ceded to the Visigoths all but the southernmost portion of Provence. After 476 this part, too, was incorporated into the Visigothic kingdom.

Thus far we have seen two facets of the ecclesial context of Faustus's treatise *De gratia*, both of which were largely brought about by the massive social upheavals in fifth-century Gaul. The first has been a theological language, redolent in some ways of Augustine's *De civitate Dei*, which enjoined Christians to look to things beyond this world and to endure with confidence the present evils. The second, seeming almost to contradict the first, has been an activistic, deeply engaged involvement on the part of the Church in responding to the social and political realities of the time. To delineate further the broad picture of the ferment that produced the *De gratia*, one must examine what was arguably the most influential force shaping Gallic Christianity from within in the fifth century: Lerinian monasticism.

Lérins: The Shape of Its Theological Culture

The island monastery of Lérins, located just off the coast near present-day Cannes, was one of two great monastic foundations of the first years of the fifth century and had considerable impact on the life of the Christian Church in Gaul in the subsequent period. It was founded by a young aristocrat, Honoratus, and his followers some years before John

Cassian founded the monasteries of St. Victor in Marseilles around 416.
While Cassian has been a more influential figure in the history of western
theology and monasticism, the practical influence of his monasteries in his
time paled in comparison with that of Lérins. Many, if not most, of the
most important bishops of southern Gaul during the fifth century were the
products of the environs of Lérins; it was, as one frequently hears, a "nursery
of bishops." In what follows, we shall examine the distinctive character of
what may be called the theological culture of this monastery. This is the
second context in which to locate the theology of the *De gratia*.[17]

Honoratus, a man of noble birth who had sojourned with his older
brother among the monks of the East, led a group of men during the first
decade of the fifth century to the small, somewhat forbidding island of
Lérins.[18] From the outset, as evidenced in its first rule, the *Regula quattuor
patrum*, the distinctive character of Lerinian monasticism asserted itself.
First, one finds a marked preference for the cenobitic over the anchoritic form
of life. Serapion, probably an Egyptian pseudonym for one of the monks
present at the founding of the monastery, speaks of a harsh desert and the

---

[17]In using the term *theological culture*, the intention is to avoid, on the
one hand, an older view in which Lérins came to be seen as a monastic school
which taught the liberal arts and classical culture. For this, which depends on a
dubious reading of the sources, see Haarhoff, *Schools of Gaul*, 177-95. On the
other hand, Riché, in his *Education and Culture in the Barbarian West*, 104-5, in
rightly rejecting this, also rejects out of hand the notion put forward by Roger in
L'enseignement des lettres classiques d'Ausone à Alcuin that Lérins was a
theological school. While Riché is correct in seeing *school* as too strong a term
to describe the influence of Lerinian thought, he does not do justice to elements of
continuity in the Lerinian theological perspective. I have therefore adopted the
term *culture* to denote this continuity of perspective, which perdures despite
particular theological differences. See also Courcelle, "Nouveaux aspects de la
culture lérinienne," 379-409.

[18]Our only narrative source for the early history of Lérins is the *Sermo
de vita S. Honorati* of Hilary of Arles (PL 50: 1249-1272), hereafter cited as *Serm.
Hon.*

terror of various monsters as arguments against a solitary life, and cites the Scriptures as to the goodness of like-minded brothers dwelling together. He concludes: "We therefore wish brothers of one mind to dwell in a house with joy; but how that unanimity and joy might be maintained in right order we must set forth with the aid of God."[19]

The fundamental principle of unity set forth in this rule is obedience to the abbot whose role is "praeesse super omnes": his rule and counsel are not in any way to be denied; one must obey him "sicut imperio Domini cum omni laetitia."[20] The common life at Lérins, therefore, was at the first seen as far more dependent upon the concrete, tangible following of precepts than upon, for example, the virtue of charity. Apart from its cenobitic emphasis[21] and the central role of obedience, the first rule of Lérins is marked by certain points of observance. In addition to a daily fast until nones and complete rest on Sundays, the monks adhered to a schedule that allowed only three hours' leisure for spiritual exercises at the beginning of the day, followed by six hours of work "sine aliqua murmuratione."[22] As Adalbert de Vogüé points out, this was quite unlike the earlier custom at Marmoutier under Martin, the founder of Gallic monasticism, in which the monks had all

---

[19]*Regula quattuor patrum* I. 8-9, in Adalbert de Vogüé, ed., *Les règles des saints pères* vol. I, SC 297: 182.

[20]Ibid., I. 10-11.

[21]Although the clear emphasis was upon the common life, the option to live a kind of quasi-eremeticism seems to have become available to Lerinian monks. While Paulinus of Nola prior to 420 refers to Lérins as a "congregatio" (*Ep.* 51. 1, PL 61: 417B), Eucherius in his *De laude eremi* of 428 confirms that some lived "divisis cellulis" after the Egyptian fashion (PL 50: 711B). The *Statuta patrum* confirms the existence of these cells.

[22]*Regula quattuor patrum* III. II (*Les règles*, 194).

their time free to read and to pray.[23] The novelty and the strength of this
new monastery lay in its emphasis on work under obedience, a practice that,
like the names of the rule's eponymous four fathers, echoes Egyptian
practice.

The first chapter of the history of Lérins ended around 427—a few
years after Faustus's arrival—when Honoratus, having been the superior for
some twenty years, left to become bishop of Arles. He was replaced by
Maximus, a monk from Riez who later became bishop there. Vogüé deems
it likely that the *Statuta patrum,* or *Second Rule of the Fathers,* was
composed at this time. While it continues along the essential lines of the
earlier rule, one finds a few changes. The superior, for example, who still
retains his authority, is now called *praepositus.* Further, the notion of charity among the members of the community grows in importance: "Ante
omnia habentes caritatem";[24] the head of the community was not simply to
be feared and obeyed but also to be loved in all things.[25] Despite such a shift
in emphasis, however, the central tenets of Lérins's communal life continued:
dutiful obedience, work in concert with prayer, and a sense of adherence to the
time-honored way of life "according to the tradition of the holy fathers."[26]

A study of *regulae* yields only a formal portrait of the fundamental
values that undergirded Lerinian monasticism. One must look to the literary
products of Lérins to gain an idea of the values that were transmitted to, and

---

[23]*Les règles,* 24.

[24]*Statuta patrum* 5 (*Les règles,* 274).

[25]*Statuta patrum* 7 (*Les règles,* 276). A. de Vogüé sees this interest in
fraternal charity as possibly influenced by Augustine's *Ordo monasterii* and
Praeceptum, both of which were written in the last decade of the fourth century in
Africa. See *Les règles,* 27.

[26]*Statuta patrum* 1 (*Les règles,* 274).

cherished by, the monks nurtured there. Drawn primarily from Eucherius of
Lyon, Hilary of Arles, and Vincent of Lérins—all older contemporaries of
Faustus—a picture emerges of the shape of Lerinian asceticism, spirituality,
and doctrinal perspective. One may isolate the following characteristics: a
positive orientation toward the monastic life as the pursuit of Christian
perfection; an activist, even quasi-military view of the ascetic life; and a deep-
seated conservatism regarding both institutions and doctrine.[27]

Eucherius in his *De laude eremi* asks rhetorically: "The love of
the desert: what must it be called in you but the love of God?"[28] Implicit in
this straight equation of the two loves is a judgment about the quality of life
in the world. The world is a place of darkness, where pleasure reigns, where
one cares for the body more than the soul; the one who befriends this world
neglects God.[29] The elect of God, however, writes Hilary, are inspired with
the desire to move away from, to flee, this world just as Honoratus did in
retiring to a barren island.[30] For those who, after his example, came to
Lérins, the flight from the world and the renunciation of its goods was not a
burdensome or dolorous matter; quite to the contrary, to escape the world is
precisely to be liberated from servitude to Pharoah and to be freed from the

---

[27]These themes are examined in detail in Pricoco, *L'isola dei santi*, 131-
207.

[28]*De laude eremi* 1: 20 (PL 50: 701D). Similarly in 3: 41: "Eremum
ergo recte incircumscriptum dei nostri templum dixerim."

[29]Ibid., 36: 394, 44: 516 (PL 50: 709C, 712B); Hilary of Arles, *Serm.
Hon.* 6: 4, 23: 31, 23: 8. Pricoco, *L'Isola dei santi*, 132, notes the idea of
rejection connoted in monastic use of *mundus* and *saeculum*. He points also (pp.
193-94) to the way in which Eucherius, in his *De contemptu mundi* (PL 50:
722BD) reprises the old theme of the world's decadence and old age, found in
Tertullian, Cyprian, Lucretius, and Seneca.

[30] Hilary of Arles, *Serm. Hon.* II: 10 (PL 50: 1254C).

entrapments of sin.[31] One finds no emphasis upon themes such as self-annihilation or mortification but rather the sense of having escaped the true locus of evil.

Pricoco speaks in this regard of a threefold fundamental optimism characterizing the disposition toward monastic life at Lérins.[32] First, one finds the sense of the monks' having been moved into a state of perfection among the perfect, in the desert which is the very house of God, the place of theophanies. Eucherius's *De laude eremi* has frequent recourse to images of the vision of God and to illuminist terminology.[33] Second and closely allied, Lerinian writers portrayed the monastic life as a condition of absolute continuity and uniformity with the way of perfection as it had been pursued since Adam; the monk enjoys the grace of Edenic innocence as a beneficiary of the new consecration wrought by Christ. For these monks—and this is especially telling for the theology of grace—both the will and the faculty to sin are completely distant: "nec magis absunt a voluntate peccandi quam a facultate."[34] There could be, therefore, no crises of discouragement, for the monk here knew nothing of a fallen will or even of a lapse in zeal. Pricoco sees here a distinction even from the contemporary enterprise of John Cassian, for "the great fear of the *infirmitas Gallicana,* which dominates the cenobitic programs of Cassian, finds no place at Lérins; here complete virtue

---

[31]Ibid. 17: 20-24 : "Nam velut educti in novam lucem, antiquum illum diu insidentem errorum carcerem detestabantur . . . amaritudo, asperitas et rabies locum dabant libertati, quam Christus obtulerat, et delectabat requies post longam et gravem Pharaoniam servitutem." Cf. 7: 3-25 and Eucherius, *De laude eremi* 32: 329f., *contempt.* (PL 50: 715CD).

[32]*L'isola dei santi,* 183-86.

[33]3: 44f., 7: 78f., 9: 101f., 13: 145f., 17: 194f., and passim.

[34]Ibid. 31: 325.

was not a privilege reserved for a few, but an ornament of all."[35] Third, while the Lerinian concept of the monastic life naturally has much to do with contemplation, it does not take on the dimensions of a negative mystical doctrine in the sense of encouraging what Pricoco calls "inerte ozio contemplativo."[36] The ascetics of Lérins were not infrequently the future bishops of Gallic dioceses whose leadership demanded practical activity and zeal. In sum, the ascetism of Lérins, despite its rhetoric of separation and perfection, did not lapse into mere introspection or passivity.

To underscore this point, consider the inclination of the monk to portray his existence and function as that of a soldier, both in the smaller scope of the quest for Christian perfection and in the broader plan of human salvation. Pricoco suggests that this tendency may be an aspect of the wider militarization of customs and consciousness that characterized late antique culture.[37] He points to the martial attitudes and practices that were increasingly taken up into monastic rules and organization. During the fourth century in Gaul, the cult of military martyrs, i.e., Christians who were executed for refusing military service, flourished in Gaul. The Christian was a *miles Christi*, a member of a *militia caelestis*, even as a deserter from the *militia Caesaris*.[38] Among the writers of Lérins, specifically Eucherius, a shift in emphasis occurs. His *Passio Acaunensium martyrum* celebrates the martyrs of Acauno, some six thousand Christian soldiers—St. Maurice and

---

[35]*L'isola dei santi*, p. 185.

[36]Ibid., 186.

[37]Ibid., 177. The thesis of this cultural militarization is the suggestion of Ramsay MacMullen, *Soldier and Civilian in the Later Roman Empire* (Cambridge: Harvard University Press, 1963).

[38]Such is the imagery in Sulpicius Severus and Paulinus of Nola. Cf. Paulinus of Nola, *Carmen* XIX.

his company—killed for refusing to persecute fellow believers.[39] Eucherius does not portray them as disloyal to the empire, nor does he suggest that monastic life is irreconcilable with service to the empire. Perhaps the changed role of imperial power, from persecutor of the Church to protector against the barbarian, shows itself here. But regardless of the attitude adopted toward military service proper, the image of the Christian as a soldier, as one who discharges a task under the authority of a superior, continues in the consciousness of the monks at Lérins.

Both because of their consciousness of being heirs of an unbroken monastic tradition and because of the perceived dependence of Christianity upon Roman society and culture, the writers from Lérins betray a marked conservatism. With regard to the spirituality of the monastic tradition, this means a tendency to avoid excess and ostentation. The corpus of Lerinian literature notably lacks stories of miracle-working or of fanatically excessive types of discipline. Again, the essential character of entry into the desert was that of liberation from the constant struggle against worldly evil—a return to innocence. Pricoco suggests, plausibly, that the tone of Lérins's ascetic conceptions may conceal some of the fundamental elements of the political ideology of the provincial aristocracy at the end of the imperial age, namely, Christian patriotism, loyalty to the monarchic institution, acceptance of the notion of *Roma aeterna*, and so on.[40]

---

[39](PL 50: 827-32).

[40]*L'isola dei santi*, 191-92. The aristocratic background and attitude of many of the monks of Lérins argues against neatly dividing Gallic bishops into "monastic" and "aristocratic" categories, as Dill has done in his *Roman Society*, 215. On the notion of the aristocratization of the Gallic bishopric, see Heinzelmann, "L'aristocratie," 75-90. See also the discussion in Markus, *Christianity in the Roman World*, 141ff.

This pervasive conservatism in the island's theological culture shows itself most clearly as a specifically theological position in Vincent's *Commonitorium*, written in 434. The only treatise known to have Lérins as its provenance, its complete title is *Tractatus peregrini pro catholica fide adversus profanas omnium haereticorum novitates*. Vincent's attitude to Christian doctrine is guided by the principle of an essentially changeless tradition; what is new is ipso facto a departure from that tradition and therefore to be condemned. Vincent speaks of "one and the same doctrine maintained through every succession of ages by the uncorrupted tradition of the truth."[41] He rails against "innovations, which are contrary to the old and to the ancient, which, if accepted, make one violate the faith of the blessed fathers, either wholly or at least for the greater part."[42] All change is a deterioration of sacred tradition: a heretic is one who "departs from the consensus of the universal and catholic church."[43] To partake of the mainstream which constitutes orthodoxy, "let us hold to what has been believed always, everywhere, and by all."[44]

A function both of the Lerinenses' putative rejection of the world and the monastery's conservatism is its bias against philosophical pursuits, inasmuch as they smack of the pagan cultural heritage. Cassian, whose influence at Lérins was important, speaks in his *Conlationes* of this heritage as "diaboli perniciosa illusio."[45] One wonders, of course, whether this

---

[41]*Comm.* 24: 2 (CCL 64: 180).

[42]Ibid. 24: 4 (CCL 64: 181).

[43]Ibid. 24: 7 (CCL 64: 181).

[44]Ibid. 2: 5 (CCL 64: 149).

[45]*Conl.* II. 24, 2 (SC 42).

attitude is more a rhetorical posture than a matter of practice, since it has often been observed that Christian writers urge the renunciation of classical learning with all the force and style of that same learning. Nevertheless, the writers of Lérins would take pains not to flaunt classical learning and to stress the life lived philosophically over the reading of philosophers. As Eucherius writes to his son Valerian: "But rather, away from those repudiated precepts of the philosophers, to whose reading you accomodate your work and intelligence, you should apply the effort of your mind to what must be imbibed from Christian dogmas . . . . Hence one may say that while others have usurped the name of philosophy, we have taken up its life."[46]

Lérins, then, in its distinctive blending of an ascetic ethos with a principled theological perspective, presents us with the contours of a culture whose values and intuitions helped to shape the mind of Faustus of Riez. The world with its blandishments and entanglements, not some tragic flaw in the human constitution, is the occasion for human involvement in sin. Once having escaped the world's seductions, the Christian is utterly free, able in Edenic innocence to keep the divine precepts. These commands are to be kept by means of devoted and obedient service; a Christianity lacking such obedience is utterly foreign to the Lerinian mind. And further, just as this ascesis has always been the one path to holy living, so too, on a doctrinal level, the one unchanging faith has been passed on purely, by universal consensus. Such was the frame of mind carried into the world by those like Faustus, Eucherius, or Hilary of Arles, men who as bishops in the troubled

---

[46]*De contemptu mundi* (PL 50: 724A).

years of fifth-century Gaul translated their Lerinian formation into a deep engagement in worldly affairs, and who in doing so earned vast prestige.[47]

Gaul's Reception of Augustinianism

The question of the reception in Gaul of the thought of Saint Augustine is exceedingly complicated and involves several variables. The first is the sheer range of Augustine's thought, which could almost lead one to speak of several different Augustines. Further, *Augustinianism*, or even *Augustine's thought* may refer either to the corpus of his own writings or to the systematizations of later disciples. One must also ask the chronological question, for while Augustine is virtually ignored in Gaul during the first decade of the fifth century, his works become a source of controversy by the end of the third decade. Further, one must acknowledge a diverse audience: the monastic culture described above certainly dominated, but did not monopolize, the theological climate of southern Gaul. Precisely, then, the question is this: How was Augustine's anti-Pelagian teaching on grace received in southern Gaul from 427 onward, both inside and outside the milieu of the new monastic foundations?

An imperial rescript of 30 April 418, very likely issued due to the efforts of Augustine and the African bishops, banned Pelagius, Coelestius, and their disciples from the city of Rome.[48] An imperial letter of 9 June

---

[47]On the increased importance of monk-bishops in the fifth century, see Heinzelmann, *Bischofsherrschaft in Gallien,* 73-98. Also see P. Rousseau, "The Spiritual Authority of the 'Monk-Bishop,'" 380-419.

[48]PL 45: 1726-28; PL 48: 379-86. The circumstances surrounding its promulgation are discussed by Burns in "Augustine's Role in the Imperial Action Against Pelagius," 67-83, and in more detail by Wermelinger, *Rom und Pelagius: die theologische Position der römischen Bischöfe im pelagianishche Streit in den Jahren 411-432,* which is the best history of the controversy.

419 extended the ban to the entire empire.[49] Coupled with the somewhat reluctant condemnation by Pope Zosimus in the summer of 418, this meant effectively that the doctrine of divine grace taught by Augustine and at this time contained in five or six works had the force of civil and ecclesiastical law.[50] We possess no real evidence of either approval or disapproval of this new situation in the church of Gaul. Certainly Pelagius would have been seen as a notorious heretic, and we find no equivalent in Gaul to the strident opposition to Augustine found in Julian of Eclanum and the bishops of Aquileia. On the other hand, an undercurrent of implicit opposition must have flowed under the surface of the eastward-tending orientation of the monks of Lérins and Marseilles, for through eastern eyes Pelagius's teaching was unobjectionable, as was proved by his acquittal at the council of Diaspolis in December 415. Some bishops in Gaul must have merited at least the accusation of Pelagian sympathies, for a bull of the emperor Valentinian III in July of 425 threatened banishment to Gallic bishops who followed the "nefarium Pelagiani et Coelestiani dogmatis errorem," unless they recanted within twenty days.[51] On the whole, however, whatever opposition Augustine's doctrines may have encountered in Gaul remained largely submerged.

The year 427 was a watershed. In this year Augustine's small treatise *De correptione et gratia* arrived in Marseilles. Originally written to

---

[49]Augustine, *Ep*. 201. 1 (CSEL 57: 299-301).

[50]*De peccatorum meritis et remissione, De spiritu et littera* (412), *De natura et gratia contra Pelagium, Liber de perfectione iustitiae hominis* (415), *De gestis Pelagii* (417), *De gratia Christi et de peccato originali libri duo* (418). Cf. the strong case made by Evans that Augustine did not write specifically against Pelagius until 415, in *Pelagius: Inquiries and Reappraisals*, 70ff.

[51]PL 48: 409-11.

quell the doubts of monks at Hadrumetum in northern Africa, it was Augustine's attempt to reconcile his stress upon the radical incapacity of human nature to do good works apart from divine grace with the phenomenon of admonition (*correptio*) found in the Scriptures. The letter of the law, says Augustine, can show a person what the good is but cannot aid him or her in its accomplishment. For this task grace, the special gift of God, is needed.[52] The obvious rejoinder to such a view was put to Augustine by the Hadrumetan monks: If one's ability to do good works depends upon a gift, how can one be reproved for lacking this gift?[53] Augustine's doctrine could be taken to imply that God, rather than the human subject, is in the final analysis the agent of human obedience to divine precepts, and so much of his treatise aims to salvage the role of human accountability. A further consequence of this radical stress upon the divine *initium* in all things, and one that Augustine does not hesitate to assert, is the doctrine of absolute predestination. Those who believe and obey are "those who have been predestined to the kingdom of God, whose number is fixed such that not one can be added to them or diminished from them."[54] Despite his protests to the contrary, Augustine's scheme with its rigid *numerus clausus* of the elect is hard-pressed to allow a really decisive role for human will and action in the divine economy.

In letters written to Augustine sometime between 427 and 429, two of his ardent followers in Gaul alerted him to the division generated in

---

[52]*De corrept. et grat.* I. 2 (PL 44: 917).

[53]Ibid. IV. 6. (col. 919): "Quomodo, inquit, meo vitio non habetur, quod non accepi ab illo, a quo nisi detur, non est omnino alius unde tale ac tantum munus habeatur?"

[54]Ibid. XIII. 39 (col. 940): ". . . qui praedestinati sunt in regnum Dei, quorum ita certus est numerus, ut nec addatur eis quisquam, nec minuatur ex eis."

Marseilles and environs by the reading of *De correptione*. Tiro Prosper of Aquitaine, who was close to the monastic community of Cassian in Marseilles, reported that "multi servorum Christi," meaning monks, were of the opinion that Augustine's doctrine of election was "contrary to the opinions of the fathers and to the interpretation of the Church."[55] Prosper noted that some had been uneasy with Augustine's earlier work against Julian of Eclanum but had assumed their own ignorance and withheld judgment. The *De correptione*, however, caused a real division between those who became more allied with Augustine and others who "departed more opposed than they had been."[56] Prosper urged that this separation be seen as dangerous "lest the spirit of Pelagian impiety run riot."[57] One should note that Prosper's ascription of Pelagian tendencies to those in southern Gaul comes on the basis of their opposition to some apparent excess in Augustine's anti-Pelagian teaching and not because of any known acceptance of Pelagius's doctrine.

Prosper's letter also summarizes the doctrinal position of those about whom he writes. To begin with, they believe that all have sinned in Adam, and that regeneration can come only with divine grace. In addition, propitiation in the blood of Christ is offered indiscriminately to all; therefore anyone willing to approach toward faith and baptism may be saved. Further, God has forseen from all eternity those who would believe, who would be worthy of being called, and whose faith would then be aided by grace.

---

[55]*Ep.* 225. 2 (CSEL 57: 455): ". . . contrarium putant patrum opinioni et ecclesiastico sensui."

[56]Ibid. (456).

[57]Ibid.: ". . . metuenda est . . . ne . . . spiritus Pelagianae impietatis inludat."

Everyone is therefore directed both to believe and to act upon the divine precepts, so that no one should despair, since a reward is prepared in return for
willing devotion.[58]

Apart from the formal critique of Augustine's doctrine of election,
i.e., that it represents an unwarranted exegetical innovation, one finds in
Prosper's account a twofold material criticism growing out of the theses
sketched above. First, a doctrine of predestination wherein some are made
vessels of honor and some of dishonor has disastrous consequences for the
character of human life. The doctrine of divine election

> both deprives the fallen of a concern for rising up again and gives
> the saints occasion for lukewarmness, for in either case labor is
> superfluous, since one rejected cannot enter in by any effort, nor can
> one of the elect be cast out for any negligence. However people
> might act, their outcome cannot be other than what God has defined;
> and in uncertain hope there can be no constant course, for if the
> choice of the predestiner determines otherwise, the intention of one
> who strives is in vain.[59]

Second, absolute predestination's consequences held dire implications
about the universal salvific will of God. What was being taught under the
name of predestination was taken by many in the Massilian monastic

---

[58]*Ep.* 225. 3 (CSEL 57:457).

[59]Ibid. (458): "et lapsis curam resurgendi adimere et sanctis occasionem
teporis adferre eo, quod in utramque partem superfluus labor sit, si neque reiectus
ulla industria possit intrare neque electus ulla negligentia possit excidere. quoquo
enim modo se egerint, non posse aliud erga eos, quam deus definiuit, accidere et
sub incerta spe cursum non posse esse constantem, cum, si aliud habeat
praedestinantis electio, cassa sit adnitentis intentio."

community as nothing more than a kind of fatalism; even worse, it made God out to be a capricious creator of different natures for different people.[60]

Prosper clearly regarded the opponents of the most radical aspects of Augustine's doctrine of grace as stubborn, disingenuous, and predisposed to Pelagianism. He complains of their tactic of defending their position by an appeal to tradition, noting that on Augustine's interpretation of the celebrated passage Rom. 9:14-21 they declare "it has been understood in this way by not one teacher of the Church."[61] In their doctrine of grace they do not turn away from "Pelagian ways"; even in admitting the primacy of grace, they define grace in terms of the original granting of free choice and reason, such that one can discern good and evil and direct the will toward knowledge of God and obedience. One attains to the grace by which we are reborn in Christ through the use of this original gift, and God calls all to salvation, whether through natural law, written law, or the preaching of the Gospel.[62]

While Prosper never mentions by name those who question Augustine's teaching, a main target is clearly the monastic circles influenced by John Cassian. The locale, Marseilles, and the reference to *servi Christi*, that is, monks, can only mean Cassian and his readers. Cassian's *Conlationes* enjoyed great popularity; they were known, read, and esteemed at Lérins—the second portion was in fact dedicated to Honoratus and Eucherius[63]—and publication of the second and third portions was occasioned by popular demand. At least the second, containing conferences XI-XVII,

---

[60]Ibid.: ". . . sub hoc praedestinationis nomine fatalem quandam induci necessitatem aut diversarum naturarum dici dominum conditorem ..."

[61]Ibid. (459): "a nullo umquam ecclesiasticorum ita esse intellecta."

[62]*Ep.* 225. 4 (CSEL 57: 460).

[63]*Conl.* XI, *Praef.* (SC 54: 98).

was in circulation in 426.[64]   The work is not a theological treatise proper, but a series of conversations with personages representing Egyptian monks. *Conlatio* XIII, the third conference of abbot Chaeremon on divine protection, gives clear examples of the doctrine that moved Prosper to petition Augustine.

On the one hand, Cassian, through the mouth of the Egyptian abbot, affirms the absolute necessity of divine grace: "It is clearly proved that the effort of one who labors can accomplish nothing without the aid of God."[65]   As the conference progresses, however, Cassian describes the mysterious characer of the working of divine grace. One cannot reduce God's gift to any neat schema, for "it is not easily discerned by human reason how the Lord gives to those who ask, is found by those who seek, and opens to those who knock, and yet is found by some who do not seek, appears visibly among those who did not ask him, and extends his hands all the day to a people who disbelieve and speak against him."[66]

Nor is the working of grace merely a logical conundrum; it is a problem of biblical exegesis. In Conference XI, 9 and 10, Cassian multiplies examples of places where Scripture affirms either the free human will or the absolute divine initiative. The Bible confirms both the freedom of our will and its *infirmitas*. The two, grace and freedom, "are, so to speak,

---

[64]Argument for dating is given by Pichery in his introduction in SC 42: 28ff.

[65]*Conl.* XI, 3 (SC 54: 149): ". . . evidentius adprobatur nihil posse perficere sine adiutorio dei laborantis industriam."

[66]Ibid. XI, 3 (158-59): ". . . non facile humana ratione discernitur quemadmodum dominus petentibus tribuat, a quaerentibus inveniatur aperiatque pulsantibus, et rursus inveniatur a non quaerentibus se, palam adpareat inter illos qui eum non interrogabant, et tota die expandat manus suas ad populum non credentem sibi et contradicentem ."

indiscriminately mixed and intermingled."[67] While in XIII, 18, Cassian affirms as settled the notion that the human *arbitrium* is not in itself sufficient for salvation, he clearly denies that one can, on the basis of Scripture, invariably claim either a divine or a human origin for the good will.[68] Although the *Conlationes* were written before the arrival in Gaul of Augustine's *De correptione*, one can readily find inchoate here the kind of criticism that according to Prosper was leveled at Augustine. It is entirely possible, in fact, that Cassian had already found in Augustine's earlier works a tendency toward one-sided exegesis, for Augustine had begun to adduce certain passages in a predestinarian fashion as early as 396.[69]

Prosper's estimate of the Massilian resistance to Augustine's doctrine of grace found an echo in the letter of his associate Hilary—not the bishop of Arles, but a layman—to Augustine. To our knowledge of the situation he adds explicitly that the erroneous views in question were aired not only in Marseilles, but elsewhere in Gaul.[70] He also notes that the opposing forces were buttressing their arguments with Augustine's own writings, notably the *Expositio quarundam propositionum ex epistula ad Romanos* and the *De libero arbitrio*.[71] Having heard of Augustine's

---

[67]Ibid. XI, 11 (162): ". . . quodammodo indiscrete permixta atque confusa."

[68]Ibid. XI, 12 (164): "Nec enim talem deus hominem fecisse credendus est, qui nec velit umquam nec possit bonum. Alioquin nec liberum ei permisit arbitrium si ei tantummodo malum ut velit et possit, bonum vero a semet ipso nec velle nec posse concessit."

[69]Cf. *De diversis quaestionibus ad Simplicianum* (PL 40: 11ff).

[70]*Ep.* 226, 2 (CSEL 57: 469): "Haec sunt itaque, quae Massilae vel etiam aliquibus locis in Gallia ventilantur."

[71]Ibid. 226, 3 (471-72); 226, 8 (477). Reference is to *Expos. quarund.* 60, 62 and *De lib. arb.* III, 23. In both of these earlier works, Augustine

proposed *Retractiones*, Hilary expresses hope of seeing this work soon, expecting that the bishop of Hippo will thereby defuse some of the ammunition of Hilary's opponents in Gaul.[72]

One should note that the frequent use of the term Pelagian to describe the dangerous leanings of those in southern Gaul shows that already for Prosper and Hilary the term had become a slogan for putatively defective views of grace as measured by the standard of Augustine's anti-Pelagian writings. Moreover, reaction in Gaul was not completely isolated or sectarian; the very fact of the writing of two letters to Augustine testifies to the magnitude of the problem. Indeed, the care that Prosper took in his language shows that he did not wish to risk charging some of Gaul's more notable Christians with heresy. He speaks of "remnants of the Pelagian depravity," of "Pelagian ways," and of the "spirit of Pelagian impiety," and so on, but always as a lurking danger rather than an outright accusation. After all, among the number of those mentioned is Hilary, the saintly bishop of Arles, whom Prosper portrays as generally favorable to Augustine's doctrinal teaching.[73] Therefore the situation in Gaul was neither an isolated problem nor one of essential anti-Augustinianism. Further, despite Prosper's portrayal of his opponents as deceptive in their appeal to tradition, we know from having examined the monastically shaped theological culture of

---

interpreted passages in defense of free will which he would later use in defense of predestination.

[72]*Ep.* 226, 10 (479): "Libros, cum editi fuerint, quos de universo opere moliris, quaeso habere mereamur, maxime ut per eorum auctoritatem, si qua tibi in tuis displicent, a dignitate tui nominis iam non trepidi sequestremus."

[73]*Ep.* 225, 9 (467): "nam unum eorum praecipuae auctoritatis et spiritalium studiorum virum, sanctum Hilarium Arelatensis episcopum, sciat beatitudo tua admiratorem sectatoremque in aliis omnibus tuae esse doctrinae. . . ."

southern Gaul that the criterion of continuity lay very near the heart of the doctrinal ideals espoused by the Gallic monks.

So from the writings of Prosper and Hilary one gains a picture of the status of Augustine's doctrine of grace in southern Gaul at the end of the 420s. On the one hand, it had ardent defenders like Prosper and Hilary; one might also recall that a bishop from a more northern area of Gaul, Germanus of Auxerre, was sent to Britain to combat Pelagianism in 429. On the other hand, a significant and influential number of Gaul's Christians, Cassian prominent among them, motivated neither by explicit antipathy to Augustinian teaching nor by adherence to Pelagian doctrine, saw the extreme limits of Augustine's anti-Pelagian predestinarianism as exegetically and theologically new. Two forces collided: the manifest prestige of Augustine as champion of orthodoxy—all the more so in the immediate aftermath of the Pelagian controversy—and the monastic tendency to equate innovation with heterodoxy. From this collision would emerge over the course of the following decades a new polarization of theology in Gaul, and, in the minds of some at least, a new heresy.

Augustine responded to Prosper and Hilary in 428-429 with a bipartite work consisting of *De praedestinatione sanctorum* and *De dono perseverantiae*. In the first of these he argued for the gratuity of the beginning of faith (*initium fidei*) against those who would argue for some movement toward faith on the part of the human will prior to a special gift of grace. From a series of biblical prooftexts, with brief references to Cyprian and Ambrose, Augustine built his case for the utter prevenience of the movement of grace, and thus for predestination. Those in Provence troubled by his writings were "novos haereticos" against whom one had to defend the faith "nova solicitudine,"[74] he argued in the *De dono perseverantiae*. For

---

[74]*De dono persev.* XXIII, 64.

Augustine, predestination became in this work something like the *sine qua non* of orthodoxy. To dissent from it was simply to be a Pelagian, captive to human pride:

> Therefore, just as the other gifts are to be preached so that the one who preaches them may be heard obediently, so predestination must be preached, so that the one who obediently hears it may glory not in man, and thus not in himself, but in the Lord. For this too is a command of God, and to hear this command obediently—"let him who glories glory in the Lord"—is a gift of God. . . . I do not hesitate to say that one who does not have this gift possesses in vain any others he may have. We pray that the Pelagians may receive this gift, but that our own might have it even more.[75]

Such were the battle lines drawn by the aged Augustine in his penultimate theological work: one could easily conclude from his words that orthodoxy and predestinationism were coterminous. After Augustine's death in 430, Prosper and those who followed him continued to make precisely this judgment.

The increased radicalization of the Augustinian position by Prosper began around 431 with his journey to Rome to obtain from Pope Celestine I a condemnation of his opponents in Gaul. Celestine's letter addressed to the bishops of southern Gaul in May of 431 adopted a cautious line, telling the

---

[75]Ibid., XXIV, 66: "Sicut ergo cetera praedicanda sunt, ut qui ea praedicat obedienter audiatur, ita praedestinatio praedicanda est, ut qui obedienter haec audit, non in homine, ac per hoc nec in se ipso, sed in Domino glorietur, quia et hoc Dei praeceptum est et hoc praeceptum obedienter audire, id est, ut qui gloriatur in Domino glorietur, similiter ut cetera, Dei donum est . . . Quod donum qui non habet, non dubito dicere, alia quaecumque habet, vaniter habet. Hoc Pelagiani, optamus, ut habeant; isti autem nostri ut plenius habeant. "

bishops that the teaching of doctrine is their affair, warning them not to leave preachers to their own fancies, and instructing them to exercise authority and to oppose doctrinal novelties.[76] To the letter is appended a series of *auctoritates* taken either from Celestine's predecessors or from African councils whose decisions had found favor in Rome. It ends with the injunction to hold to such teachings of the apostolic see in doubtful matters.

Around the same time Prosper wrote two polemical works; one was a poem, the *Carmen de ingratis*, which was a ringing denunciation of Pelagian teaching on grace and of the "ingrates" who professed it. The second work, more pointedly polemical, took aim at Cassian. This *De gratia Dei et libero arbitrio contra Collatorem* set out to refute twelve propositions culled from *Conlatio* XIII (which one suspects was being circulated independently from the other Conferences).[77] The work is addressed to Cassian ("vir quidam sacerdotalis") in the second person throughout. Prosper demonstrates that, apart from the catholic meaning of the first proposition, Cassian's remaining eleven theses are either Pelagian or aid the Pelagian cause and "disrupt the peace of the victorious Church by again taking up petty questions from the school of those condemned."[78] Prosper concludes, having shown that the "reprehensores sancti Augustini" made hollow objections, impugned correct doctrine, and defended corruptions.[79] Cassian's suggestions of a *bona voluntas* or a capacity of human free choice apart from

---

[76]PL 50: 528ff.

[77]Prosper finds the offensive passages "in libro cuius praenotatio est, de Protectione Dei," and makes no clear reference to other *Conlationes*. Cf. *Contr. Coll.* II, 1 (PL 51: 218A).

[78]Ibid., XIX, 1 (col. 265C): ". . . et pacem victricis Ecclesiae, resumptis de damnatorum schola quaestiunculis, inquietant."

[79]Ibid., XXIII (col. 276B).

the special help of grace meet, throughout the treatise, with the accusation of Pelagianism. Such was the rigid Augustinianism championed in Gaul after 430.[80]

On the other side, which one may call the native monastic-theological culture of southern Gaul, one finds continued expression of the objections noted in Prosper's and Hilary's letters to Augustine. If Cassian's *Conlatio* XIII was circulated as a tract, its dissemination would indicate some attempt at galvanizing resistance to the more radical aspects of the Augustinian scheme. A more certain instance of such resistance may be found in the *Commonitorium* of Vincent of Lérins, written c. 434. While Vincent's language is not on the whole polemical and the recurring theme of the treatise is the fullness and continuity of Christian doctrine, at certain points in the text an opponent comes briefly into view whose main offenses seem to be (1) a misleading use of Scripture, which is used to support (2) a novel doctrine of grace.

In *Commonitorium* 26 Vincent refers to the devil's use of Scripture to tempt Christ and notes that the same phenomenon has continued and is now carried on by the members of the devil, i.e., heretics, toward the members of Christ. "But if anyone should ask one of the heretics who urges such things upon him: 'Whence do you prove, whence do you teach that I should abandon the ancient and universal faith of the Catholic Church?' he will immediately say, 'For it is written.' Then he will set before you a thousand testimonies, examples, and authorities . . . by the new and

---

[80]Similar teaching, not directed at Cassian, is found in the *Hypomnesticon Augustini contra Pelagianos sive Caelestianos haereticos*, which is very likely also the work of Prosper. Cf. John E. Chisholm, *The Pseudo-Augustinian Hypomnesticon Against the Pelagians and Celestians*, Paradosis nos. 20 and 21 (Fribourg: University Press, 1967 and 1980). The second volume contains a thorough critical text.

immoral interpretation of which the unfortunate soul might fall from the catholic fortress into the depths of heresy."[81] And as to the nature of this heresy:

> They dare to promise and to teach that in their Church, that is, in the small circle of their communion, there is a sort of great, special, and wholly personal grace of God such that without any labor, without any zeal, without any effort, even if they neither ask, seek, or knock, those who belong to their number are so divinely arranged that, borne by angelic hands, i.e., preserved by angelic protection, they can never dash their foot against a stone, that is, they can never be scandalized.[82]

Vincent's comments are pointed. Such a doctrine of grace reduces the catholic Church to a *conventiculum*, a select *numerus* upon whom grace has been poured. The biblical reference to asking, seeking, and knocking may in fact echo a passage from Augustine's *De dono*

---

[81]*Comm.* 26, 6-7 (CCL 64: 185, 21-28): "Ac si quis interroget quempiam haereticorum talia sibi persuadentem: Unde probas, unde doces, quod ecclesiae catholicae universalem et antiquam fidem dimittere debeam? Statim ille: Scriptum est enim. Et continuo mille testimonia, mille exempla, mille auctoritates parat . . . quibus novo et malo more interpretatis, ex arce catholica in haereseos barathrum infelix anima praecipitetur."

[82]Ibid. 26, 8-9 (185, 30-37): "Audent etenim polliceri et docere quod in Ecclesia sua, id est, in communionis suae conventiculo, magna et specialis ac plane personalis quaedam sit Dei gratia, adeo ut sine ullo labore, sine ullo studio, sine ulla industria, etiamsi nec petant, nec quaerant, nec pulsent, quicumque illi ad numerum suum pertinent, tamen ita divinitus dispensentur ut angelicis evecti manibus, id est, angelica protectione servati, nunquam possint offendere ad lapidem pedem suum, id est, nunquam scandalizari."

perseverantiae .[83] Already for Vincent in 434, whether in fact or in his own perception, aspects of a radical Augustinianism were being pushed in an elitist and quietist direction. Vincent does not hesitate to label those who hold such views "heretics."

In *Commonitorium* 28 Vincent prescribes a remedy for heretical excesses, following his usual rule of consensus:

> Indeed, whatever a person has thought—whether he be a saint and a learned man, whether a bishop, whether a confessor and martyr—which is beyond or even contrary to all, should be kept among his own personal, hidden, and private opinions, quite apart from the authority of the common, public, and general opinion, lest, at the greatest peril for our eternal salvation, having rejected the ancient truth of universal dogma according to the sacrilege of heretics and the custom of schismatics, we should follow the new error of one man.[84]

The only heretic mentioned by name in this connection is the Pelagian Julian of Eclanum. Still, one can see that a new heresy, whose tenets seem precisely the opposite of Pelagianism, has also attracted the attention of Vincent.

---

[83]*De dono persev.* XXIII, 64: "Adtentant ergo quomodo falluntur, qui putant esse a nobis, non dari nobis, ut petamus, quaeramus, pulsemus. "

[84]*Comm.* 28, 8 (CCL 64: 187, 33-40): "Quidquid vero, quamvis ille sanctus et doctus, quamvis episcopus, quamvis confessor et martyr, praeter omnes aut etiam contra omnes senserit, id inter proprias et occultas et privatas opiniunculas a communis et publicae ac generalis sententiae auctoritate secretum sit; ne cum summo aeternae salutis periculo, juxta sacrilegam haereticorum et schismaticorum consuetudinem, universalis dogmatis antiqua veritate dimissa unius hominis novitium sectemur errorem."

The enigmatic work known as the *Praedestinatus*, not of Gallic provenance, gives further evidence that an extreme version of radically predestinarian Augustinianism was taken to be heresy in some quarters. It is thought to have been written by Arnobius the Younger at Rome between 432 and 435.[85] The work consists of three books. The first is a catalogue of ninety heresies, beginning with Simon Magus and ending with the three most recent, namely, Pelagianism, Nestorianism, and that having "the name of the *praedestinati*."[86] This last heresy, which is, says the author, carried on under the name of Bishop Augustine, teaches that divine election or reprobation has nothing to do with human behavior and that grace precedes the free choice of the will, so that one receives before asking, finds before seeking, and is opened to before knocking.[87] The second book purports to be a pamphlet circulated by the *praedestinati* falsely under the name of Augustine, and the third refutes this pamphlet.

By the mid-430s, then, some two decades after the Pelagian controversy, a polarized theological situation existed in Gaul. On one side was the condemned teaching of Pelagius or, rather more often, its caricature: the denial of a need for grace and an excessive optimism regarding human capacities for free choice and good works. On the other side stood the radicalized version of Augustinianism attacked in the *Commonitorium*, with an echo in Italy in the *Praedestinatus*. This too may well have been a caricature, but certainly one very much alive in the minds of many in Gaul.

---

[85]Arguments for the date and authorship of the *Praedestinatus* can be found in Abel, "Le 'Praedestinatus' et le pélagianisme," 5-25. The text of the work appears in PL 53: 587-672.

[86]PL 53: 620.

[87]Ibid.

Those in southern Gaul influenced by the monastic writers of Lérins and Marseilles most probably saw both these two stances as theologically defective.[88] Pelagianism, officially condemned and easily refuted, was a simple enough target. The heresy of the *praedestinati*, however, was all the more insidious because, first, it could advance under the banner of anti-Pelagianism and claim Augustine's prestige and, second, because it seemed to encourage passivity in a place whose theological culture and historical situation demanded zealous effort. After the mid-430s the polemical battle submerges, only to surface again in the 470s in the affair that brought Faustus of Riez to write the treatise *De gratia*.

Faustus and the Circumstances of the De gratia

Faustus of Riez (c.405-c.490) was by the seventh decade of the fifth century a widely revered, though somewhat controversial, figure in the Gallic church. Probably a Briton by birth, he had entered the monastery at Lérins around 424 and was elevated to its abbacy c.433, thus becoming the community's third abbot.[89] He was therefore a younger contemporary of Vincent, whose *Commonitorium* dates from around 434, and a good deal younger than Cassian, whose death is generally placed around 435.

After having been elevated to the see of Riez around 457, Faustus gained fame both as a preacher and as a writer of letters.[90] More to the point

---

[88]Cf. Simonetti, "Il *De gratia*," 125ff.

[89]Our only primary sources for Faustus's life are his own letters, edited by Engelbrecht in CSEL 21, some letters of Sidonius Apollinaris (*Ep.* VII, IX, XI), and the *Carmen eucharisticum ad Faustum Reiensem episcopum* (PL 58: 718-22), also of Sidonius. The most complete critical discussion of the dating of Faustus's life is in Weigel's dated but useful *Faustus of Riez*. We have accepted his dates as probable.

[90]While the critical status of Faustus's letters is relatively sure, the question of his homiletical output is completely unsettled. The latest attempt at a

of our present discussion, he also wrote a few theological treatises.
Sometime during his episcopacy he wrote a polemical treatise, *De spiritu
sancto libri duo,* against "Arian and Macedonian" errors.[91] In the late 460s,
in response to questions of one of his correspondents, Faustus wrote a small
tract that, by alleging the corporeality of the soul, became the source of some
controversy, though it did nothing to impugn Faustus's reputation for
orthodoxy.[92]

The chain of events that led to the writing of the *De gratia* began in
471 or 472 when a priest, Lucidus, came to Faustus's attention.[93] Lucidus
seems to have come into danger of disciplinary action by the bishops of Gaul
in connection with his doctrine of grace. He had apparently requested, either
in person or by letter, a letter from Faustus on the matter. Faustus's reply,

---

solution may be found in the critical edition of the so-called pseudo-Eusebian
homilies in CCL 101-101B. The editor, Fr. Glorie, regards these homilies,
formerly attributed by many to Faustus, as having been written or redacted by
Caesarius of Arles or one of his disciples, then collected at a later date. Glorie's
thesis has not been universally accepted (cf. Griffe, "Nouveau plaidoyer pour
Fauste de Riez," 187-92), and the matter remains in doubt.

[91]CSEL 21: 101-57.

[92]In this epistle (*Ep.* 3, CSEL 21: 168-81), Faustus asserted that all
things outside of God, whether heavenly or earthly, were "corporeal" (*corporea*).
The notion is drawn from Cassian's *Conl.* VII, 13, which he cited at length.
Faustus did not mean, as he expressly asserted, the kind of physical materiality
one customarily associates with the term; rather, it is intended as a statement of
divine transcendence over against the finite and contingent character of creation.
Nevertheless, his imprecision occasioned a response by the more philosophically
astute Claudianus Mamaertus, whose *De statu animae* (CSEL 11: 18-197) refuted
the tract at length, without identifying its author.

[93]Our only sources for information about Lucidus are the letter written to
him by Faustus (*Ep.* 1, CSEL 21: 161f) and Lucidus's letter of retraction (*Ep.* 2,
CSEL 21: 165f), which seems to have been written by Faustus. Koch, *Der heilige
Faustus,* 18 n. 1, says that Lucidus "ohne Zweifel war . . . Priester der Diözese
Riez," but this is in fact speculation.

alternately sharp and conciliatory, shows that he had previously tried to dissuade Lucidus from what were regarded as heretical views:

> How can I speak of this interpretation with your Unanimity through letters, as you wish, since I was not at all able to draw you back to the way of truth in person by many persuasive and humble conversations? When we speak of God's grace and human obedience we must always take a position such that neither prone to the right nor rebellious on the left we rather walk the royal way. I marvel that your Veneration has uttered what no one at all by way of religious profession has written or preached contrary to the catholic faith, although there have been very many who gloried in the Christian name and believed that their various profane errors should be set down in written documents.[94]

One might hear in this the echoes of the allegation that predestinarian views were being falsely ascribed to Augustine. As the essential content of the "royal way," Faustus enjoined Lucidus to attach Christian obedience to divine grace and to shun any doctrine of predestination that denies human labor, for this is just as dangerous as Pelagius's doctrine.[95]

---

[94]*Ep.* 1 (CSEL 21: 161-62): "quid possum de hoc sensu, sicut vis, cum unanimitate tua per litteras loqui, cum te presens multa et blanda et humili conlocutione numquam potuerim ad viam veritatis adtrahere? loquentes ergo de gratia dei et oboedientia hominis id omnimodo statuere debemus, ut neque proni in sinistram neque inportuni in dexteram regia magis gradiamur via. illud autem venerationem tuam dixisse miratus sum, quod nullus umquam sub religiosa professione contra catholicam fidem vel scripserit vel praedicaverit, cum plurimi multiplices et profanos errores suos etiam scriptorum monumentis crediderint inserendos, qui tamen Christiano nomine gloriabantur."

[95]Ibid. (162).

Faustus's letter continued with a list of six anathemas, first condemning those who, "among the lingering impieties of Pelagius," deny the need of grace, then denouncing several assertions of absolute predestination.[96] To these anathemas and to the explication that followed, Faustus demanded Lucidus's subscription prior to the matter's coming before a council of bishops. This council was the annual episcopal conference at Arles in 473.[97] Lucidus seems to have refused to subscribe, for the bishops condemned his doctrine. A *libellus subiectionis,* probably also from Faustus's hand, was issued that contained a list of anathemas slightly different from the first, probably reflecting matters that came to light during the council's deliberations.[98] Lucidus now put his name both to Faustus's original letter and to the conciliar *libellus.*

The bishops of the council of Arles commissioned Faustus to write a treatise setting forth in detail the consensus of the Church concerning grace, to be submitted at the next annual council of Arles. Prior to this next council, however, another gathering took place at Lyons, of which we know almost nothing. From the witness of Faustus's prefatory letter to the metropolitan of Arles, Leontius, we know only that the council of Lyons dealt with new errors which may or may not have had to do with Lucidus: "in which treatise the synod of Lyons has driven out the newly discovered errors that somehow came about after the subscription of the council of

---

[96]Ibid. The phrase "reliquas Pelagii impietates" mirrors a term used by Prosper to describe Gallic opposition to Augustine's teaching (*Ep.* 225, 465): "in istis Pelagianae reliquiis pravitatis . . ."

[97]Denzinger, 330-42.

[98]*Ep.* 2 (CSEL 21: 165-66).

Arles."[99] The treatise *De gratia*, therefore, represents Faustus's theological

exposition of two episcopal synods' deliberations. Despite any idiosyncrasies

that the work may possess, it is essentially the portrait of what one must

regard as the mainstream, centrist doctrine of grace in southern Gaul in the

latter fifth century. To examine its argument, its sources, and its theological

affirmations is therefore to learn in its historical particularity the nature of

Gallic Christianity at this time.

*   *   *

One must read the *De gratia* against the backdrop of historical and

theological controversy and tension.   Gaul's rapidly disintegrating

sociopolitical order brought about calls in the Christian community for

repentance and moral earnestness, and for political and military resistance. It

further produced a generation of bishops who, while nourished largely on the

rhetoric of contemplation and renunciation, were compelled by events and

inclined by their accustomed civic status to involve themselves in an

immediate and active way in a changing world.   Theologically, the

Arianism—whatever it may have been—of the Goths provided a constant

polemical opponent and the newer heresy, Pelagianism, had allied against

itself both the prestige of the bishop of Hippo and the force of imperial and

ecclesiastical law. At the same time, the fervor of anti-Pelagianism, as

expressed by its champions like Prosper, seemed in the eyes of many to court

the danger of an even newer heresy: predestinationism. Whether a pre-

destinarian heresy existed anywhere but in the minds of its opponents is a fair

question, just as it is for Pelagianism. Nevertheless, a theology that could be

---

[99]Ibid.

perceived as enjoining passivity, even indolence, would appear to be both
novel and repugnant to a theological culture whose heroes and leaders pursued
virtue through ascesis and offered themselves as human barter to barbarian
kings.

One must, further, read the *De gratia* without an anachronistic
evaluation of Augustinianism. The theological culture of southern Gaul,
which took its sustenance from the new monastic foundations under Cassian
and Honoratus, appealed—ostensibly at least—to broad lines of tradition and
consensus. Despite the widespread prestige of Augustine and the presence of
his ardent disciples, the evidence suggests that his theology, particularly on
the question of grace, was not on all points regarded as normative, and
certainly not as a benchmark of orthodoxy. Statements like that of Weigel—
"The Fathers [at Arles and Lyons] were anti-Augustinian by education and
environment and therefore spontaneously Semipelagian"[100]—fail to reflect
the doctrinal configuration of the time. The issue was not so much
Augustinianism against Pelagianism as it was finding a measure of
theological stability in an atmosphere of decadent and extreme alternatives.

---

[100]Weigel, *Faustus of Riez*, 95.

CHAPTER TWO
THE STRUCTURE AND ARGUMENT
OF THE *DE GRATIA*

In the aftermath of the conciliar condemnations of Lucidus at Arles and Lyons in 473-474, Faustus wrote his treatise on grace. Its goal was to clarify the theological rationale which lay behind those condemnations and to persuade the reader of the truth of that doctrine in the face of new errors.[1] The work thus demands to be understood both as a structured, systematic, coherently developed theological presentation and as an argument employing rhetorical techniques. The two categories cannot, of course, be strictly separated, since structure and arrangement contribute to the process of persuasion. In this chapter we shall examine how Faustus constructs and develops his argument.

Such analysis is complicated by the fact that the undergirding structural logic of the *De gratia* is not immediately evident even upon close reading. The most obvious structural division of the work, for example, that of the two books, does not correspond to any major shift in subject matter. Indeed, throughout the treatise Faustus's argument seems to return repeatedly

---

[1]*De grat.*, prol., 4. 22-29.

to a few main points in apparently desultory fashion. Despite such difficulties, however, it is possible to show that in the *De gratia* Faustus has adapted the polemical material taken from the dispute with Lucidus into the form of a coherent treatise which rests upon two broad lines of argument. No attempt will be made to argue for systematic neatness, but only for an identifiable consistency of thought which can be found imbedded in the structure of the text.

Structural Elements

This passage from Faustus's letter to Lucidus in anticipation of the episcopal conference at Arles in 473 provides an important clue to understanding how Faustus came to choose the doctrinal topics that frame the *De gratia*: "Now when you come to us in Christ's name, or when you have been summoned by the holy bishops, then if the Lord allows we will set forth testimonies appropriate to their topics, in which catholic teachings are made clear and their contraries demolished."[2] Faustus drew up for the synod a series of doctrinal *testimonia*, that is, written evidences, which would become a kind of canon against which Lucidus's teaching was to be measured. What were the topics of these *testimonia?* The same letter provides six probable foci in the list of anathemas to which Lucidus is directed to subscribe:

Let him be accursed, who among Pelagius's lingering impieties, contends with condemned presumption that man is born without sin

---

[2]*Ep.* 1 (CSEL 21: 162-3): "Cum autem ad nos in Christi nomine veneris aut cum a sanctis sacerdotibus evocatus fueris, tunc oportuna, si dominus iusserit, locis suis testimonia proferemus, quibus et catholica sunt manifestentur et quae catholicis contraria destruantur."

and able to be saved by labor alone, and who believes that he can be liberated without the grace of God.

... who asserts that a person solemnly baptized with a faithful confession and asserting the catholic faith, who later fell away by the various blandishments and temptations of this world, had perished in Adam and original sin.

... who says that a man is forced into death by God's foreknowledge.

... who says that one who has perished did not receive the ability to be saved.

... who says that a vessel of dishonor cannot arise to become a vessel of honor.

... who says that Christ neither died for all, nor wanted all to be saved.[3]

Because these were the very items on the conciliar agenda regarding Lucidus, they were assuredly the subject matter of at least some of the *testimonia*.

As a result of the council's deliberations came the *libellus subiectionis* to be submitted by Lucidus. Its list of nine condemned propositions corresponds with the earlier anathemas only on four points. The

---

[3]Ibid. (162): "Anathema ergo illi, qui inter reliquas Pelagii inpietates hominem sine peccato nasci et per solum laborem posse salvari damnanda praesumptione contenderit et qui eum sine gratia dei liberari posse crediderit ... qui hominem cum fideli confessione solemniter baptizatum et adserentem catholicam fidem et postmodum per diversa mundi huius oblectamenta et temptamenta prolapsum in Adam et originale peccatum perisse adseruerit ... qui per dei praescientiam hominem deprimi in mortem dixerit ... qui dixerit illum, qui periit, non accepisse, ut salvus esse posset ... qui dixerit quod vas in contumeliam non possit adsurgere, ut sit vas in honorem ... qui dixerit quod Christus non pro omnibus mortuus sit nec omnes homines salvos esse velit."

five new topics may reflect new issues that arose during the conciliar discussions, or they may be the material of additional *testimonia* written by Faustus prior to the council. The nine anathemas of the *libellus* are as follows:

> With you I condemn that interpretation which says that the labor of human obedience is not to be joined to divine grace,
>
> ... that after the fall of the first man the will's power of choice is utterly extinct,
>
> ... that Christ our Lord and savior did not undergo death for the salvation of all,
>
> ... that God's foreknowledge forcibly compels a man to death, or that one who perishes does so by God's will,
>
> ... that whoever falls away after legitimately receiving baptism dies in Adam,
>
> ... that some are assigned to death, others predestined to life,
>
> ... that from Adam until Christ no one from among the nations had been saved by the first grace of God, that is by the law of nature, in anticipation of Christ's coming, because free will perished from everyone in the first parent,
>
> ... that the patriarchs and prophets, or even the greatest of saints before the times of redemption were unable to come into the life of paradise,
>
> ... that fire and hell do not exist.[4]

---

[4]*Ep.* 2 (CSEL 21: 165-6): "damno vobiscum sensum illum, qui dicit laborem humanae obedientiae divinae gratiae non esse iugendum . . . post primi hominis lapsum ex toto arbitrium voluntatis extinctum . . . quod Christus dominus et salvator noster mortem non pro omnium salute susceperit . . . quod praescientia

We do not know the precise reason for the difference between the two sets of anathemas; however, the two lists when combined supply the main doctrinal loci of the chapters of the *De gratia*. All but one of the epistular condemnations—that concerning fire and hell—find their way materially into Faustus's treatise as chapter topics. Of the thirty *capitula* of the *De gratia*, eighteen may be said to have been drawn from the two epistles. These polemics, therefore, account directly or indirectly for the majority of the doctrinal components that define the structure of the work: I. 1, 3, 7, 8, 10-14, 16-18, and II. 2, 3, 5, 10-12.

Of the remaining twelve chapters, eight (I. 4, 5, 6, 9, and II. 1, 4, 6, 7) concern themselves directly with the exegesis of problematic biblical passages. Such exegetical sections may also have been among the *testimonia* compiled by Faustus for the councils at Arles and Lyon, but this cannot be proved. The four remaining chapters consist of a polemic against Pelagius's baptismal doctrine (I. 2), two replies to particular species of defective doctrines of free will (I. 15, II. 8), and a reply to a heresy centered on the notion of *imago Dei* (II. 9).

From a structural view, the elements of the *De gratia* thus fall into three categories. The core probably consists of *testimonia* compiled by Faustus, corresponding to the condemnations found in the two epistles of 471/2 and 473/4. The second main group of topics are the eight chapters of

---

dei hominem violenter conpellat ad mortem vel quod dei pereant voluntate, qui
pereunt . . . quod post acceptum legitime baptismum in Adam moriatur, quicumque
deliquerit . . . alios deputatos ad mortem alios ad vitam prae-
destinatos . . . ab Adam usque ad Christum nullos ex gentibus per primam dei
gratiam, id est per legem naturae in adventum Christi fuisse salvatos eo, quod
liberum arbitrium ex omnibus in primo parente perdiderit . . . patriarchas ac
prophetas vel summos quosque sanctorum etiam ante redemptionis tempora in
paradisi habitatione deguisse . . . ignes et inferna non esse."

biblical exegesis, which may also have originated in the context of the conciliar polemics.[5] Third come four chapters of a topical nature. The *De gratia*, then, represents a redaction of all these loci according to the needs of Faustus's organizational scheme.

In terms of its literary genre, this treatise occupies a curious position between polemical tractate and systematic treatise, with frequent homiletic or hortatory overtones. Yet on its own testimony, as we shall see, it purports to be primarily an appeal to the scriptural record. The polemical aspect of the text is the most readily apparent, since the work was occasioned by a controversial situation. But to characterize the work simply as polemic is to miss the real force of the work as an expression of a positive theological stance. In summarizing the content and argument of the *De gratia,* we shall gain some appreciation of this stance.

The Treatise and Its Argument

The *De gratia* was written in two books, of eighteen and twelve chapters respectively, and was prefaced with a short introductory letter to Leontius, the metropolitan of Arles who had summoned and presided over the episcopal council. This prefatory letter gives in brief scope the central concerns that control Faustus's writing of the treatise. These concerns are both positive and negative.

---

[5]Evidence of an original setting in the polemic against Lucidus, and perhaps also of a hasty redaction of the treatise, may be found in the frequent lapse into use of the second-person singular in the course of argument. Such passages, which contrast with the impersonal and third-person constructions of most of the treatise, may be either vestiges of writings directed against a single opponent or merely Faustus's rhetorical use of an imagined interlocutor.

Faustus puts forward as the controlling positive metaphor of the interplay of grace and human effort the relationship between a patron or lord and a servant. This image in fact becomes something of a topos in the body of the treatise: "One takes up the task of asserting grace competently and wholesomely when he adjoins the obedience of a servant's labor, just as if a subservient footman might cling inseparably to his patron or lord . . . just as it is unfitting for a helmsman's rower to fail him, or a bishop's attendant, or a commander's soldier, so it is fitting that grace and its foster child obedience should be inseparably linked together by servitude."[6]

One must, in order to do justice both to divine aid and to human effort, tread a precarious *via regia*, on either side of which the dangers of heresy threaten. Faustus's words show his awareness that some aspects of the doctrinal climate of Gaul, still in the shadow of the Pelagian controversy and the campaign of Prosper, incline toward one side of that royal way, and so a more negative concern shows itself; Faustus himself had to avoid being tainted by the appearance of Pelagian sympathies:

> . . . since Pelagius impiously proclaimed the task of building a tower of pride to heaven, we deemed it necessary to summarize and refute his blasphemies with a brief discourse, lest perhaps one who excludes the gift of labor, that is, the precept of the lawgiver, when we are asserting that God's mercy must be furthered by faith and works, might unknowingly connect a catholic voice to Pelagius's

---

[6]*De gratia*, prol., 3. 18-21; 4. 4-7: "studium asserendae gratiae conpetenter et salubriter suscipit qui oboedientiam famuli laboris adiungit, tamquam si patrono vel domino inseparabiliter pedisequus minister inhaereat . . . sicut deesse non convenit gubernatori remigem suum, sacerdoti ministrum suum, imperatori militem suum, ita oportet ut gratia alumna oboedientia inseparabili servitute conexa sit."

sense of discretion. Then, having left the royal way by falling to
the right, he might believe that we are falling to the left, and by
speaking of labor as the servant of grace we may seem to place a
stumbling block before the feet of the blind.[7]

The way to proceed, Faustus tells Leontius, is by a straightforward
appeal to the witness of the authoritative texts, the *testimonia*: "May it not
offend those who delight in the ornaments of words that we, content with the
strength of the testimonies, have set forth the light of truth without
sublimity of speech."[8]

On Faustus's own evidence, then, the work seeks, on grounds of the
biblical witness, to follow the mainstream course in setting forth the doctrine
of grace. The subtle allusion to one who has left the road "by falling to the
right" underscores our   earlier assertion that for some at least, predestinarianism appeared as a pressing danger.   Faustus's aversion to the
extremes of left and right and his appeal to the notion of a continuous center
of tradition, may show the mark of the Lerinian theological ethos upon his
dogmatic theology.   Indeed, since the *De gratia* represents the consensus of
the bishops of southern Gaul, one may say that the values cherished at Lérins
coincided with those of the wider Gallic church.

---

[7]Ibid., 4. 9-18:   "... quia Pelagius ... impie praedicavit elationis
turrem in caelum conatus erigere, blasphemias eius brevi sermone praestringere et
confutare necessarium iudicavimus, ne forte is, qui donum laboris, id est
praeceptum iubentis excludit, asserentibus nobis, quod dei misericordia fide et
operibus promerenda est, catholicam vocem ad Pelagii sensum discretionis
nescius adplicaret et omissa via regia in dexteram cadens in sinistram declinare
nos crederet, et, dum de labore servo gratiae loquimur, offendiculum ante pedes
caeci opposuisse videremur."

[8]Ibid., 4. 24-27:   "non autem aliquos, qui verborum phaleris delectantur,
offendat, quod testimoniorum virtute contenti absque sublimitate sermonis lucem
protulimus veritatis ..."

Of the eighteen chapters of book one of the treatise, we lack the latter part of I. 14 and virtually all of I. 15; this is one of three significant lacunae in the extant text of the work.[9] The first two chapters are aimed against Pelagianism; the remaining sixteen, and in fact most of the remainder of the work, are directed against a species of predestinarian teaching. A summary of the contents of the chapters follows.

Book One

I. 1, "That the Interpretation of Pelagius, Which Denies Grace, Must Be Done Away With": here Faustus criticizes Pelagius in a manner which is both vituperative and cautious. On the one hand, Pelagius "has striven in the lingering abominations of his doctrine to affirm, with damnable pride, that human labor can prevail without grace."[10] Faustus spares neither invective nor ad hominem arguments; Pelagius is a "pestifer doctor," lacking both piety and judgment. On the other hand, even in responding to such a notorious heretic Faustus takes care to do so "ex parte aliqua in medium"[11] because of the danger of a total rejection of the role of human effort. Response to Pelagianism cannot take the form of mere reaction. Faustus's critique of Pelagius is therefore qualified to a small degree by his insistence

---

[9] Regrettably, the sole extant manuscript witness to the *De gratia* is the codex conserved in Paris, Bibliothèque Nationale, 2166, dating from the ninth century. Engelbrecht, in his critical edition of the text, cites alternate readings from various printed versions. Other lacunae are from the mid-fourth paragraph of II. 6 to the third-last of II. 8 (thus eliminating all of II. 7) and from the mid-second paragraph of II. 11 until to ninth-last of II. 12. It would appear that the nine paragraphs of II. 12 make up almost the whole of the chapter.

[10] I. 1. 6, 21-23: "...inter reliquas dogmatis sui abominationes etiam laborem hominis valere posse sine gratia elatione damnabili adfirmare conatus est."

[11] I. 1. 6, 24.

upon characterizing the opposite pole—advocates of a *sola gratia* position—
as imbibing the same heretical spirit as the Pelagians: "They hiss with the
spirit of one serpent."[12]

The *via regia*, the royal mean invoked by the author in the prefatory
letter, becomes early on in the treatise a kind of leitmotif that allows him to
stigmatize radical predestinarian teaching by making it the equal and opposite
error of Pelagianism. Similarly, Faustus makes good rhetorical use of the
Chalcedonian Christological decisions which were reached in his own
lifetime. The respective positions of, if you will, *solo labore* and *sola gratia*
are likened to doctrines regarding Christ as either solely human or solely
divine.[13] Faustus invokes the Virgilian metaphor of Scylla and Charybdis to
warn of the heretical dangers threatening on left and right for unwary
sailors.[14] As an argumentative technique, such bipolarity is applied not only
to left and right, but to another crucial juxtaposition: creator and redeemer.
Proper doctrine requires equal reverence for God under both aspects, and
Pelagius reveals his essential impiety by denying both: by asserting Adam's
original mortality he attaches death to the creator, and by denying original sin
he trivializes the redeemer's work.[15] By instituting a fundamentally bipolar

---

[12]I. 1. 7, 11-12: ". . . spiritu unius serpentis insibilant."

[13]I. 1. 8, 5-7: "pari modo in petram scandali offendunt vel illi, qui
Christum dominum solum deum, vel illi, qui solum hominem amissa discretionis
luce asserere praesumpserunt."

[14]I. 1. 7, 24-28: "sed quia velut temerarii remiges sine magistro
inexplorato mari vela conmittunt ac temperare moderamina nesciunt et
gubernacula tractare non norunt, hic tamquam in Scyllae male dextrum fertur
periclum, ille in laeuum Charybdis tendit abruptum."

[15]I. 1. 11, 2-4: "quod cum dicit, duplici impietate blasphemat, dum et
mortem ad auctoris invidiam revocat et negando originale vinculum gratiam
reparatoris evacuat."

scheme, then, I. 1 becomes, as we shall see, programmatic for book one and to some extent for the entire treatise. While the formally theological purpose of I. 1 is to exclude Pelagianism and to warn of its opposite, the chapter's more important strategic purpose is to establish a rhetoric of the middle, a kind of doctrinal Archimedian point from which to evaluate competing views.

I. 2, "Against Pelagius's Objection, in Which He Says Infants Do Not Need Baptism," brings the broader condemnation of Pelagius into narrower focus by responding to a putative statement of Pelagius about baptism. From Pelagius's mouth comes the question how baptized parents could transmit original sin to their offspring, since they themselves have been cleansed from sin. Faustus answers first with a distinction between generation and regeneration, the former having to do with parents' agency and with the concupiscence by which original sin is transmitted. Parents can transmit only what pertains to natural generation. Lest he be accused of denigrating marriage, Faustus affirms his praise of matrimony as derived from a blessing while condemning the stain of concupiscence which has deprived marriage of its original chastity. Faustus's acceptance here of Augustine's position on the transmission of original sin through concupiscence bolsters his anti-Pelagian credentials.[16]

This chapter marks the end of Faustus's abbreviated refutation of Pelagius. It bears repeating here that Pelagius's notoriety as heresiarch in the fifth-century West made him an easy target. He had been amply refuted by Augustine and censured by Church and empire. The fact that only about 10 percent of the *De gratia* is aimed toward Pelagianism should not, therefore, lead one to suppose that Faustus is disingenuous in claiming to pursue a

---

[16]Augustine had similarly taught that parents could only pass on what they possess by nature, not by grace. Cf. Augustine, *De nupt. et conc.* II, 34, 58; I, 19, 21 and *De grat. Chr. et de pecc. orig.* II, 40, 45; II, 39, 44.

centrist course. It would be more surprising if he felt compelled to rehearse every argument of the anti-Pelagian case. Rather, the two initial chapters suffice for the author's purpose, namely, to establish his own ethos as a mouthpiece of orthodoxy.[17]

I. 3, "Against What They Say: That Every Person Is Saved by Grace Alone, Without Any Labor," marks the beginning of Faustus's extended attack upon the anti-Pelagian, predestinarian camp. It also signals the start of a notably impassioned engagement of Faustus's argument. Two theses present themselves as the objectionable core of the defective view: first, the assertion that grace is granted to some but denied to others, and second, that devoted service is not required for worship of God. Faustus's answer to the first thesis is essentially a charge of inconsistency: its proponents rely on slogans like "everything is by grace alone,"[18] but they deny this by limiting the scope of grace to only a part of the human race. Indeed, they deny the gift of grace, just as Pelagius does. It would be more fitting that such a slogan exalting grace be applied to Faustus's scheme, for those who hold his view regard the benefits of grace as "extended not to a part, but to the whole, of the human race."[19] Having ironically turned the slogan on its head, Faustus cites Gen. 2:5 to heighten the inconsistency of his opponents' position: How could one take a respite from work and lapse into leisure, when even in Paradise Adam was commanded to tend the earth?

---

[17]Simonetti, "Il *De gratia*," 128, makes the important point that while a denial of divine aid would be unacceptable even to a superficially educated Christian, the *sola gratia* position could easily accommodate itself to traditional language and piety, and therefore required a more detailed refutation.

[18]I. 3. 14, 26-7: "totum, inquiunt, solius est gratiae."

[19]I. 3. 14, 28-29: ". . . qui non in partem, sed in totum genus humanum gratiae beneficia fatemur extendi."

Faustus's first use of Scripture in the antipredestinarian argument is significant in its reference to the primal human condition. The duty of service has always been a necessary constituent of human existence in the divine plan, and to deny its role is to err at the most basic anthropological level of creation.

In the second part of I. 3 Faustus first uses the creator-redeemer pairing to carry his attack from the realm of creation to that of redemption, then argues from the standpoint of Christian religious practice. First, he shows that the predestinarian scheme truncates the doctrine of redemption as surely as it devalues created human capacities:

> When they say "everything is from God's grace," who is not inclined with the affect of his whole heart toward so revered a term? Yet when we answer: "Clearly everything is from grace, but the creator and redeemer offers it to all and pours it out for the salvation of all," to this they retreat far from the path of piety and presume to answer: "The savior did not grant it to all, for he did not die for all." Behold: immediately in the second statement appears the impugner of grace, who in the first was thought to be its champion.[20]

Second, he pursues the argument from the Christian practice of prayer. To pray is incumbent upon the Christian; yet if one's fate has been sealed by predestination, the biblical exhortations to prayer are unjust, and

---

[20]I. 3. 15, 10-17: "Cum dixerint: totum gratiae dei est, quis non ad tam reverendum nomen omni cordis inclinetur affectu? sed cum responderimus: totum plane gratiae est, sed omnibus eam offert atque ingerit ad salutem omnium conditor ac redemptor, ad haec illi longe a pietatis tramite recendentes respondere praesumunt: non eam salvator omnibus dedit, quia nec pro omnibus mortuus est. ecce statim in secundis apparet gratiae impugnator, qui in primis putabatur assertor."

this particular exercise of piety is fruitless: "Do you think that I should knock and then despair of its being opened to me?"[21] The twin pillars of Faustus's argument, then, are what one might call (1) the "doctrinal," i.e., that which argues for the necessity of human action in the orders both of creation and of redemption, and (2) the "practical," which focuses upon the disastrous effect of predestinarian teaching upon Christian religious practice.

Chapters I. 4, I. 5, and I. 6 are three of the straightforwardly exegetical chapters of the treatise. That is, they begin by posing a problematic text or series of texts, then resolve the problems by exegetical argument, usually by using Faustus's favored technique of amassing other biblical texts to illumine the one in question. In this case, the three chapters are grouped immediately after Faustus's refutation of the *sola gratia* position and are aimed at passages that have been adduced—perhaps by Lucidus—in favor of such a position. While one might suppose that Faustus is merely appending a series of prooftexts to his own doctrinal analysis, Simonetti argues that the opposite is true. For him, the discussion of such passages constitutes the fabric of Faustus's discourse, the structure that supports the more technically dogmatic assertions in the treatise.[22] It is difficult to say whether Simonetti is correct on this score, but, in his favor, the interplay and juxtaposition of scriptural passages certainly permeate the fabric of the treatise, even if they might not supply its structure as such.

In I. 4, "The Works of the Law are Destroyed and Those of Grace Commended, or, Against What They Most Unlearnedly Propose as Evidences

---

[21]I. 3. 16, 9-10: "pulsare debere me iudicas et aperiendum mihi esse desperas?"

[22]Simonetti, "Il *De gratia*," 135, further characterizes Faustus as the one writer who more than any other in the controversy over grace was able to take account of all the pertinent biblical passages.

for the Assertion of Grace Alone," Faustus answers a number of prooftexts
that had been adduced in favor of a *sola gratia* position, among them Rom.
4:4f. and 11:6. Against these are counterposed other New Testament texts,
such as Jas. 2:17f. and several Pauline citations that commend human works
even to those under the regime of grace. Scripture proscribes not works in
general but only the works of the law, which are really to be identified with
the pride of the Jews.[23]

In I. 5, Faustus interprets 1 Cor. 15:10 as Paul's threefold
perspective on grace and human works. It is in a sense an exegesis of the
Apostle's own psychology. First Paul, as piously submissive, credits the
origins of his Christian existence to grace ("by God's grace I am what I am"),
then, teaching obedience, he gives credit to his own labor ("I labored more
than all of them"), and in the end he speaks of the cooperation of the two
("yet not I, but God's grace with me").[24] Faustus acknowledges that the two
are not in every place portrayed in such a balanced way but, citing an exegetical rule of "Bishop Augustine," asserts that not all on which Scripture is
silent should be denied.[25] In his summary, Faustus inveighs against those
who rebel against the Apostle and against Christ by removing both service
and prayer. He charges that those who do so have avoided Pelagius's doctrine
only to fall "ad Manichaeorum dogma pestiferum"[26] in their denial of free
will.

---

[23] I. 4. 18, 26-7: "opera legis destrui legimus, cum Iudaeorum conprimit
elationem . . ."

[24] I. 5. 20, 3-6.

[25] I. 5. 20, 11-14: "cum unum sine altero dicitur, tacetur alterum, non
negatur secundum illam regulam, quam antistes Augustinus insinuat: non omnia
quae tacentur negantur."

[26] I. 5. 21, 1.

Faustus's citation of Augustine here marks the first of two times the bishop of Hippo's name is invoked. More significantly, though, it is the second time his teaching is used. We recall that Faustus clearly regarded Augustine's doctrine of concupiscence and original sin to be important ammunition against Pelagius in I. 2. Now Faustus cites this curious *regula* to argue against the other extreme. The author certainly wishes to claim Augustine as a fellow occupant of the centrist position for rhetorical purposes, regardless of whether he actually was thought to be such.[27] The rule itself commands interest because it does in fact express a main tenet of Faustus's approach to exegesis, namely, to counterbalance the ostensible extremity of one text by the use of others.

In I. 6 Faustus begins from Eph. 2:8-9: "By grace you have been saved through faith, and this not from yourselves. It is the gift of God, not from works, lest anyone glory." The chapter does not immediately attempt a straightforward interpretation of the passage but uses a number of others to show that faith is itself a kind of work. The fundamental distinction supporting Faustus's argument is that between two *tempora gratiae*, which might best be translated "occasions of grace." Referring to Abraham as Paul's exemplar of faith in Gal. 3:6, the author notes that the occasion of grace in which we are redeemed has no regard for human works, but only for the devotion of faith.[28] He illustrates by citing Gal. 3:6 then immediately turning to Heb. 10:38, creating a chiasm which introduces the second occasion of grace. The writer of Hebrews says: "The righteous one lives by

---

[27]Cf. *Ep. 7 ad Graecum* (CSEL 21: 201) in which Faustus asserts Augustine's essential orthodoxy but warns that he is suspect on some matters.

[28]I. 6. 21, 11-13: "tempus gratiae, quo redempti sumus, merita hominum non expectavit, opera penitus non quaesivit, sola deus fidei nostrae devotione contentus fuit . . ."

my faith, but if he shrinks back, he will not be pleasing to my soul." For Faustus this passage demonstrates that righteousness and faith are granted to one who seeks God, and that one can willfully neglect such divine gifts. As Hebrews 11:6 further asserts, God rewards those who seek him. The second occasion of grace, then, is the human movement of will and action that inheres in belief. Faustus illustrates the two *tempora gratiae*, which he finally labels "vocation" and "consummation," with reference to baptism and confirmation: "You see that the steps of vocation and of consummation are distinct. He expects faith from infants, and requires works along with faith from those who have been confirmed, such that he increases the affect of belief in those who progress, and that he who gives daily help might assist those who labor."[29]

This last passage goes to the real root of Faustus's argument, for despite the exegetical purport of the chapter, the author's case is built upon *affectum*, the subjective attitude of the believing person. The bulk of Faustus's scriptural citations illustrate the phenomenon of willing human action in concert with divine economy. Predestinarians give attention only to the first occasion of grace, that appropriate to infants.

The discussion in I. 7 moves away from the general theme of grace and human effort to the specific question of the free human power of choice (*liberum arbitrium*) or, as one commonly calls it in shorthand, "free will." Faustus's polemical opponents argue that the free will has been totally removed from the human being. To such a doctrine he replies that loss of the *liberum arbitrium* would reduce the one who is "rich with understanding,

---

[29]I. 6. 22, 23-26: "agnosce distinctos esse gradus vocationis et consummationis. fidem expectat a parvulis, opera etiam cum fide a confirmatis requirit ita tamen, ut credulitatis affectum proficientibus augeat et laborantibus adiutor cotidianus adsistat."

endowed with reason, and decorated with the honor of the divine image"[30] to
a level of existence indistinguishable from that of the brutes. Scripture and
experience are full of examples of the human quest for virtue and
righteousness, but if human beings are without freedom or will, such
pursuits are ruled out a fortiori. Faustus admits that the dignity of original
righteousness has been tarnished by sin, but insists that the pursuit of
holiness and sanctification is still incumbent upon human beings.

Having argued against a total loss of the *liberum arbitrium,* Faustus
must explain in I. 8 "How the Infirmity of Free Choice of the Will Should
Be Understood." The human predicament is not a loss, but a weakening
(*infirmitas*), of free will. Freedom must therefore be restored to its full vigor
through a kind of convalescence—Faustus compares it to recovery from
illness, dissipation, or habitual drunkenness[31]—that involves both personal
effort and assistance from another. A number of biblical texts enjoining a
willful choice of obedience supply the exegetical force to Faustus's argument,
and the chapter ends with an extended interpretation of Luke 9:23, "If anyone
wills to come after me, let him deny himself, take up his cross, and follow
me." The interpretation of Jesus's words here again partakes of the strong
dialectical bipolarity in the treatise: "This means let one thing be brought
about by its opposite. Let patience conquer irascibility; let temperance
restrain concupiscence; let humility drive away pride; let the cross destroy
pleasure-seeking. Who would suppose that these things are to be conferred

---

[30]I. 7. 23, 4-6: ". . . hominem intellectu locupletatum, ratione
praeditum, divinae imaginis honore decoratum . . ."

[31]I. 8. 24, 21-25: "sicut homo longe infirmitate confectus . . . sicut
post inveteratam luxuriae consuetudinem . . . sicut longo temulentiae usu
captivata."

upon himself as he sleeps, through grace alone, with no labor of the heart, no fleshly affliction . . .?"[32]

In this scheme the virtues properly comprise the opposite pole from human evils. The notion of an inert or extinguished human will is tantamount to an invitation to laziness, which would allow the evil, vice-ridden side of the dichotomy to have free reign. Against the threat of such indolence, Faustus enjoins the laborious, even pugnacious, effort of the will. Ever mindful, perhaps, of the accusation of Pelagian tendencies, Faustus adds that he would not make grace and labor coequal; rather, "We have given preference to grace as utterly beyond comparison."[33]

Having given both a negative and a positive treatment of the human will, Faustus in I. 9 moves again to a discussion of problematic biblical passages, in this case Rom. 9:16 and Mt. 9:13, two texts that seem precisely to deny any role for human will or action. In the Romans passage, Paul writes with regard to salvation that "it is not of him who wills, nor of him who runs, but of God who has mercy." Faustus's strategy, by now familiar, is to counterpose other Pauline texts that clearly delineate a place for human "running," namely 1 Cor. 9:24f., Gal. 5:7, and 2 Tim. 4:7. Understood in a broader context, passages like Rom. 9:16 are really meant as a hedge against pride and presumption in the works of the law. Similarly, Jesus's words in Mt. 9:13, "I did not come to call the righteous, but sinners, to repentance,"

---

[32] I. 8. 26, 10-15: ". . . id est, alter efficiatur ex altero. patientia vincat iracundiam, temperantia refrenet concupiscentiam, humilitas exturbet superbiam, crux conterat voluptatem. quis haec sine labore cordis, sine adflictione carnis . . . dormienti sibi per solam gratiam aestimet conferenda?" This image of a battle between the virtues and the vices had earlier been portrayed by Prudentius in his *Psychomachia* (CSEL 61: 167-211).

[33] I. 8. 26, 20-21: ". . . sed omnino gratiam sine comparatione praeponimus."

are aimed sarcastically against those Jews who presume upon their own illusory righteousness.

The important question in divine dealings with the human race is not one's vocation but one's actions, which must involve the use of the will. God, creator of both the interior and the exterior person, has allotted a realm of will and action analogous to one's power over the bodily members. Just as each person has a hand or an eye which can be put to any use, so it is with the human will. Because one's exercise of virtue on the way to righteousness and thence to salvation depends on proper employment of the *liberum arbitrium*, universal access to the means of salvation follows directly from Faustus's theological anthropology: "Righteousness in humankind, therefore, is not a personal, but a general and public, gift of God. Access to taking hold of salvation is as a kind of fountain set in the midst of this world, given in common for all to draw from, so that one who neglects to do so stands justly accused before the one who gave it."[34]

The question of human salvation finally depends, not originally but proximately, upon one's will, for the criterion of judgment before God is one's proper use of one's given capacities. The actions arising from devotion are of far more consequence than is predestination. Again, the *sola gratia* schema turns out in the end to deny the efficacy of grace, since one who fails to be vigilant may fall in the day of judgment.

In I. 10 a similar error provides the opposition. Here the suspect position holds that "free choice of the will is prone only toward evil in man, and not at all toward good."[35] In his accustomed manner Faustus compiles

---

[34] I. 9. 30, 9-13: "iustitia ergo in homine non personale, sed generale et publicum dei munus est. aditus capessendae salutis quasi fons quidam in medium mundi huius expositus et in commune concessus ad hauriendum universis patet, ut largitori merito reus sit, qui haurire neglexerit."

[35] I. 10. 32, 11-12.

biblical texts; in this case he deploys primarily New Testament exhortations. Does not, argues Faustus, the phenomenon of exhortation to obedience and repentance imply the capacity for response? Holy deeds have the highest honor because the kingdom of heaven is promised to those who give dutiful service with the cooperation of grace. Pursuit of such an arduous path of virtue offends the otiose and indolent, but the Church is built by the labors of those who in the Apostle's words are "God's helpers" (1 Cor. 3:9). When people fail to serve—to their own condemnation—blame lies with their own disobedience, not with a fatal flaw inserted by God into human nature.

The focal point of I. 11, Rom. 9:21 might be seen as justifying the notion of absolute predestination, since it asks, "Does not the potter have power over the clay, to make from the same lump one vessel in honor and another in dishonor?" The chapter is directed against those who say that a *vas in contumeliam* cannot rise up to become a *vas in honorem*. For Faustus, such use of this text does violence to the broader context of Scripture, for it ignores the fact that the making of a "vessel" takes place over the course of a lifelong struggle: "For when, by grace, a person has begun to be a vessel of honor, he or she must be especially watchful, so that the honor received may be kept safe with divine cooperation, so that the chosen person will not be changed into a vessel of dishonor when sin arises."[36] The capacity to turn in either direction always attends human existence. One's own choice, not the *vis praedestinationis*, determines the direction of the will, and such a choice can move one either to the side of the devil or to the side of God, as Scripture frequently attests.

---

[36] I. 11. 36, 20-23: "nam cum homo per gratiam esse coeperit vas honoris, invigilandum est, ut acceptus honor divina cooperatione servetur, ne adquisitus homo postmodum in vas contumeliae culpa exsistente vertatur."

This chapter contains some interesting rhetorical features. The author first applies a kind of rhetorical analysis to Rom. 9:21: the passage regarding the making of vessels, he says, is written by Paul as a conclusion (*conclusa elocutione*), which taken alone does not give account of the preceding causes (*praecedentes causas*) by which a person actually comes to be a vessel of honor or of dishonor.[37] The human being, by willing obedience or disobedience, determines the kind of vessel that he or she is to be. Faustus then extends the language of Paul, saying that "in order to become a vessel of mercy, one must first be a vessel of obedience, so that the sentence of the just judge may follow from the preceding causes."[38] He makes even further use of the Pauline metaphor to turn the predestinarian interpretation completely on its head: "vessel" really has reference "to the substance of man" (*ad substantiam hominis*), which—perhaps Faustus alludes to 2 Cor. 4:7—is stored in a vessel. This substance is, namely, the type and diversity of the will (*genus ac diversitatem ... voluntatis*).[39] So by transferring the biblical imagery, Faustus gives this text precisely the opposite referent from that used by his opponents. The "vessel" is not the divinely prefixed character of people, but the realm of the will's freedom to choose, by which people form themselves for honor or for dishonor.

Chapter I. 12 is an extended compilation of biblical texts illustrating the point just made, i.e., that the human power of choice is capable of movement in either direction. Scripture frequently promises consequences either for obedience or for disobedience. Toward the end of this chapter two

---

[37]I. 11. 36, 18-20.

[38]I. 11. 37, 8-10: ". . . ut fiat vas misericordiae, prius futurus est vas oboedientiae, ut praecedentibus causis iusti iudicis sententia subsequatur."

[39]I. 11. 38, 4-5.

problematic texts arise, each of which affords Faustus an opportunity to refine his argument. He notes the heretical use of Rom. 9:15, "I will be merciful to whom I wish and will show mercy to whom I have mercy," and asks rhetorically whether what God wills is just or unjust. When the obvious answer is given, Faustus asserts that a passage of this kind must be interpreted as reflecting divine justice. Seen in this way, the object of divine mercy is one who is known to be righteous, whose faith is seen by God. To such a one the increase of faith is granted.[40] Divine justice thus becomes a hermeneutical criterion.

Rom. 9:18-19 supplies the second problem text: "Therefore he has mercy on whom he wishes and hardens whom he wishes. You will then say to me: 'What more does he seek, for who can resist his will?'" Faustus sees the passage as allowing an erroneous opinion—that of an utterly irresistible will of God—to be voiced by an imagined interlocutor. Paul then responds (Rom. 9:20), "O man, who are you to answer back to God? Does not the potter have the power over the clay, to make from the same lump one vessel in honor and another in dishonor?" Paul's answer first restrains the faithless by the use of authority. But the second and most important point is the phrase "out of the same lump" (ex eadem massa). Augustine's division of humanity into two massae, one of perdition, the other of salvation, was certainly a commonplace, though it was apparently overstated by Augustine's opponents.[41] Faustus's interpretation here strikes very near the center of the textual arsenal of radicalized Augustinians, as the author himself

---

[40]I. 12. 43, 6-25.

[41]The division is found in Augustine's De diversis quaestionibus LXXXIII, 68. 3, Ep. 194. 22 and elsewhere, passim, in the anti-Pelagian works, most notably for the Gallic scene in De corrept. et grat. 16 and 25. Among the "Pelagian" charges against Augustine mentioned by Prosper is that he believes in "duas humani generis massas, duas naturas" (Ep. ad Rufinum III, PL 51: 79A-B).

is well aware: "When he says here 'out of the same lump,' whoever of you might believe that there are two 'lumps' of the human race should recognize that there is but one to be found in the Holy Scriptures. Depravity of intentions and diversity of wills causes two to exist. So it is because of their qualities, and not by the impulse of God, that this or that person is made a vessel either of honor of dishonor."[42]

Again Faustus's scheme of dualities comes into play: the human race is fundamentally a unity in the divine ordination, and its division results from a defect of human wills. Augustine too had really posited a unity of the human race, but as a *massa damnationis*; out of this some were elected, thus creating a second *massa*. For Augustine, divine mercy produces a diversity out of the unity in Adamic sin, whereas for Faustus, human sin produces diversity out of a creational unity.

I. 13, "Where the Grace of God and the Human Will Are Joined Together by the Assertion of Testimonies," is a brief collation of biblical texts showing the dual affirmation of the power of grace and the assent of the human will. The chapter is shot through with a polemical tone directed against those who fail to see the manifest doctrine of free will on every page of Scripture. A noteworthy feature here is the prominence of the Psalms; of the chapter's fifteen citations, eleven are from the Psalter.

In I. 14 Faustus seizes upon a perceived internal inconsistency in the argument of an opponent. This opponent, who seems to have admitted that some people perish in their sins despite having been baptized, has explained that they must not have fully believed in their baptism. For Faustus this is a

---

[42]I. 12. 44, 12-17: ". . . dum dicit ex eadem massa, quicumque duas generis humani massas esse arbitrabaris, unam sacra ex lectione cognosce. duas autem facit pravitas studiorum et diversitas voluntatum. ita pro earum qualitatibus, non pro inpulsu dei unusquisque aut contumeliae vas aut honoris efficitur."

tacit confession that God's grace depends for its efficacy upon the cooperation of the human will. If one grants the validity of trinitarian baptism, one can only account for falling-away by referring to human negligence. The chapter breaks off as Faustus invokes the example of children who, though reared by devoted parents, later fall away. Though truncated, the chapter gives another example of Faustus's argumentative technique of exposing the incoherence of his opponents' argument.

Unfortunately the bulk of I. 15 is also lost, save for the last fifteen lines. Its announced topic concerns the fall of the angels and the possession of the angels' likeness, against a certain person's opinion. One can only speculate, but probably someone had put forward a view likening the human condition to that of angels, i.e., as irrevocably divided into two camps. What remains of Faustus's argument has moved away from the topic of angels to that of the gentiles being grafted into Israel, but his line of reasoning here could plausibly apply to the question of angels as well: even those apparently cut off (i.e., gentiles, fallen angels) may still have hope because of God's magnanimity, while those grafted in (Israel, the Church, angels) may still fear being cut off.[43]

The longest chapter of book one, I. 16 argues against another consequence of a radically predestinarian scheme: the notion that Christ did not die for all. Such teaching is for Faustus utterly execrable, since Scripture clearly asserts the universal scope of Christ's redemptive death. Against the practical objection that some people are evidently not redeemed, since they live in sin, Faustus uses the analogy—undoubtedly from personal experience—of a captive city set free from servitude by the effort of a priest

---

[43] I. 15. 48, 17-19: ". . . humilitatem, ut et qui insertus est frangi timeat, magnanimitatem, ut spem remunerationis et qui fractus est non deponat."

or legate. The fact that some may be bribed or enticed into forfeiting their
freedom detracts neither from the extent nor from the gratuity of their
redemption: "Does one who rejects his freedom cause some lessening of the
redeemer's benevolence? Not so!"[44]

The second half of I. 16 is directed against a misuse of John 6:44,
"No one comes to me unless the Father who sent me draws him." Faustus
insists that the mercy of the one who draws is not violent or impetuous;
rather, it is freely and generally given. The predestinarian, by contrast, sees a
one-sided and excessive picture of a God who draws whomever he will
regardless of human labor. God draws, "but to the Lord who assists and calls
the servant extends the hand of faith, by which he may be drawn."[45] The one
drawn is a willing and acting person, not merely senseless matter. The
drawing of the Lord comes often in Scripture as a loving invitation. God
draws all but embraces those who respond by keeping the divine precepts.
Faustus's remarks here, which are grouped around the idea of the verb "to
draw" (*adtrahere*), have broader doctrinal implications which will be
addressed in chapter 4. One can say in general that the target at which
Faustus aims is a notion of divine drawing that usurps or overrides innate
human powers. Augustine's late position is capable of such an interpretation.[46]

---

[44]I. 16. 50, 27-28: "numquid aliquam benivolentiae redemptoris intulit
deminutionem, qui respuit libertatem? Non ita est."

[45]I. 16. 52, 4-5: "sed adsistenti et vocanti domino famulus manum
fidei, qua adtrahatur, extendit . . . "

[46]*De corrept. et grat.* 14. 45: "intus egit, corda tenuit, corda movit,
eosque voluntatibus eorum, quas ipse in illis operatus est, traxit." Cf. the
discussion of this point in Tibiletti, "Libero arbitrio e grazia," 259-85.

Against the opinion that God hardens a person's heart so as to render him or her incapable of salvation, Faustus in I. 17 again pleads for a more careful look at the Scriptures. To close off access to salvation would be to revoke something that, as we have seen, is constitutive of human existence. Numerous texts show that hardening of the heart comes as a result of human sin, not of divine harshness; in fact, precisely the divine goodness frequently occasions a sinful human response. God brings about hardening only in the sense of allowing, for a time, an increase of human rebellion.

The final chapter of book one, I. 18, continues against the most extreme theological implication of dual predestination, namely, the idea that people are impelled into death by God's will. Faustus's defense is twofold: first, Scripture clearly speaks of God's desire that people not perish; second, the biblical accounts assign blame not to God, but to human beings, for their deaths in sin. At stake here, among other things, is God's trustworthiness. Referring to Jesus's lament over Jerusalem in Mt. 23:37, Faustus reasons: "If the Lord had closed off access to salvation for those about to perish, he merely pretended to cry over their ruin."[47] God requires a human will ready to do good works and would not require good works unless such a will had been given.

So ends book one. Faustus's strategy, as reflected in his argument, has been to establish a middle stance by excluding error on either side. His primary opponents are those who hold to a predestinarian scheme that emphasizes divine power to the exclusion of human effort. The burden of book one is therefore to establish the necessity of human will and action in the divine economy, and his argument, always scriptural in its fabric, is built

---

[47]I. 18. 57, 3-4: "si dominus perituris salutis intercluserat aditum, ergo falso istorum defleuit exitium."

upon two pillars: (1) a theological anthropology—often implicit—which emphasizes created human capacity, and (2) the data of Christian piety and the religious affections—prayer, obedience, ascesis in the pursuit of virtue.

Book Two

Book two represents a subtle shift of emphasis. The predestinarian view still provides the opposition, and Faustus continues to provide an apologia for human capacities. Now, however, the author, having established his stance, begins to treat human freedom of will and action less in terms of their necessity in the economy of salvation, and more with respect to their gratuity, which has its origin in the divine intention toward humanity. Despite the polemical material contained in book two, the overall purpose is positive: to focus upon the *prima gratia*, the grace that inheres in the creation of the human race. Whereas the argument of book one rested upon the two pillars of an implicit theological anthropology and Christian experience, Faustus tends in book two to ground his anthropology in the divine benevolence, keeping intact, of course, the exegetical focus. That is, he attempts to show that an appeal to human exertion in response to God is finally an appeal to divine grace.

The first chapter of book two renews Faustus's attack upon those who ascribe the hardening of hearts to God by focusing on the classical locus of the problem: the hardening of Pharoah's heart in Exodus. At issue is whether Pharoah was willingly hardened by God, in which case Pharoah was responsible, or unwillingly hardened, in which case one must blame God for Pharoah's sin and for injustice in punishing it. By framing the question in this way, Faustus demands a basic decision about the character of God: can a God who hardens Pharoah's heart be merciful and just toward humanity?

Faustus again resorts to a kind of rhetorical analysis of Scripture to make his point. Since Pharoah's will was manifestly free in refusing to obey God and release the Hebrews, what could have been meant by the statement "I will harden Pharoah's heart"? It is, says Faustus, to be likened to a common figure of speech: "In the same way we sometimes, in common conversation, adopt this manner of speaking. We may, for example, charge stubborn servants with our own mildness, saying: 'I have made you worse with my patience; I have nourished your malice and pride by my remission; I have made you stubborn by my indulgence; by my indifference I have stirred up your heart to be hardened against me.'"[48] In reality the divine attitude toward humankind is an undifferentiated benevolence. Divine mercy is as rain: it falls upon all land but brings forth good fruits from cultivated land and thorns from uncultivated. In the face of such mercy, owing to the sphere of the will's freedom, one person might improve for the better while another, like Pharoah, is hardened against God.

Having established the basic premise of unchanging divine mercy toward humanity, Faustus in II. 2 and II. 3 addresses the thorny problem of divine foreknowledge (*praescientia*) and predestination (*praedestinatio*). In II. 2 the main argument is that divine foreknowledge "forcibly urges human wills neither toward just pursuits nor toward their opposites."[49] Put differently, divine foreknowledge in no way intrudes upon or usurps the

---

[48]II. 1. 59, 10-16: "sic interdum familiariter etiam apud homines genus huius elocutionis adsumimus, sic interdum contumacibus famulis exprobramus mansuetudinem nostram ita dicentes: ego patientia mea pessimum te feci, ego remissione mea malitiam tuam superbiamque nutrivi, ego te contumacem indulgentia mea reddidi, ego dissimulatione mea cor tuum, ut contra me obduraretur, animavi."

[49]II. 2. 61, 7-8: "Quod praescientia dei nec ad iusta nec ad contraria humanas violenter urgeat voluntates."

prerogatives of the human will. To suppose that the causes of human actions
arise from foreknowledge is a fundamental misunderstanding. Causation in
fact runs precisely in the opposite direction, for "the freedom and will of the
one foreknown impose a quality upon the foreknowing God."[50] God has a
general foreknowledge regarding the state of the world; but with regard to
human beings, divine foreknowledge depends upon their actions. Guilt for
sin, then, rests squarely with the sinner, for no compulsion takes place.
Faustus places an eloquent address in the mouth of Providence: "O man, I
have not made you of the sort that I have foreknown you will become. I have
formed you to be good in keeping with the law of my justice, and lest you
should follow after evil I have admonished you; I have foreseen you to be evil
in following after the iniquity of your will."[51] The divine purpose is not a
prefixed necessity, but can be changed by prayer, as was the case with
Hezekiah (2 Kings 20:1-11), who by repenting deferred the certain death
pronounced upon him.

The root problem of those who misunderstand divine foreknowledge
is their failure to distinguish between foreknowledge and predestination. One
might point out here that those who make such an equation do so with good
Augustinian precedent,[52] but in II. 3 Faustus argues precisely that the two
are not to be seen as equivalent. His starting point is Rom. 8:29, "whom he

---

[50]II. 2. 61, 13-14: "sed magis deo praesciendi ingerit qualitatem
libertas praesciti hominis ac voluntas."

[51]II. 2. 61, 31-62, 2: "o homo, non te talem feci, qualem te futurum esse
praescivi. bonum te pro iustitiae meae lege formavi et, ne malum sequereris,
admonui, malum te pro consecutura voluntatum tuarum iniquitate praevidi."

[52]Augustine, *De dono persev.* 18. 1ff.: "Unde aliquando eadem
praedestinatio significatur nomine praescientiae . . . . " 19. 48: "Quid ergo nos
prohibet, quando apud aliquos verbi Dei tractores legimus Dei praescientiam, et
agitur de vocatione electorum, eamdem praedestinationem intellegere?" The
equation is common in the anti-Pelagian corpus.

foreknew and predestined to be conformed to the image of his son." Plainly, to foreknow is one thing, to predestine another. Faustus argues, however, that neither one involves the production or compulsion of human deeds. Foreknowledge refers to the divine power to see things beforehand; just as the human eye does not bring about the phenomena it sees, so divine foreknowledge is similarly a passive capacity: "Is one who foresees a sinner therefore the cause of sin? God foreknows adultery; does God indeed kindle bones and marrow with flames of impure passion? God foreknows a murderer; does God therefore add brutal emotions to the confused senses?"[53]

Predestination, on the other hand, is a function of divine justice, whereby God ordains a reward or punishment as the consequence of a given action. Faustus introduces, through an imagined interlocutor, the example of the Holy Innocents in Bethlehem. Looked at in a certain way, the martyrdom of these infants might be seen as having been accomplished solely by the power of the divine will. Really, though, this case illustrates the difference between foreknowledge and predestination. The deaths of the infants, though foreseen, were not compelled, but freely willed by those who committed the crime. Divine predestination nevertheless ordained the glorification of those slain. Despite willful human evil, the "author of goodness" still arranges a good outcome; divine benevolence is not compromised.

The predestinationism against which Faustus argues entails the notion that God's qualities of mercy and justice can each be exercised separately to the exclusion of the other, that is, that God could show utter mercy to the elect and utter justice to the condemned. Were this the case, it

---

[53]II. 3. 64, 10-14: ". . . qui praevidet peccatorem, ergo ipse causa peccati est? praescit adulterium deus, ergo ipse ossa et medullas ignibus obsceni furoris inflammat? praescit deus homicidam, numquid ipse bestiales motus perturbatis sensibus suggerit . . . "

would constitute an indictment of the central theological point Faustus has made thus far, namely, the undifferentiated benevolence of God toward humanity.

In II. 4 he addresses the matter by arguing for the equity of God's dealings. Divine mercy is always active, even among those who might be lost: "For he is also merciful to the lost, he who seeks and calls sinners, and who long is patient with those who fail. Just as he makes his sun to rise upon both the good and the evil, and as it rains upon the just and the unjust, so he has filled both, without partiality, with the light of reason, clothed them with the honor of his image, and called them generally to the grace of redemption."[54]

Likewise, God is also just toward the elect, "whom he receives when they turn to him, whom he does not forsake when they labor, whom he makes worthy when they freely and faithfully serve."[55] The practical consequence of God's inseparable justice and mercy is the joining of grace and human labor: one labors mightily yet always rightly ascribes any benefits to grace rather than to industry.

II. 5 takes its beginning from an ostensibly problematic text, John 12:39, "Therefore they were unable to believe." Apparently this was used to support the view that those who perish are unable, rather than unwilling, to be saved. A properly contextual reading, however, reveals that the faculty of

---

[54]II. 4. 66, 5-10: "nam misericors est et in perditos, qui inquirit et invitat errantes, qui diu sustinet delinquentes. et sicut solem suum oriri facit super bonos et malos et pluit super iustos et iniustos, ita utrosque indifferenter lumine rationis implevit, honore imaginis suae induit, ad gratiam redemptionis generaliter evocavit."

[55]II. 4. 66, 14-16: "iustus, inquam, et circa eos, quos suscipit revertentes, quos non deserit laborantes, quos dignos efficit libertate fideliter servientes."

believing had been given to many of the people in question, but they lacked the will to confess. The real lesson to be learned in the gospel passage, argues Faustus, is how easily the good gifts of the will and of faith can be corrupted. As was the case with Pharoah, the ungodly make ill use of God's mercy by their willful negligence. The first criterion for divine judgment is one's neglect of benefits received; no one, therefore, can be excluded from such blessings.

In II. 6 a similar theme, the question of divine arbitrariness, arises in connection with Rom. 9:9f., in which God's attitude toward Jacob and Esau comes "before they had done any kind of good or evil." The radically predestinarian reading of this text has God pronouncing "not with the order of a ruler but with the law of a tyrant . . . one worthy of affection, the other of hate."[56] On this view, no reason or cause for divine judgment exists. Declaring that this is a senseless view, Faustus suggests that the text must be read with an eye to what may be concordant with divine justice. The case of Esau and Jacob is in fact for Paul an illustration of the election of the gentiles, whose faith is preferred to the pride and arrogance of the Jews. Therefore the preference of Jacob over Esau does not demonstrate pure and arbitrary divine power but is the product of God's just judgment. Again, the context of Paul's words is all-important. No fatal necessity is at work, only the foreknown merit of faith.

A lacuna interrupts the text of II. 6 and extends through the whole of II. 7. We know from the *capitula* of the book that II. 7 deals with another facet of the passage just discussed, namely, the meaning of "that the promise

---

[56]II. 6. 71, 19-20: "non ordine regentis, sed iure dominantis illum affectu dignum reddat, hunc odio . . ."

of God might remain." The textual gap also encompasses the initial part of
II. 8.

In what remains of II. 8, directed against those who affirm that
Adam "utterly perished," we find Faustus arguing for the continued exercise
of human choice, even after Adam's fall. After the fall, the creator still
desired that creation be noble and that human beings should gain mastery over
sin. The consequence of the primal sin was the weakening, not the death, of
the *liberum arbitrium*. To please God is not impossible but difficult. Abel's
sacrifice shows the continuing power of the innate goodness given generally
by God in the form of an inward law which made Abel a lover of the virtues.
This inner gift is much more than a mere capacity; it is a positive datum:

> Do you see that the good of belief is not a new privilege, but an old
> one, and that in the very beginning of the world's establishment the
> human mind was endowed by the most high Author not only with
> intellect and reason, but also with faith? In fact he had already given
> a knowledge of himself to the soul then, when he agreed to commit
> his image to it.[57]

The two questions of the goodness of the creator and of human constitution
turn out to be virtually the same. Divine equity and benevolence show
themselves in the making of a creature positively oriented toward the creator.

Mention of the image leads Faustus in II. 9 to discuss "in whose
image and likeness the first man was created." This is, with II. 10 and II. 12,

---

[57]II. 8. 76, 20-25: "vides bonum credulitatis non novellum esse
privilegium, sed vetustum, et inter ipsa mundi coalescentis exordia mentem
hominis sicut intellectu atque ratione ita etiam fide a summo auctore dotatam?
itaque iam tum dedit animae notitiam suam, quando ei committere dignatus est
imaginem suam."

one of the three longest chapters of the entire treatise and comes close to the heart of Faustus's theological anthropology. First he dismisses a curious, but apparently popular, view that holds that the creator fashioned Adam after the image of Christ's humanity, which was to be assumed from the virgin.[58] The implication of such a conception would be that the order of redemption renders the order of creation secondary or even irrelevant. As Faustus's rhetorical opponent asks: "What does this connection of the image of God with freedom of choice matter to me, since the excellent creator, who was to come in later ages also as redeemer, rather made man to that image he was going to assume from man through the Virgin?"[59] For Faustus, such a devaluation of the creational referent of the image fails both on logical and theological grounds.

Logically, the principles of something prior cannot assume the image of something coming much later.[60] Reason would instead dictate that the first Adam, simply by virtue of chronological order, would transmit his

---

[58]II. 9. 76, 29-78, 25. This conception, which according to Faustus was held "a plerisque" in his own time, has been identified by Simonetti ("Il *De gratia*," 136, n. 33) as being of Asiatic origin and attested to by Tertullian. Tertullian in *De carnis resurrectione* 6 (CSEL 47: 33), speaks of those who say ". . . ad imaginem dei fecit illum, scilicet Christi." One could well imagine the appeal of such a view in Faustus's time in light of the nearly ubiquitous anti-Arian polemic. Marius Victorinus, for example, in his Adversus Arium, in order to preserve the identity between the Incarnate and the logos/imago, makes such statements as ". . . quod de Maria filius est dei et ipse imago et ipse logos . . ." (*Adv. Arium* I. 36, CSEL 83: 121). The connection is conjectural, but plausible.

[59]II. 9. 76, 28-77, 2: "quid mihi ad libertatem arbitrii iungis imaginem dei, cum ille eximius conditor futurus secuturis saeculis et redemptor ad illam magis imaginem fecerit hominem, quam per virginem erat adsumpturus ex homine?"

[60]With reference to things coming "multo posterioris" Faustus evokes the common theme of the late time of the Incarnation, seen for example in Augustine's ages of the world. It is a christianization of the old Roman theme of "senectus mundi."

image to the second Adam, rather than vice versa. In any case, it would be most unwise to suppose that the configuration of the first parent somehow anticipated that of one who did not yet exist.

The center of Faustus's argument here, however, is more directly theological, and at this point his voice reaches a crescendo. If one subordinates the order of creation to that of redemption, one really dishonors God's creature for two reasons. First, if Adam was made according to the image of the one who was to cure human sin, primal innocence would bear the taint of future sin; human ruin would in a sense lie potentially within God's pure creation.

Second, it was not necessary for the human being to be completed or perfected according to a future image, because the *imago Dei* was complete within itself, without any reference to the redemptive work of Christ: "It is therefore more reasonable that in man, to whom the reality of grace, not of nature, is handed on by God in the very likeness, *image* should rather be called what is received from one who is higher and superior, and *likeness* is better understood as conferred from the truth which the Father rightly communicates to his Son by nature."[61]

Again, as above, the human being possesses not merely neutral capacity, but positive divine life, indeed the material for adoptive filiation. Faustus plays on the terms *res* and *forma*, commonplaces in Augustine's *De doctrina christiana*, to show that Adam was constituted not as a mere "form" of a later exemplar, nor as a possessor of mere "nature," but was the recipient of the very reality of grace in the primal creation. If anything, the order of

---

[61]II. 9. 77, 21-25: "id ergo rationi magis congruit, ut in homine, cui in ipsa similitudine a deo gratiae res traditur, non naturae, imago hoc potius nuncupetur, quod a priore et superiore suscipitur, et de veritate similitudo fuisse conlata plenius iudicetur, quam tamen cum filio naturali pater iure communicat."

redemption corresponds to *forma*, and that of creation to *res*, for in creation the maker bestowed the image, while in redemption the savior took on the "form of a servant."[62]

The image of God, further, cannot refer only to the one who was to be incarnate from Mary, for the granting of the image was clearly a work of the entire Trinity. The words "Let us make man after our image and likeness" show this clearly. The image is bestowed in common by "the one divinity of the three persons."[63]

If one attends to this *prima gratia* by which the human being was honored with the divine image, one should realize, says Faustus, that humankind still possesses free will, even if attenuated. Justice, wisdom, and reason, which are natural to God, come as gifts to the human being; Faustus uses the analogy of God as gold and the human person as a gilded vessel. But these creational gifts are not simply superfluous qualities; they serve to constitute, even in their gratuity, authentic human existence: "They err, therefore, who regard justice and the other virtues of the soul to be a substance without which the soul could subsist anyway by the lifegiving power in its nature." [64]

The image, that is, the original, constitutive gifts of free will and immortality, can never be stripped away. The *imago* remains even in evil people; but the *similitudo*, the likeness, is present only in those who are

---

[62]Ibid., 26-30.

[63]II. 9. 78, 24: "trium personarum una divinitas." In all likelihood Faustus has learned his trinitarian theology from Augustine's *De Trinitate*, where it is axiomatic that the works of the Trinity *ad extra* are not divided.

[64]II. 9. 79, 20-22: "Errant ergo, qui iustitiam reliquasque virtutes animae putant esse substantiam, sine quibus utcumque potest vitali in natura sua vigore subsistere . . ."

good. One achieves worthiness to be called a child of God, that is, one makes proper use of both *imago* and *similitudo*, even by following the law of nature which preceded the written law, as witnessed by the examples of Abel, Enoch, and Noah. No less an authority than Augustine affirms that the natural law is written in human hearts.[65] The phenomenon of just laws among the heathen further testifies to the presence of natural law, as does Rom. 1:18. People who are condemned have no excuse, for by virtue of the primal gift of the divine image they have always possessed the ability to do good.

The argument here at II. 9 has reached the epicenter of Faustus's theological position. The divine philanthropy reaches its climax, and human dignity its zenith, precisely in the creational bestowal of the image of God. The categories of the doctrine of God thus become bound up inextricably with those of anthropology, such that to deny the perduring freedom of the human free will is to deny God's benevolence in creation. By extension, to deny the freedom of the will is to deny the unity of the divine purpose from creation to redemption. Human beings are not constituted as empty natures which must await a special infusion of grace; rather, the grace of redemption merely restores the fullest use of the more fundamentally important *prima gratia*.

The discussion of the *imago* under the aspect of an innate natural law or natural good leads Faustus in II. 10 to the question of the "heathen" (*gentes*). His rhetorical interlocutor is made to suggest that prior to the advent of Christ none of the *gentes* partook of salvation. This is a variation

---

[65] II. 9. 81, 19-23: "Opus itaque naturalis legis in cordibus hominum fuisse conscriptum etiam beatissimus pontifex Augustinus doctissimo sermone prosequitur ita dicens: utrumque simul currit in isto alveo atque torrente generis humani, malum, quod a parente trahitur, et bonum, quod a creante tribuitur." The citation is from *De civ. Dei* XXII. 24. 1; Faustus substitutes *alveo* for Augustine's *fluvio*.

of the argument raised in II. 9. Here the question does not concern the superiority of the image of Christ to that of Adam. Rather, Faustus's opponent grants the existence in humans of some created natural good but argues that it is irrelevant because it was of no avail prior to Christ.

Faustus's response is twofold. First, as always, one must never forget that creation and redemption are not neatly separable; one who denies the efficacy of natural goodness denies its author, who is both creator and restorer.[66] Second—and here Faustus is notably circumspect—he argues that in practice the work of grace does not rule out some initiating role for the human will: "I shall seem incautious not even in this matter if I profess that often in our dispositions—not in the origins of our life, but at least in the middle parts—the movement of our will precedes the special graces which come to us from an added generosity, because God ordains it so."[67] In favor of this assertion, Faustus adduces the scriptural example of Cornelius the centurion, whose wish for healing preceded the actual work of grace. Several other examples more pertinent to the matter of those prior to Christ are also cited: Abraham, Job, and Rahab.

Further, some have argued that prior to the time of grace (*gratiae tempus*) knowledge of the one God had not been given to the heathen. Yet

---

[66]II. 10. 83, 20-21.

[67]II. 10. 83, 29-84, 3: "Ne in hoc quidem videbor incautus, si profitear, quod aliquotiens in dispositionibus nostris non quidem in vitae nostrae primordiis, sed dumtaxat in mediis gratias speciales et ex accedenti largitate venientes voluntas nostra deo ita ordinante praecedat." Faustus's rapid denial that the precedence of the human will refers to the "origins" of our life is certainly evidence of the extent to which Augustinian sensibilities govern his discourse. Augustine's thought had evolved from the early *Expositio quarundam propositionum ex epistula ad Romanos*, in which he saw the wholly human *initium fidei* as explaining divine election, to the position of his anti-Pelagian works, in which even the *initium fidei* was a gift of grace. Faustus makes clear, by his qualifications, that grace is ultimately antecedent to the human will, even if experientially later.

the Apostle Paul has clearly said that knowledge of God's attributes is available to all, even the gentiles. Human neglect of the inward law or perverse use of the sense of religion do not undermine the creator's generosity in giving such things. The God-given freedom of the will to accept or reject knowledge of God endures as a creational gift even in the disobedient.

II. 11, which speaks of the gentiles' natural knowledge of God, is interrupted by a lacuna after twenty-four lines. The chapter begins with the prophet Daniel prophesying against Nebuchadnezzar (Daniel 4:24ff.), telling him that he can redeem his sins by the exercise of mercy and generosity. Faustus argues that Nebuchadnezzar's ability to choose in the realm of salvation shows both his proximity to the divine mercy and the continuing power of the will. Similar support is drawn from the story of Belshazzar.

Jonah's mission to the Ninevites supplies the material for II. 12, "De Ninivitis," of which the first lines are missing. The argument here continues Faustus's case for the innate divine gifts. Jonah, after all, did not teach or encourage the Ninevites; he pronounced an immutable sentence upon them. Nevertheless, those in the city believed, as Rom. 4:18 has it, "against hope, in hope." By Jonah's concealment of divine munificence, "faith is proved, striving is exercised, the disposition is made manifest; an inner fire does all of this in man, [a fire] implanted in man by God and nourished by man with God's grace."[68]

The case of the Ninevites therefore demonstrates that in the very order of creation all the gifts necessary for salvation, including faith, have always flourished. Jonah's seemingly immutable decree against the Ninevites is in fact a kind of "holy lie" (*pio mendacio*) that was intended to induce the

---

[68]II. 12. 90, 18-21: "dum munificentia absconditur, fides probatur, exercetur ambitus, manifestatur affectus, totumque hoc in homine ignis interior a deo insitus et ab homine cum dei gratia nutritus operatur."

condemned to bring the remedy of penitence to bear against sin; this inducement assumes the ability to repent. The divine dealings with humanity, then, are always, as it were, bipolar: even to invoke the term "aid" or "help" (*auxilium*) implies both a worker and a helper. Righteousness on earth still depends upon human zeal and virtue. One is granted the virtues as a reward for earthly toil and is rewarded for virtues in the life to come.

Such an arrangement, in which human will and reason find a major role in the divine economy, represents the best possible result of the divine counsel in creation. Faustus presents at the end of II. 12 an imagined dialogue among four divine virtues—Power, Goodness, Wisdom, and Justice (*potentia, bonitas, sapientia, iustitia*)—in which each asserts her concerns in the fashioning of the human creature. Would it not, for example, be better for humanity to be created without the ability to sin? Such a situation would not accord with the divine plan, which is in the final analysis inscrutable. But there will come a time beyond time when we shall not struggle to live sinlessly, and those who are now embroiled in this battle will then know "a joy without fear, a reward without envy, and a kingdom with no enemy."[69]

So Faustus's argument in the second book of the *De gratia*, which has consistently argued from the divine benevolence, equity, justice, and so on, culminates in a kind of all-encompassing parenthesis. Before all time stand the divine virtues, from whose collective dialogue and plan the human being emerges endowed with freedom, will, and reason in God's own image. At the end of time, or beyond it, will stand the same creature, delivered from this life's struggles as the crowning vindication of the creator's wisdom.

* * *

---

[69]II. 12. 96, 21-22: "sine metu gaudium, sine invido praemium, sine hoste sit regnum."

The treatise *De gratia* is a skillful, if somewhat uneven, reshaping of the controversial topics of the episcopal councils at Arles and Lyon into a coherently argued treatise. The opponent is no longer Lucidus alone, but those who "dicunt," "aiunt," "asserunt" the suspect theses. Book one, with its pervasive use of the rhetoric of polarity, primarily takes up the negative task of excluding error in order to establish a center. Using the data of the devotional life and a mostly implicit theological anthropology, its argument aims to demonstrate the inevitable existence of human cooperation in the divine plan. This focus upon the concrete experience of piety lends the treatise a distinctly inward and psychological emphasis.

Book two buttresses the underpinnings of Faustus's theological anthropology by grounding them in an explicit portrayal of God's philanthropy. This line of thought reaches its theological and rhetorical peak in the discussion of the *imago Dei* in II. 9. At the risk of overstatement, one could also characterize the program of book two as positive, in contrast to the polemical thrust of book one.

Throughout both books the author makes the interpretation of scriptural passages the main battleground. His exegetical approach, which will be treated in more detail later, bears the mark of his argumentative technique: just as one excludes radicalized doctrines of left or right in order to find an integrated center, so one scrutinizes passages of Scripture in light of other, complementary passages to arrive at the fullness of truth. At times Faustus uses Scripture simply as oracular prooftexts to corroborate a point; at other times he devotes extended analytical attention to individual passages.

St. Augustine occupies a curious place in the argument of the treatise. He is cited twice by name—the only non-biblical writer to be so cited—and in both cases is regarded positively as an authority. In several instances, however, predestinarian interpretations virtually identical, or at least traceable, to those of the late Augustine are refuted without his being mentioned. This ambivalence certainly reflects the broader ambivalence toward Augustine in Gaul noted in chapter 1.

Whether Faustus had a particular *animus* toward Augustine is impossible to say. He was certainly willing to cite the bishop of Hippo to his own advantage. His unwillingness to attach Augustine's name to any predestinarian excesses was either purely politic or based upon a conviction that Augustine's doctrine had been badly served by such teachers as Lucidus.

Features of Faustus's Lerinian background show themselves in several places. His emphasis on created human capacities calls to mind the motif of a return to Edenic innocence expressed by some of the monks of Lérins. His focus on prayer, ascesis, the pursuit of virtue, and even his abundant use of the Psalter give the *De gratia* a distinctive monastic character. His conviction of the need to stay on the central path of doctrine echoes his older contemporary Vincent and agrees with the general comportment of the Lerinian monks in their rejection of excessive pieties. The general theme of Christian life as an active struggle, rather than a passive contemplation, also would have been a common one at Lérins.

Particular evidences of Faustus's episcopal life do not make themselves greatly felt in the structure and argument of the work. The most noteworthy is his allusion to the role of a legate interceding for a captive city. Thus we know at least one very concrete influence of Faustus's practical life on the doctrine of grace. One might also note a certain similarity of perspective between Faustus and Salvian of Marseilles, who, admittedly in a more moralistic manner, directed the thoughts of his readers away from blaming the mysteries of divine Providence for their difficulties and toward their own moral comportment.

In the matter of style and expression, the treatise also occupies a kind of middle ground. The most obvious feature to some readers is the prolixity of the work. E. Amann, ill-disposed toward Faustus anyway, refers to the *De gratia* as "un ouvrage de longue haleine," lacking structure and tending toward obscurantism in its prose style.[70] The present chapter has shown such a statement to be excessive, if understandable. On the other side from Amann are those who would see Faustus as a master stylist. Faustus's contemporary Sidonius Apollinaris praised Faustus's style with characteristic excess.[71] Between the two extremes one might best term his style as serviceable. Erasmus, we recall, praised it for its clarity and aptness for teaching. Faustus does not write with elaborate ornamentation or with frequent allusion to classical authors; his use of Scylla and Charybdis and a possible oblique reference to Cicero in I. 1 are the only hints in this direction, and may well have been the residue of his boyhood schooling in grammar. But while no Lactantius, he writes with clarity and force, with nicely balanced sentence structures, making frequent use of antitheses, alliterations, and assonances. The defects of his Latin are only those characteristic of the late fifth century in Gaul, and even at that he avoids the bombast that characterized the writings of an author like Sidonius.[72] In any case, his treatise is not, for all its tendency to longwindedness, without moments of terse, eloquent argument.

In all respects, then, the *De gratia* was a work of its time, a time somehow still in the long shadow of great theological figures. The principals of the Pelagian controversy—Augustine, Pelagius, Julian—were

---

[70]"Semipélagiens," 1833.

[71]*Ep.* IX, 3, 9 (PL 58: 618C, 624C).

[72]A helpful discussion of Faustus's style is found in Hårleman, "La littérature gallo-romaine," 164ff.

all long dead. Even those who took up the cudgels at the end of the Pelagian controversy—Prosper, Hilary, Vincent, Cassian—were no longer living. It was an age more of *compendia* and *florilegia* than of original theological works. Faustus's theology was undoubtedly formed not only by Scripture and his own immediate surroundings but also by those luminaries who had gone before him. Our next task will be to identify those sources and to illustrate the use to which Faustus put them.

CHAPTER THREE
THE SOURCES OF THE *DE GRATIA*

Faustus of Riez, who clearly saw himself and portrayed himself as an advocate of the theological center, knew the importance of authority in fashioning doctrinal assertions. Authority for him meant the *auctoritates*, authoritative texts, either of Scripture or of a reputable teacher of the Church. So he denigrates Pelagius's teachings as "confused in their erudition and trite in their authority."[1] Against another set of opponents who argue that baptism can be rendered invalid by imperfect belief, he asks: "In what author do you read this? On the strength of which teacher do you presume to assert this?"[2] Faustus's use of *praesumere* in this connection points to the essence of his position: to claim a position without authoritative warrant is to presume. The present chapter will, in a limited way, put Faustus's own question to his treatise: Upon what authority or authorities do its arguments rest? To answer this question, we must identify at least the main literary sources which he employed. Having done so, we will be better equipped to

---

[1] I. 1. 6, 19-20: ". . . eruditione confusas, auctoritate calcatas . . ."

[2] I. 14. 46, 17-18: ". . . in quo auctore hoc legis, de quo doctore hoc asserere praesumis . . ."

locate Faustus's theological culture more precisely. The first chapter of this study set Faustus against the backdrop of the broad historical and theological factors shaping his own perspective. The second demonstrated the way in which Faustus molded the controversial materials of the synods at Arles and Lyons into a persuasive treatise. The task before us now is to ask with even more specificity which writings Faustus had at hand or in mind while writing the *De gratia.*

His most obvious authority is Holy Scripture; the treatise contains more than 250 explicit biblical citations, and several clear allusions. Faustus's biblical exegesis and argumentation therefore merit close attention. Because his biblical interpretations frequently contrast with those of others, his use of Scripture as a polemical tool will also come into focus. This raises the further question of Faustus's use of other Christian writers. While his only cited nonbiblical authority is St. Augustine, Faustus shows familiarity with, and occasionally direct dependence upon, several other Christian authors. Non-Christian sources merit only a brief note. While we will not undertake the daunting philological task of isolating every possible source that Faustus may have known, we can pursue the more modest goal of identifying those which figure most prominently.

Faustus's Use of Scripture

Manlio Simonetti, in his important 1977 study of the *De gratia,* places his strongest emphasis upon Faustus's use of Holy Scripture; biblical passages make up the main structure and fabric of Faustus's discourse, to which the more technical theological assertions are appended.[3] Certainly

---

[3]"II *De gratia* ," 135.

from a formal perspective Simonetti's assertion is patently true; Faustus quotes Scripture 255 times in the extant text, which runs to ninety pages of text in the Vienna edition. The extent to which one can portray the treatise as primarily interested in Scripture cannot be measured, however, simply by noting the prominence of biblical citations. One must also consider in some detail how Faustus deploys the arsenal of biblical texts.

First, from a purely quantitative point of view, Faustus favors certain books of Scripture. From the Old Testament, nearly half his citations (45 percent) are from the Psalms; the Psalter is in fact the most frequently cited book in the entire treatise.[4] If one adds the books of Genesis, Isaiah, Jeremiah, and Ezekiel, the five books supply more than three-quarters of Faustus's Old Testament quotations. Wisdom is cited three times; Ecclesiasticus twice. In the New Testament, Faustus's most frequently cited book is the Epistle to the Romans, cited thirty-five times, followed by Matthew, 1 Corinthians, John, Galatians, Luke, and Hebrews. These seven books supply roughly three-quarters of the New Testament citations. New Testament passages outnumber Old Testament passages 158 to 102.

Such quantitative observations have limited worth. They suggest the prominence of the Psalms, Romans, and the Gospels (excluding Mark) as Faustus's favored scriptural loci, but do little to illustrate his active engagement as an interpreter of Holy Scripture. To do this we must give attention to his method of biblical exegesis.

---

[4] Out of 101 or 103 OT citations (two may be taken from NT passages), 44 are from the Psalms. In the text as we have it, 23 of these correspond verbatim to the so-called Gallican Psalter, 19 vary only on minor points, and 2 seem to preserve a different reading from both the Gallican and Hebrew Psalters. The Gallican Psalter, Jerome's correction of the Old Latin to agree with the LXX was in common use in Gaul at the time of Alcuin, and became through his influence the Vulgate Psalter. Faustus's citations would seem to be a witness to the currency of this Psalter in the late fifth century, though one cannot rule out a "cleaning up" of such texts in our sole ninth-century MS.

Just as the rhetoric of the *De gratia* is essentially bipolar, excluding extreme positions in favor of a middle way, so Faustus's use of Scripture aims at inclusiveness and equilibrium. Scripture must be interpreted and understood in the broadest way, taking into account the whole of sacred writ. The failure to adhere to such a global method of interpretation leads one to propose extreme, one-sided readings, and this rash extremity characterizes the heretic, whether a Pelagian or one of the *praedestinati*.[5] This intertwining of Faustus's rhetorical purpose with his biblical hermeneutic is crystallized in the only interpretive rule set forth in the *De gratia*: "When one thing is asserted without the other, the other is unmentioned, not denied, according to that rule which bishop Augustine introduces: 'Not everything which is unmentioned is denied.'"[6] This rule seems to be a kind of summary or epitome drawn from Augustine, rather than an actual rule quoted verbatim.[7] In making use of it, Faustus is able to lend the weight of Augustine's prestige to an enterprise that aims to undercut some of the more radical consequences arising from Augustine's own anti-Pelagian works. It is conceivable, in fact, that Faustus was not being disingenuous, but that he

---

[5]Hence Faustus's likening in I. 1 of heretical extremists to rash oarsmen who foolishly brave Scylla and Charybdis without a captain.

[6]I. 5. 20, 11-14: "cum unum sine altero dicitur, tacetur alterum, non negatur secundum illam regulam, quam antistes Augustinus insinuat: non omnia quae tacentur negantur."

[7]The rule as cited does not appear to be contained among Augustine's writings. The general principle, that things concealed in one part of Scripture are manifest elsewhere, has ample attestation in Augustine. In *De doct. chr.* II. vi. 8 Augustine speaks of the Holy Spirit's modulating Scripture such that open passages give access to the hungry, and obscure passages deter the proud. In II. ix. 14 he counsels that one must know the whole of Scripture in order to apply what is manifest to what is obscure. Several other passages of Augustine's great hermeneutical work accord with Faustus's rule, though none matches it precisely.

saw himself as a hermeneutical ally of the bishop of Hippo, even as he questioned the direction of some of the latter's exegesis.

To illustrate Faustus's method of biblical interpretation, let us first examine how he treats the set of texts adduced in favor of his opponents. The main "problem passages" taken up by Faustus are: Rom. 4:2ff., I Cor. 15:10, Rom. 9:16, Matt. 9:13, Ps. 126:1, Rom. 9:21, Rom. 9:18, Jn. 6:44, Exod. 4:21, Rom. 8:29, John 12:39, and Rom. 9:9. This stockpile of texts, mostly Pauline, was apparently being used by Faustus's predestinarian opponents—perhaps by Lucidus himself—to buttress their position. By employing his hermeneutic of equilibrium and emphasizing the broader context of Scripture, Faustus is able to blunt the one-sidedness of his opponents' assertions.

In Rom. 4:2ff. the Apostle Paul invokes the example of Abraham to argue for justification through faith, saying that if the divine reward is given in return for works, it is not grace, but something owed. Faustus portrays the opposition as citing this passage in order to assert the operation of "grace alone," apart from human works.[8] Against this interpretation, Faustus asserts that two kinds of works exist, one of which, works of the law, was done away with the coming of Christ, the other of which still endures. To substantiate his claim, Faustus appeals to the fundamental consonance of Scripture:

> We certainly will not maintain that the testimonies of the apostles
> are incompatible or contrary to one another when another apostle
> says "Faith without works is dead," and "show me your faith

---

[8]Augustine made use of this passage in several places to underscore the gratuity of divine grace but did not make the kind of extreme assertions Faustus's opponents putatively make, such as an outright denial of the need for works. Cf. *De grat. et lib. arb.* V. 11, XXII. 43; *De pecc. mer. et remiss.* XXVII. 42.

without works and I will show you my faith by works ..." Yet neither does Paul, teacher of the gentiles, seem to be self-contradictory when he says: "In all things let us show ourselves as ministers of God, in many sufferings, in tribulations, in hardships, in distresses, in beatings, in imprisonments, in tumults, in labors" and: "each will receive his own reward according to his labor."[9]

So by marshalling the evidence of a broader sampling of Scripture, including both James[10] and Paul, Faustus seriously challenges his opponents' selective use of a Pauline passage, putting before them the choice of either affirming discord within Scripture or bowing to a more "catholic" interpretation: "To the ignorant and unlearned, and to those who resist the truth with an obstinate spirit, these appear to be discordances. But indeed, according to the catholic rule the works of the law, which are according to the letter, are to be abandoned, while those works which after grace must take place with the accompaniment of grace, are affirmed."[11] Faustus completes

---

[9]I. 4. 18, 6-10: "neque enim apostolorum testimonia conpugnantia et contraria sibi esse dicemus, cum alius apostolus dicat: fides sine operibus mortua est, et iterum: ostende mihi fidem tuam sine operibus et ego ostendam tibi ex operibus fidem meam . . . sed nec ipse doctor gentium Paulus diversus sibi et contrarius apparebit ita dicens: in omnibus exhibeamus nosmet ipsos sicut dei ministros in multa patientia, in tribulationibus, in necessitatibus, in augustiis, in plagis, in carceribus, in seditionibus, in laboribus, et iterum: unusquisque propriam mercedem accipiet secundum suum laborem."

[10]It is a curiosity worth noting that James 2:14-26 is not cited once in the entire corpus of Augustine's anti-Pelagian works.

[11]I. 5. 18, 20-24: "quae imperitis indoctis et his, qui veritati obstinato spiritu reluctantur, discordantia videbuntur. verum iuxta catholicam regulam opera legis evacuantur, quae secundum litteram sunt, et ea, quae post gratiam comitante gratia gerenda sunt, asseruntur."

his attack with a number of passages which both condemn the works of the law and enjoin Christian good deeds.

The polemic entailed in Faustus's treatment of 1 Cor. 15:10 is less obvious, since he mentions no opponent who has misused the passage. To appreciate Faustus's interpretation we should first see the verse in full: "But by the grace of God I am what I am, and his grace in me was not in vain; rather, I labored more than all of them, yet not I, but God's grace with me."[12] For Faustus, this passage illustrates the equilibrium or moderation in the Apostle's own thought:

> Note how he always subjoins the service of labor to the gift of grace. "Yet not I." Since he introduced mention of labor alone, he quickly rushed back as if to the embrace of Mother Grace saying: "but God's grace with me." He says, "by the grace of God I am." As one piously subject, he ascribes the beginnings to grace alone; as the teacher of obedience, he credits the middle parts to labor; and in the consummation, being restrained, he conjoins both grace and labor. He did not say, "I apart from grace," nor "grace apart from me," but "God's grace with me." How well he connected at the end of his discourse what he set forth singly and distinctly at the beginning![13]

---

[12]I. 5. 19, 26-28. Citation is verbatim from the Vulgate.

[13]I. 5. 19, 29-20, 9: "vide quomodo ad gratiae donum semper subiungit laboris obsequium: non ego autem. quia mentionem solius laboris intulerat, cito quasi ad amplexum matris gratiae recucurrit dicens: sed gratia dei mecum. gratia, inquit, dei sum. primas partes soli gratiae pie subiectus adscripsit, media quaeque labori magister oboedientiae deputavit, utrumque in consummatione moderatus gratiam laboremque coniunxit. non dixit: ego sine gratia rel gratia sine me, sed gratia dei mecum. quae prius singillatim distincta protulerat, quam bene in sermonis fine conexuit."

The exegesis of this passage, while it contains no overtly polemical language, bears within itself a rather sharp rebuke aimed at those predestinationists who regard Augustine as their authority, for its words readily call to mind Augustine's interpretation in *De gratia et libero arbitrio*:

> Lest the will itself, without God's grace, be regarded as capable of any good, when he had said, "His grace in me was not in vain, but I labored more than all of them," he subjoined the statement, "yet not I, but God's grace with me," that is, not alone, but God's grace with me, and by this he means neither the grace of God alone nor he himself alone, but God's grace with him. But that he should be called from heaven and be converted by so great and efficacious a calling was [the work of] God's grace alone.[14]

Faustus's announced intention of adhering to Augustine's hermeneutic seems to be matched in this instance by an exegesis of 1 Cor. 15:10 very similar to that of Augustine. While the text does not warrant concluding direct dependence upon Augustine's interpretaion of this verse, one must admit the striking affinity between the two and note that Faustus's invocation of Augustine occurs at the end of this very passage in the *De gratia*. Insofar as it is possible, Faustus certainly wishes to enlist Augustine's name in his cause.

---

[14]*De grat. et lib arb*. XII (PL 44: 889): "Tamen ne ipsa voluntas sine gratia Dei putetur boni aliquid posse, continuo cum dixisset, Gratia eius in me vacua non fuit, sed plus omnibus illis laboravi; subjunxit atque ait, non ego autem, sed gratia Dei mecum; id est, non solus, sed gratia Dei mecum ac per hoc nec gratia Dei sola, nec ipse solus, sed gratia Dei cum illo. Ut autem de coelo vocaretur, et tam magna efficacissima vocatione converteretur gratia Dei erat sola." Cf. *De gest. Pel*. XXXV-XXXVI.

What we have called Faustus's hermeneutic of equilibrium did not always make it so easy to stand with St. Augustine in matters of biblical interpretation. This difficulty becomes especially clear when one examines Faustus's attempt to explain several passages in the Romans chapter 9, a chapter which has been a kind of predestinarian commonplace in the history of Christian thought. Simonetti has correcly pointed out how Augustine, in the years after 396, habitually treated the rapport between divine grace and free will on the basis of a stockpile of Pauline quotations, often taken out of context.[15] Among the most prominent of these were a series of texts taken from the ninth chapter of Romans, texts which also supply us with some of the more telling illustrations of Faustus's use of Scripture.

The first of these passages to merit Faustus's attention in the *De gratia* is Rom. 9:16, "It is not of him who wills nor of him who runs, but of God who has mercy." Faustus refers to this text twice (I. 1. 11, 23ff.; I. 9. 26, 26-27, 15). In the first instance he uses it against Pelagianism, as a warning against presuming upon one's own works; the Holy Scriptures strike out against "the presumption of [Pelagius's] arrogance,"[16] since he exalts labor as sufficient for salvation. The more detailed and important discussion of the passage, however, arises against an overemphasis on divine grace such that "nothing is from man."[17] Faustus's opponents, ever mindful of the danger of presuming upon one's own works, as the "Jew" does upon the law, or Pelagius upon the free will, cite Rom. 9:16 much as Faustus did in I. 1, but with much more radical results. Faustus responds, once again, by counterposing other Scriptures. For him, it is quite clear that Rom. 9:16 is

---

[15]"Il *De gratia*," 132.

[16]I. 1. 11, 24: ". . . contra huius arrogantiae praesumptionem . . ."

[17]I. 9. 26, 26: ". . . nihil est hominis . . . "

addressed as a rebuke to one who "regards himself alone as sufficing in himself without the hand of a helper."[18] But Paul's words here are not aimed at those who join their own effort to divine mercy. Paul says something very different to them: "Run in such a way that you may understand" (1 Cor. 9:24); "You were running so well. Who impeded you from obeying the truth?" (Gal. 5:7); "Therefore I run, not as if in uncertainty" (1 Cor. 9:26); "I have finished the course, I have kept the faith" (2 Tim. 4:7). Again, Faustus's method of weighing Scripture against Scripture proves a hedge against excess, even excess with some claim to an Augustinian warrant.[19]

A second passage, Rom. 9:9-13, concerns Jacob and Esau: "Now the word of promise is this: 'After this time I will come, and a son shall be born to Sarah'; not only that, but Rebecca, from one union with Isaac our father. So when they had not yet been born, or done any kind of good or evil, in order that God's purpose regarding election might remain, not by works, but by the one who calls, it was said that the older should serve the younger, as it is written, 'Jacob I have loved, but Esau I have hated.'" Again in this case, Faustus decries his opponents' immoderate use of Scripture, for some use this passage to teach the impious belief that God "without any moderator's judgment between good and evil, not with a ruler's order but with

---

[18]I. 9. 26, 31-27, 1: ". . . qui solum se sibi sufficere sine manu adiuvantis existimat."

[19]Rom. 9:16 is one of the more frequently cited passages in Augustine's anti-Pelagian works, used always to show the utter inability of human capacities to obtain merit apart from divine grace. Cf. *De grat. et lib. arb.* VII, 16; *Contr. duas ep. Pel.* V, 10; *De gest. Pel.* XIV, 35, 37; XV, 38; XXVI, 51; *De grat. Chr.* X. vi, 51. It is used with particular force in arguing for the predestination of infants in *De dono persev.* XI, 25. Twice, in *De grat. et lib. arb.* VII, 16 and *De gest. Pel.* XIV, 35, Augustine, like Faustus, counterposes 2 Tim. 4:7; in both instances he tends to subsume this passage beneath Rom. 9:16, arguing that Paul's "running" was done by divine power. Augustine had begun to interpret Rom. 9 in a predestinarian manner as early as 396 in *De diversis quaestionibus ad Simplicianum.*

a tyrant's law, renders one worthy of affection, the other of hate."[20] In such
a state of affairs, God gives no consideration to human devotion or ascetic
labor, but makes an arbitrary choice. Faustus's response to this extreme
predestinarianism[21] takes up almost the whole of II. 6, and is remarkable in
its detail and in its insistence upon Paul's authorial intention.

As adduced by predestinarians, this Scripture seems to impugn
divine justice. Faustus therefore urges an interpretation consonant with a
portrayal of a just God. His main contention, and one that to a modern
exegete would seem reasonable and appropriate,[22] is that Paul's teaching here
concerns the calling of the gentiles, and is not a general discussion of divine
grace and free will. Faustus indicts the interpretive methods of his
opponents, who ignore both the context and the particulars of Paul's
argument:

> So this very one draws clouds of ignorance over himself, who does
> not so much accommodate himself to following the meaning of the
> Holy Scriptures as violently drags the Holy Scriptures to his own
> understanding and tries presumptively to apply them. And, having
> left out the preceding and following argument, he persuades himself
> according to his own understanding of something that the Apostle

---

[20]II. 6. 71, 18-20: ". . . absque ullo inter malum et bonum moderatoris
examine non ordine regentis, sed iure dominantis illum affectu dignum reddat,
hunc odio . . ."

[21]This passage is another of Augustine's favorite Scriptural loci in the
anti-Pelagian works, finding treatment in *De anima et eius orig.* III, vi, 8 and vii,
9; *De pecc. mer. et remiss.* XXI, 29, 30; *De praed. sanct.* XIX, 38. Particularly in
the latter passage, Augustine uses the passage to deny that any prior or foreseen
human merit can explain divine predestination. He roundly rejects the notion of a
foreknown faith prior to the divine calling.

[22]Simonetti makes this point in "Il *De gratia*," 132.

did not at all set out to say. Now if you return to the introduction
of the passage in question, you will easily avoid the ambiguity. If
the teacher of the gentiles had begun his treatment from the
beginning of man and were speaking of the whole course of human
life as predetermined from its origin and as under necessity, rather
than as having free choice of the will given it, because the Lord of
all, according to a powerful command and violent decree, had
relinquished some to perdition and elected others to salvation, then
perhaps . . . such a perverse belief could declare itself.[23]

Those who use Paul's narrative of Jacob and Esau to teach absolute
predestination are thus guilty both of ignorance and of presumption. Their
ignorance consists in the simple inability to read Paul's discourse as a whole;
Faustus clearly sees the Jacob-Esau narrative as proceeding from an initial
exordium to a conclusion whose validity lies only within Paul's own
rhetorical occasion. Faustus's opponents demonstrate the hermeneutical sin
of presumption in their unwillingness to allow the testimony of Scripture to
modify their opinions. They attribute to the Apostle an argument more
suited to their own unbalanced understanding than to his actual line of
thought.

---

[23]II. 6. 72, 1-15: "itaque ipse sibi obducit ignorantiae nebulas, qui non
tam scripturis sanctis sequaci sensu se accommodat, quam scripturas sanctas ad
intellectum suum violenter adtrahere et praesumptive nititur applicare et id sibi
pro captur suo omissa praecedentium vel sequentium ratione persuadet, unde
penitus loqui apostolus non instituit. quod si ad capituli ipsius, de quo agitur,
recurras exordium, omne absque ulla difficultate declinabis ambiguum. si magister
gentium de genesi hominum tractare coepisset et diceret homini totius vitae
cursum origine praefinitum et magis necessitati subditum, quam libero arbitrio
fuisse commissum eo, quod dominus omnium pro potestatis nutu violentoque
decreto alios relinqueret ad perditionem, alios eligeret ad salutem, tunc
forsitan . . . hunc iniqua persuasio posset asserere."

Properly understood, says Faustus, Paul's words point us to the ancient examples of Jacob and Esau "to suppress the presumption of the Jews, who impudently took pride in the works of the law."[24] God's preference of the younger to the older people was not a matter of mere divine caprice, but of justice; God foresaw the impiety of the Jews and the obedience of the gentiles. While an inept or depraved interpretation of this passage could call divine justice into question, a moderate and circumspect exegetical approach keeps God's manifest equity in view.[25] Once again Faustus's theme is balance or equilibrium: one does not make rash statements about God's ways with humanity on the basis of a scriptural passage taken out of context.

A third portion of Rom. 9 sheds further light on Faustus's exegetical method. Certain of those against whom Faustus writes asserted that a "vessel of dishonor" (*vas in contumeliam*) could not rise up to become a "vessel of honor" (*vas in honorem*), that is, presumably, that the reprobate cannot become acceptable to God. In support of this assertion they have cited Rom. 9:21: "Does not the potter have power over the clay, to make from the same lump one vessel in honor, the other in dishonor?" Faustus's response to this abuse of Scripture occupies all of I. 11.

Again applying a kind of rhetorical analysis to the passage, Faustus argues that the Apostle presents rather an incomplete picture: "In this passage, he has suppressed, in the conclusion of his discourse, the preceding

---

[24]II. 6. 72, 17-19: ". . . Iudaeorum praesumptionem . . . conprimere . . . qui inprobe de legis operibus intumescebant . . . "

[25]Unfortunately, Faustus's discussion of the passage breaks off in our MS just as he begins to discuss manifest reasons for God's preference of Jacob over Esau; cf. II. 6. 75, 6f.

causes by which a man may be turned either into dishonor or into honor."[26] Left unsaid in this instance by the Apostle but corroborated elsewhere in Scripture is the fact that becoming a vessel either of honor or of dishonor depends upon continual human effort. Faustus continues: "For when a man, by grace, has begun to be a vessel of honor, he must be especially watchful, so that the honor he has received may be kept safe with divine cooperation; otherwise this chosen person might be turned into a vessel of dishonor when sin arises."[27] The remainder of I. 11 finds Faustus deploying a vast arsenal of Scripture citations—twenty-one in number—which show by their exhortations to repentance and cleansing that human beings are not pressed into sin or into righteousness by some fatal necessity. To move from one state to another is a matter of human choice. Once more, attention to the immediate context of a passage and its rhetoric, as well as to the broader witness of Scripture, equips Faustus for avoiding what he would certainly regard as a tendentious reading of the Bible.[28]

Not only the Pauline letters, but the Gospels as well, have been aimed in a predestinarian direction by those whom Faustus opposes. Most prominent among these gospel passages is John 6:44, which Faustus takes up in I. 16: "No one comes to me unless the Father who sent me draws

---

[26]I. 11. 36, 18-20: "hoc loco praecedentes causas, quibus vel in honorem vel in contumeliam homo transeat, conclusa elocutione suppressit."

[27]I. 11. 36, 20-23: "nam cum homo per gratiam esse coeperit vas honoris, invigilandum est, ut acceptus honor divina cooperatione servetur, ne adquisitus homo postmodum in vas contumeliae culpa exsistente vertatur."

[28]Rom. 9:21 is not prominent among the biblical passages used by Augustine in the polemic against the Pelagians. While he cites it in a clearly predestinarian sense, it did not enjoy the same pride of place as other passages and certainly not the centrality it seems to have had for Faustus's opponents. Cf. *De nupt. et conc.* II, iii, 8 and iv, 30; *Ep.* 214, 3; *Contr. duas ep. Pel.* XIII. Faustus's treatment of this passage bears a remarkable resemblance to that of Origen-Rufinus in *De princ.* III. i. 21-24; see the discussion of Origen-Rufinus below.

him." For Faustus, these words are meant as a rebuke to anyone who makes excessive claims about his own powers apart from divine aid. For Faustus's opponents, Jesus' words here indicate God's decision to draw only some toward salvation. The work of human salvation would thus rest entirely with God. The fault of such an interpretation lies precisely in its one-sidedness: "One credits the salvation of the one drawn to the violence of the one who draws. Clearly, one who is ignorant of the bonds of devoted love recognizes only the chains of a burdensome servitude . . . when one person says everything is to be attributed to labor, and another that everything is to be attributed to grace, the Greek saying is fulfilled in both: 'Excesses are inequities.'"[29] The kind of "drawing" done by the Father must be seen in a way that better accords with a balanced portrayal of divine grace and human labor, and which is consonant with the whole testimony of Holy Scripture. The Father's drawing is an invitation demanding response, not a unilateral action: "He is not, is he, like stupid, senseless matter, one who must be moved about and pulled from place to place? Rather, the servant extends the hand of faith, by which he may be drawn, to the Lord who assists and calls, and he says, 'I believe, Lord; help my unbelief.' [. . .] So the Lord invites the one who wills, draws the one who desires, raises up the one who leans on him. What is it to draw but to preach, to excite with the consolations of the Scriptures . . . ?"[30] Faustus then turns the reader to other passages of

---

[29]I. 16. 51, 12-19: ". . . adtracti salutem adtrahentis putat esse violentiam. apparet illum non nosse nisi catenas obnoxiae servitutis, qui devotae nescit vincula caritatis . . . cum inter haec unus totum labori, alter totum gratiae indicet deputandum, impletur in utroque Graeca sententia: nimietates, inquit, inaequalitates sunt."

[30]I. 16. 52, 2-13: "numquid velut insensibilis et inepta materies de loco ad locum movendus est et trahendus? sed adsistenti et vocanti domino famulus manum fidei, qua adtrahatur, extendit et dicit: credo, domine, adiuva incredulitatem meam . . . ita dominus invitat volentem, adtrahit desiderantem, erigit adnitentem.

Scripture that portray God's universal invitation: "Hear the Lord drawing, not with harsh bonds but with hands of hope, and inviting with arms of love."[31] So Faustus's moderating hermeneutic allows him to blunt the force of a verse that had been used to buttress the most radical of predestinarian conclusions regarding free will.[32]

The Psalms, to whose numerical predominance in the *De gratia* we have already drawn attention, serve a distinctive purpose in Faustus's argument. Virtually without exception, Faustus cites passages from the Psalms which illustrate the willing and affective response of human beings to God. The pervasive interweaving of the Psalter into Faustus's theological discourse thus continually underscores the need of human will and action in the economy of salvation. One can appreciate the rhetorical force of his use of Psalms by a simple observation: book one, in which, as we have maintained, Faustus argues from the practice of Christian piety for the necessity of human effort, contains thirty-nine of the forty-four Psalm citations in the entire treatise. So the exigencies of the author's argument seem largely to determine his deployment of Psalm texts. Book two, in which Faustus tends to argue for the gratuity of created human endowments, has fewer Psalm citations, in accord with its slightly different argument. This is not to say that the Psalms are more supportive of one argument

---

quid est autem adtrahere nisi praedicare, nisi scripturarum consolationibus excitare . . .?

[31]I. 16. 52, 15-16: "Audi dominum non duris nexibus, sed spei manibus adtrahentem et dilectionis brachiis invitantem . . ." He then cites Hosea 11:4, Song 1:3, and Mt. 11:28.

[32]Augustine uses John 6:44 in *De praed. sanct.* VIII, 15 to support his assertion that some are given the wherewithal to believe, while some are not. He uses it in precisely the same way in *Contra duas ep. Pel.* III, 6 and IX, 37, and somewhat less forcefully in *De grat. Chr.* X, 11.

against another, but only that their devotional setting is especially fitting in an argument that focuses on the practice of piety.

On at least one occasion the Psalter provides a matter of serious contention. In I. 10 Faustus brings up an especially troublesome text that had easily lent itself to predestinarian interpretation, Ps. 126:1: "Unless the Lord build the house, they labor in vain who build it."[33] Those against whom Faustus writes have construed the verse as a radical denigration of human effort; to this he replies:

> Those who ignorantly bring this up as an objection, believing that everything human must be denied, cannot move their understanding beyond the mere sound of the words. Does the Lord ever administer the salvation of the human race all by himself, as if to procure it alone? Of course not. Rather, since the body is disposed through its members to follow the leadership of the head, the Lord builds his house through the priests and pastors of the Church, through those who say, "We are God's helpers." The one who takes to himself the care for human salvation is the redeemer's helper.[34]

---

[33] Augustine had cited the verse as part of the discourse between Pelagius and John, the archbishop of Jerusalem, in *De gest. Pel.* XIV, 37. He used it himself in *De praed. sanct.* VII, 12, to assert the uselessness of human works apart from the special gift of faith. He did not, however, deny the value of good works, provided they arose from faith.

[34] I. 10. 35, 9-17: "qui hoc inperite obiciunt et totum homini denegandum credunt, primum secundum sonum litterae intellectum suum expedire non possunt. numquid enim dominus per se tantum velut solitaria procuratione salutem humani generis administrat? non utique. sed cum corpus per membra dispositum capitis exsequatur imperium, aedificat <dominus> domum suam per ecclesiae praesules atque pastores, per eos, qui dicunt: dei enim adiutores sumus. qui enim curam suscipit salvandi hominis, adiutor est redemptoris."

Faustus goes on to explain the building of the Church through the dutiful labors of priests, apostles, and martyrs, illustrating from the scriptural example of King Saul the need for continual devoted service. This Scripture was not, then, written to deny the manifest need of human effort, but to curb the pride of one who attributes either the beginning (*initium*) or the end (*finem*) of his works to himself.[35]

To summarize: Faustus's use of Scripture meshes neatly with the mode of argument he employs in the treatise *De gratia*. His exegesis in general, like the treatise itself, aims at identifying excesses of left and right in order to establish a solid middle ground. Simonetti has rightly spoken of Faustus's inclusive, global approach to Scripture, and has noted the similarity to John Cassian's manner of reading Scripture.[36] The more difficult question, however, is to what extent Faustus's doctrinal argument emerges from his exegesis. This question may finally be insoluble, but one must point out that Faustus's global approach to Scripture is not simply the disinterested method of an exegete attempting to deal equitably with the Scriptures. The method itself, for all its apparent equanimity, is also demonstrably a function of Faustus's persuasive and polemical intention. Without doubt, the use of Scripture in the *De gratia* actualizes the centrist ideal expressed, for example, by Vincent of Lérins in the *Commonitorium*. But this very ideal, as we have seen, took shape against the perceived threat of predestinarianism. So to Simonetti's contention that the *De gratia* is primarily a discussion of biblical passages to which doctrinal assertions are

---

[35] I. 10. 35, 25-26.

[36] "Il *De gratia*," 131. Cassian had, in *Conl.* XIII, displayed the difficulty of the question of free will and divine grace by alternately citing passages in favor of each.

grafted, one may add the caution that the mode of discussion employed is already determined by Faustus's doctrinal argument.

Certainly the silent partner in much of Faustus's biblical argumentation is St. Augustine. Faustus purports to follow a method of scriptural interpretation taken from Augustine, and indeed, one could make a case that Faustus's alleged Augustinian rule resembles currents of thought in the *De doctrina christiana*. At the same time, the results of Faustus's interpretation of Scripture frequently tend in a different direction. While he never directly disputes with the bishop of Hippo, Faustus certainly joins battle precisely at the point of some of Augustine's favored anti-Pelagian prooftexts. On comparing the exegesis directly with Augustine's on these texts, however, one finds Faustus aiming not at Augustine but at a kind of hyper-Augustinian predestinarian use of the Bible. It may well be that Faustus regarded such radical interpretations to be abuses of Augustine's own hermeneutical canons.

For the most part, Faustus does not strike one as an exceptionally original interpreter of Scripture. His ability to marshal a wide array of biblical texts in the controversy is noteworthy but not unprecedented. He is cautious, attentive to the context and rhetoric of the biblical writings, and not on the whole given to allegory.[37] At many points his use of Scripture depends upon that of earlier writers, the most important of whom we may now identify.

---

[37]Some measure of allegorical interpretation is, of course, to be expected. His use of the "house" built by the Lord in Ps. 126:1 to exemplify the Church affords one example. Another may be seen in his exegesis of Lk. 15:7 in I. 9, in which the "ninety-nine righteous" are shown by the imperfection of the number ninety-nine to be actually unrighteous and proud.

Faustus's Use of Christian Writers and Other Sources

Apart from two mentions of Augustine and the many scriptural quotations, Faustus of Riez does not explicitly identify any sources of his theology in the *De gratia*. He was not, however, as original a thinker as this fact might suggest. He draws considerably upon other Christian writers of antiquity, sometimes very directly and at other times perhaps with only a distant familiarity. To identify every possible source would, of course, be a mammoth undertaking, but we can at least enumerate the most prominent and influential authors whose thought helped to shape the *De gratia*, and we can illustrate Faustus's manner of employing their thought. Most obvious among them, not surprisingly, are Augustine and Cassian. Less evident but of real importance is Origen, in the translation of Rufinus. A case can also be made for the influence of Hilary of Poitiers.

Augustine

Carlo Tibiletti's work has brought about a new awareness of Augustine's positive significance in the *De gratia*. Now untenable is the notion of some earlier critics that Faustus was a deceptive anti-Augustinian.[38] It is true, of course, that Faustus regarded Augustine as suspect, or at least fallible, in some matters.[39] We have also noted instances

---

[38]Tibiletti, "Libero arbitrio e grazia," 263, n. 29. Iacobus Basagnius, in his prolegomena to the works of Faustus (PL 58: 777-84), styles him, citing the sixteenth-century historian Caesar Baronius, as one who changes his skin (*versipellis*), a little fox (*velpecula*), given to shrewdness (*subtilitas*). He cites no less an authority than Isidore of Seville as having termed him a man of profound cleverness or deceitfulness (*vir profundae calliditatis*). Cf. the discussion above in the introduction to this study.

[39]In Faustus's epistle to the deacon Graecus (*Ep.* VII, CSEL 21: 200ff.), he assures his reader of Augustine's orthodoxy on the matter at hand—

in which Faustus does exegetical battle with biblical interpretations having at least some Augustinian warrant. Still, Tibiletti has argued that Augustine's thought is used positively by Faustus, with the exception of the former's doctrine of predestination.[40] This has certainly proven true in Faustus's explicit use of Augustine's hermeneutical rule. We will now demonstrate more broadly that much of Augustine's thought has been assimilated, such that Faustus often uses its categories as his own.

First, Faustus was acquainted with *De civitate Dei*. Apart from his citation of the elusive Augustinian rule just mentioned, his only other explicit attribution to Augustine is a passage from *De civitate Dei* XXII, 24, 1: "Even the most blessed pontiff Augustine agrees that the work of the natural law has been written in human hearts when he says in a most learned discourse: 'Both run simultaneously in the stream and current of the human race: evil, which is handed on by the parent, and goodness, which is given by the creator.'"[41] One finds no other explicit citations of *De civitate Dei* in the treatise; a possible allusion to XXII, 1 occurs in *De gratia* II. 3. 65, 7-10, where Faustus speaks of God's ability to draw good from human evil. But

---

Christology—but mentions in passing that something in the holy bishop's writings is "regarded as suspect among very learned men" ("apud doctissimos viros putatur esse suspectum"); 201, 12-13.

[40]"Libero arbitrio e grazia," 263.

[41]II. 9. 81, 19-23: "Opus itaque naturalis legis in cordibus hominum fuisse conscriptum etiam beatissimus pontifex Augustinus doctissimo sermone prosequitur ita dicens: utrumque simul currit in isto alveo atque torrente generis humani, malum, quod a parente trahitur, et bonum, quod a creante tribuitur." Courcelle, in "Nouveaux aspects de la culture lérinienne," 404, n. 9, has drawn attention to Faustus's substitution of *alveo* for Augustine's *fluvio*. The meaning of *malum* here for Faustus has been a matter of some contention; cf. chapter 4 of the present study.

while this notion can be traced back to Augustine,[42] there is really no compelling textual reason to suppose that Augustine lies behind its use here.

The first two chapters of the *De gratia* as well as a brief allusion in the prologue provide us with the clearest and most extended dependence upon Augustine's thought, but in a paradoxical way. On the one hand, Faustus clearly reproduces Augustine's portrayal of, and response to, Pelagianism, as well as his account of original sin and concupiscence. Indeed, one may well suspect that Faustus's doctrinal centrism may be drawn as much from Augustine as from his own Lerinian ethos. On the other hand, this obvious dependence is not direct in the sense of being textually precise; Faustus distills rather than quotes. So one may say that in this most unambiguously Augustinian portion of the treatise, Faustus assimilates the broad perspective of certain of Augustine's anti-Pelagian writings without entering into the intricacies of his argumentation.

In the prefatory letter to Leontius, which serves as a prologue to the treatise, Faustus speaks of the need to confute Pelagius's doctrine so that Faustus's own insistence on faith and works will not be misconstrued. He worries that someone, having been cautioned against an excessive predestinationism, might mistakenly regard Pelagius's view as the catholic view: "Then, having left the royal way by falling to the right, he might believe that we decline to the left, and in speaking of labor as the servant of

---

[42]Besides *De civ. Dei* XXII, 1, Tibiletti finds the same thought expressed in *Enchir.* 8, 27 and 28, 104. Cf. "Libero arbitrio e grazia," 263. Very similar terminology is found in *De pecc. mer. et remiss.* I, xxix, 57, in connection with the good use of concupiscence in marital union. The distinction between good and evil uses of things is a commonplace in Augustine's discussions of concupiscence.

grace we may seem to place a stumbling block before the blind."[43] In adopting this metaphor, Faustus seems to be taking up the language of Augustine's *Ep.* 215 to Valentinus, which accompanied the treatise *De gratia et libero arbitrio* to the monks at Hadrumetum. With reference to the straight path to be walked by the godly person, Augustine writes:

> Indeed, that one is understood as declining to the right, who wishes to assign his own good works, which pertain to the right-hand paths, to himself and not to God. . . . For which reason, most dearly beloved, whoever says "My will suffices for me to do good works" declines to the right. But on the other hand, those who think that a good life is to be forsaken when they hear God's grace preached so as to believe and understand that he by himself makes human wills good from evil, and guards what he has made, and thus they say "Let us do evil, that good might come," these people decline to the left.[44]

So the attempt to tread a middle path between Pelagianism and solagratianism was made by Augustine in addressing the concerns of the monastic community. Faustus's use of the same metaphor, including some of the

---

[43]Prol. 4. 15-18: ". . . et omissa via regia in dexteram cadens in sinistram declinare nos crederet, et, dum de labore servo gratiae loquimur, offendiculum ante pedes caeci opposuisse videremur."

[44]*Ep.* 215. 7-8 (CSEL 57: 393-95): "declinare quippe ille est intellegendus in dextram, qui bona ipsa opera, quae ad vias dextras pertinent, sibi vult adsignare non deo . . . Quapropter, dilectissimi,quicumque dicit: 'Voluntas mea mihi sufficit ad facienda opera bona,' declinat in dextram. sed rursus illi, qui putant bonam vitam esse deserendam, quando audiunt sic dei gratiam praedicari, ut credatur et intellegatur voluntates hominum ipse ex malis bonas facere, ipsa etiam, quas fecerit, custodire, et propterea dicunt: Faciamus mala, ut veniant bona, in sinistram declinant."

same terminology and the assigning of the "right-hand" error to Pelagius, strongly suggests a familiarity, whether at first hand or not, with this letter.

Faustus's portrait of Pelagius is certainly drawn from Augustine. The Pelagian position is adduced in its most radical formulation: "Pelagius therefore says that human nature is, in itself, sufficient for obtaining salvation. So the pestiferous teacher affirms these things, as if the makeup of our condition still remained in its unimpaired state."[45] Against such a position Faustus cites two favorite Augustinian prooftexts, John 15:5 and Psalm 126:1. While he clearly takes this portrayal, directly or indirectly, from Augustine, it is sufficiently general as to be derivable from any of several of the anti-Pelagian works.[46] This same phenomenon obtains through much of I. 1-2: we find unmistakably Augustinian affirmations given in a way that suggests that they have been integrated into the shape of Faustus's own thought rather than slavishly copied from Augustine's writings.

Faustus's second accusation against Pelagius has to do with Adam's created mortality: "Pelagius continues that Adam was made a mortal, who, whether he had sinned or not, would have been liable to death. Yet since the Apostle says, 'Therefore just as through one man sin entered this world, and through sin death,' you understand this to mean that if sin had not gone first, death would not have followed, and the bestowed immortality would have

---

[45]I. 1. 8, 23-26: "Dicit ergo Pelagius, quod ad obtinendam salutem natura hominis sibi sola sifficiat. ita haec pestifer doctor adfirmat, quasi adhuc factura conditionis nostrae in statu suo inlibata permaneat."

[46]Among many examples, one could cite *De nat. et grat.* XI, 6, in which Augustine speaks of those who try to show that "human nature needs no physician" ("naturam humanam neque . . . medico indigere"). Without directly attacking Pelagius, Augustine speaks in the same work (II. 2) of the notion that human nature "might be sufficient in itself" ("si potest sibi sufficere") to fulfill the law. Cf. also *Ep.* 215. 8, *De grat. et lib. arb.* IV, 6.

perdured."[47] In addition to the citation of Rom. 5:12, Faustus invokes Gen. 2:17 to show that death is not of the natural order but is the consequence of sin. Again, Faustus's discussion is redolent of Augustine's treatment. In this instance Augustine's discourse can be identified with somewhat greater certainty. Augustine confutes those who argue for Adam's original liability to death in only one place: *De peccatorum meritis et remissione* I, ii-ix. He notes that some say Adam would have died even apart from sin. These assert that Gen. 2:17, "On the day you eat thereof, you will surely die," refers to the death of the soul, not bodily death. He distinguishes among the terms *mortale* (capable of dying), *mortuum* (dead), and *moriturus* (liable to death); Adam was created *mortale*, but not *moriturus*. His mortality was destined to be superseded by incorruption, had not sin intervened.[48] Augustine cites Rom. 5:12 to underscore the physical death that results from sin. So Faustus's brief characterization of Pelagius's view here encapsulates Augustine's more extensive and detailed treatment, using some of the same Scripture references and terminology (e.g., *moriturus*). The use of Augustine is not precise or detailed, but the source is clear enough.

In seeing Adam as having been created liable to death, says Faustus, Pelagius makes the notion of death as a penalty for sin appear false: "Man is God's work; sin is the devil's work: death is the penalty for sin. The Apostle did not say 'the will of God is death,' but 'the wage of sin is death.'"[49] The

---

[47]I. 1. 9, 4-9: "Prosequitur adhuc Pelagius Adam mortalem factum, qui, sive peccasset sive non peccasset, esset moriturus. sed cum dicat apostolus: propterea, inquit, sicut per unum hominem in hunc mundum peccatum intravit et per peccatum mors, intellegis, quia, si peccatum non praecessisset, mors secuta non esset et donata inmortalitas perdurasset . . ."

[48]*De pecc. mer. et remiss.* I, v.

[49]I. 1. 10, 28-30: "homo enim opus dei, peccatum opus diaboli, mors poena peccati. nam apostolus non dixit: voluntas dei mors sed: stipendium peccati mors."

language of Faustus's little formula here seems to have been drawn from Augustine's language in *De nuptiis et concupiscentia* I. 1: "For just as sin, whether contracted by infants from this source or that is the devil's work, so man, whether born in this way or that, is God's work."[50] Augustine does not add the third component, the citation of Rom. 6:23, to the formula; this would suggest either Faustus's own addition or perhaps his repetition of a common formula already in circulation.

Faustus's treatment of Pelagius's denial of original sin could, again, have been drawn from any of a number of Augustine's works. Certain ones, however, readily suggest themselves. Pelagius's refusal to recognize original sin in infants, a defect alleged by Augustine in several places,[51] is noted, too, by Faustus, who goes on to chide Pelagius for his inability, or unwillingness, to recognize the results of original sin in the human race: "Is it any wonder that he does not recognize that tree by its fruits that he has been unwilling to recognize in its roots?"[52] This allusion to Mt. 7:16 mirrors Augustine's use of the passage in precisely the same context in *De nuptiis et concupiscentia* II, xxvi, 41-43.

At the beginning of I. 2, Faustus portrays Pelagius as posing a troubling question: "Pelagius also adds: 'If through the gift of baptism original sin is removed, then those born of two baptized parents should be

---

[50]"nam sicut peccatum, sive hinc sive inde a parvulis trahitur, opus est diaboli, sic homo sive hinc sive inde nascitur, opus est dei." Cf. also *De nupt. et conc.* II, xxvi, 43.

[51]*De nat. et grat.* viii, 9; *De pecc. mer. et remiss.* I, xvi, 21; I, xxviii, 56; III, i, 1; III, ii-48. The long discussion in *De pecc. mer. et remiss.* III specifically attributes the erring view to Pelagius and refutes it in detail. Cf. also *De nupt. et conc.* II, iii, 9ff.

[52]I. 1. 11, 7-9: "quid mirum si arborem illam in fructibus non agnoscat, quam noluit in radice cognoscere?"

without this sin. How,' he asks, 'do they transmit to their offspring what they did not have at all in themselves?'"[53] For Faustus this problem is irrational and easily refutable. There are, he says, two kinds of birth, one of generation, by which the parents pass on what is of nature and proper to them, and one of regeneration, which has nothing to do with parental agency. Parents can pass on what is of nature, but not what is of grace.[54] This had already been the teaching of Augustine, employed against Pelagius in two works, *De gratia Christi et de peccato originali* and *De nuptiis et concupiscentia*: "The regenerate man does not regenerate children of the flesh but generates them. [. . .] Original sin remains in the offspring, even if in the parent the guilt of that same sin has been washed away by the remission of sins."[55] But while for Faustus, Pelagius's case was easily (*facile*) answered, Augustine declares that the matter was "not to be found out by easy argument."[56] Such was the benefit, for Faustus, of relying upon another's argument.

As Tibiletti has pointed out, Faustus is at one with Augustine in seeing carnal concupiscence as the mode of transmission for original sin. From parents, whether baptized or not, original sin passes on to the offspring, such that we cry out with the Prophet, "Behold, I was conceived in

---

[53]I. 2. 12, 6-9: "Adtendit etiam Pelagius: si per baptismi donum tollitur originale peccatum, de duobus baptizatis nati debent hoc carere peccato. quomodo, inquit, mittunt ad posteros quod ipsi in se minime habuerunt."

[54]I. 2. 12, 9-29.

[55]*De grat. Chr. et pecc. orig.* II, xl, 45: "regeneratus non regenerat filios carnis, sed generat." II, xxxix, 44: "manet in prole originis vitium, etiamsi in parente reatus eiusdem vitii remissione ablutus est peccatorum."

[56]*De nupt. et conc.* I, xix, 21: ". . . non facili ratione indagatur."

iniquity, and in sins my mother bore me."[57] Specifically, the bondage of sin is passed on through the desire involved in sexual union: "If you should ask whence comes the bond that drags down one's offspring, without doubt it is through the arousing ardor of cursed procreation, and through the enticing embrace of the two parents. For when you see that he alone is immune from the original contagion who was conceived not by the flesh but by the spirit ... be aware that the cause of original evil comes from the delight of conceiving a child and from the sin of pleasure."[58] Augustine's notion of the role of concupiscence may be easily recognized here;[59] Faustus's use of *ardor* to describe the culpable passion simply repeats an Augustinian commonplace. Further, Augustine, depending upon Ambrose, attributed Christ's sinlessness precisely to his exemption from concupiscent procreation. Before quoting Ambrose's commentary on Isaiah, Augustine summarized the late bishop of Milan's position: ". . . the reason why Christ's birth in the flesh was free from all sinful fault [was] that his conception was not the result of the union of the two sexes; but there is not one among human beings conceived in such a union who is without sin."[60]

---

[57]Faustus's reading of Ps. 50:7 here is interesting. The usual Vulgate reading of the Psalm is "et in peccatis peperit me . . ." but Faustus has "et in delictis peperit me . . ." This reading, found in Ambrose, *De poenitentia* i, 2, 3, was used only once by Augustine, when quoting from Ambrose in *De grat. Chr.* XLI, 47. Elsewhere in Augustine's citations of this verse, he has *peccatis*.

[58]I. 2. 13, 2-9: "unde autem veniat nexus iste, qui posteros trahit, si requiras: sine dubio per incentiuum maledictae generationis ardorem et per inlecebrosum utriusque parentis amplexum. nam cum illum solum videas ab originali inmunem esse contagione , qui non carne, sed spiritu . . . conceptus est, agnosce causam mali originalis de oblectamento naturam conceptionis et de vitio voluptatis."

[59]Cf., inter alia, *De nupt. et conc.* I, xxxii, 37; II, xxxiv, 58.

[60]*De nupt. et conc.* II, v, 15: ". . . cum Christi carnalem nativitatem . . . expertem esse delicti, quia conceptus eius utriusque sexus commixtionis est

The sin that originated in Adam and Eve was rooted in proud disobedience. Its immediate consequence, says Faustus, was twofold, a loss of control over the bodily members and the sense of shame which accompanied this loss:

> But when in his intention to be God, he desired a taste of the deadly fruit and extended his damnable desire even to the ambition for majesty, heedless of the law and of its mandates, he was punished by an attack in the rebellion of his members and, when he presumed equality with his Lord, he lost the power over his body. From pride is born incontinence. For he showed what was striken in him by the way he hid the shameful parts.[61]

These two consequences of Adam's sin—loss of control over the body and shame in leaving uncovered the organs of procreation—are the same given by Augustine. In a passage that very nearly parallels Faustus's discussion, Augustine writes:

> Should not the freedom of the human will be ashamed, that by its contempt of God the ruler it should lose its own rule in its own members? Where could the rightful depravation of human nature for its disobedience be more fittingly shown than in those disobedient

---

expers; nullum autem hominum esse sine delicto qui de illa commixtione conceptus sit."

[61]I. 2. 13, 19-25: "cum vero illo animo, ut deus esset, gustum cibi letalis adpetit et damnandam cupiditatem in ambitum maiestatis extendit, inmemor legis et mandatorum legis rebellis multatur inpugnatione membrorum et, dum aequalitatem domini sui praesumit, corporis sui perdidit potestatem. de superbia nata est incontinentia. nam quid in eo percussum esset ostendit, quando verecunda contexit."

parts from which, through succession, nature itself subsists? [. . .] When the first people had experienced in their flesh this motion, which was indecent because disobedient, and were ashamed in their nudity, they covered those same members with fig leaves, so that at least the shameful thing could be veiled by choice.[62]

Once more, Faustus's dependence upon Augustine's thought is evident, even if it is a step removed from direct textual quotation.

In the matter of original sin and concupiscence, a final instance of adherence to Augustine shows itself. At the end of I. 2 Faustus meets the objection that he seems to condemn marriage in condemning concupiscence. In response he distinguishes between the office of marriage, which comes from divine precept, and the adulteration of that office by sin. Marriage has been stained by concupiscence but is still good. Had not sin intervened, procreation in marriage would have been chaste and unadulterated.[63] Augustine's concern in *De nuptiis et concupiscentia* was, similarly, "to distinguish the evil of carnal concupiscence . . . from the goodness of marriage."[64] Further, it is not dependent upon human sin; rather, "marriage

---

[62]*De nupt. et conc.* I, vi, 7: ". . . non erubesceret humani libertas arbitrii, quod contemnendo imperantem deum etiam in membra propria proprium perdidisset imperium? ubi autem convenientius monstraretur inoboedientiae merito humanam depravatam esse naturam quam in his inoboedientibus locis, unde per successionem subsistit ipsa natura? [. . .] hunc itaque motum ideo indecentem, quia inoboedientem, cum illi primi homines in sua carne sensissent et in sua nuditate erubuissent, foliis ficulneis eadem membra texerunt, ut saltem arbitrio verecundantium velaretur . . ." Cf. *Contr. duas ep. Pel.* xxxi; *De grat. Chr.* xxxvi, 41; *De pecc. mer. et remiss.* I, xxi, 21.

[63]I. 2. 13, 28-14, 18.

[64]*De nupt. et conc.* I, i, 1: "carnalis concupiscentiae malum . . . discernere a bonitate nuptiarum." Similarly, I, v, 6; vii, 8; xvi, 18; *De grat. Chr.* xxxiii, 38.

... would still have existed, even if no one had sinned. For the procreation of children in the body of that life would have taken place without that disorder, without which one cannot now come to be 'in the body of this death.'"[65] So the passage in *De gratia* I. 1-2, from beginning to end, depends extensively on the thought of Augustine in his anti-Pelagian works, especially *De nuptiis et concupiscentia*. The broad material agreement is not matched by detailed textual dependence or the one-to-one correspondence of parallel passages, some similar vocabulary notwithstanding. The impression obtains that Augustine's works have been learned at secondhand, or, more likely, that his sensibilities have simply been well assimilated on the matter of original sin and its effects.

Faustus's dependence on Augustine's doctrines of original sin and concupiscence is certain. In a much less clear, but suggestive, way, Faustus may have imbibed Augustine's thought on the Trinity, even though Augustine is by no means cited on this doctrine, and indeed, doctrines of God and Trinity do not loom large in the *De gratia*. Some hints, however, of Faustus's trinitarian thought emerge, *sotto voce*, in the dense anthropological chapter II. 9. Faustus speaks of the granting of the *imago Dei* to humankind as specifically referring to the image of the Trinity: "whatever the Trinity bestows in common upon humankind is derived from the likeness of the deity. . . . Since, therefore, this image is conferred by the Father, Son, and Holy Spirit, undoubtedly the one divinity of the three persons has granted the dignity of its image to the first man."[66] This passage recalls two themes in

---

[65]*De nupt. et conc.* I, i, 1: ". . . nuptiae vero essent, etiamsi nemo peccasset; fieret quippe sine isto morbo seminatio filiorum in corpore vitae illius, sine quo nunc fieri non potest in corpore mortis huius." Tibiletti, in "Libero arbitrio e grazia," 262, cites *De nupt. et conc.* II, xxii, 37 and II, vii, 17.

[66]II. 9. 78, 12-25: ". . . ex deitatis similitudine derivatur, quidquid homini trinitas in commune largitur . . . cum ergo imago haec a patre et filio et

Augustine's *De Trinitate*. In *De Trinitate* I, v, 8, Augustine voices the assertion that "the Trinity works indivisibly in everything God works"[67] and proceeds to illustrate this principle using the example of the divine image in humankind in I, vii, 10. Elsewhere in the treatise Augustine elaborates on the specifically trinitarian character of the impress of God's image in humans through his notion of *vestigia Trinitatis*, which he elaborates in *De Trinitate* IX-XIV. In both the inner and outer human life, one may find traces of God's triune existence by virtue of creation in the *imago Dei*. Hence the mind, its knowledge, and the love it has of itself and of its knowledge—or human memory, understanding, and will, and so on—mirror the divine being in an imperfect way. Certainly Faustus, in his exposition of the image of God, has something much like this in mind when he writes that "man therefore is called the image of God because the truth kindly and graciously implanted justice in him; and reason, wisdom; and perpetuity, eternity. It is from the image of God that man understands, that he knows what is right, that he discriminates between evil and good with the scrutiny of judgment."[68] Despite the clear differences from Augustine's versions of the *vestigia Trinitatis*, it is not farfetched to suggest that Faustus's threefold formulas here are imitative of Augustine.

To conclude this consideration of Augustine's contribution to the *De gratia*, we may concur with Tibiletti that it was considerable. Besides

---

sancto spiritu conferatur, suae absque dubio trium personarum una divinitas primo homini suae imaginis tribuit dignitatem."

67". . . inseparabiliter operari trinitatem in omni re quam deus operatur . . ." CCL 50: 36.

68II. 9. 78, 28-79, 2: "imago ergo dei homo dicitur, quia ei indulgenter ac dignanter inseruit veritas iustitiam, ratio sapientiam, perennitas aeternitatem. de imagine dei est, quod intellegit, quod rectum sapit, quod inter malum et bonum iudicio examinante discriminat."

Faustus's two overt citations of Augustine, one finds almost complete reliance upon Augustine for the material of the two first chapters of the treatise. Faustus was familiar, whether at first or second hand, with some of Augustine's anti-Pelagian works. While he uses these positively against Pelagianism, he also uses them selectively. One finds no positive use of the bipartite *De praedestinatione sanctorum* and *De dono perseverantiae*, which were directed against the monks of Gaul in 428/429; indeed, the preceding section on Faustus's exegesis suggested that he may have regarded as suspect some of the interpretive tendencies found in these works. Further, Faustus knew at least some of *De civitate Dei* and may have known *De doctrina Christiana* and *De Trinitate*. Because he did not make precise and detailed citations of Augustine, we simply cannot know the exact sort of access he had to the writings of the bishop of Hippo. Certainly Prosper of Aquitaine helped to make fifth-century Gaul a treasury of Augustinian *florilegia*,[69] and so one can with good cause question any apparent first-hand contact with Augustine. While there are those who would argue, for example, that Lérins must have possessed an entire Augustinian library,[70] a more prudent suggestion would be that many of Augustine's categories and sensibilities had begun to become the *lingua franca* of the Gallic church a

---

[69]E.g., *Pro Augustino responsiones ad excerpta Genuensium, Pro Augustino responsiones ad capitula objectionum Gallorum calumniantium, Pro Augustino responsiones ad capitula objectionum Vincentianarum*, to name but a few.

[70]So Courcelle in "Nouveaux aspects de la culture lérinienne," 404, n. 9. He records his agreement with J. Madoz, who published what he termed excerpts "ex universo beatae recordationis Augustini episcopi in unam collecta" (PL, Supplementum, III: 23-45). Courcelle argues that Vincent of Lérins had at hand an entire library of Augustine's works. This seems to me an extreme conclusion in light of the prevalence of works like those of Prosper.

generation after his death. Augustine's prestige and genius made recourse to him inevitable.

John Cassian

The work of several scholars has shown Faustus's dependence upon John Cassian. Well before the composition of the *De gratia* Faustus had established his doctrine of the human soul largely on Cassian's authority.[71] In light of Cassian's remarkable stature as one of the great monastic figures of his time and the likelihood of relations between the monasteries of St. Victor and Lérins,[72] Faustus's use of his work is hardly surprising. Most of this dependence, however, is not witnessed in the *De gratia*. Michael Petschenig, editor of the Vienna edition of John Cassian (CSEL 13 and 17), noted seven instances of derivation from Cassian, of which only one is from the *De gratia*.[73] Engelbrecht, editor of Faustus for the same series, added only two loci to Petschenig's list, one of which is from the *De gratia*.[74] More recently, Tibiletti has suggested that certain anthropological features of the *De gratia* derive from Cassian,[75] and Yves-Marie Duval finds some

---

[71]In *Ep.* 3 (CSEL 21), 176, 7, Faustus refers to *Conl.* VII, wherein the "corporeality" of the soul is upheld, as "quidam receptissimus patrum tractatus."

[72]So Tibiletti, "Libero arbitrio e grazia," 267, n. 47.

[73]*Wochenschrift für klassische Philologie* 8 (1891): 1426, cited in Weigel, *Faustus*, 33. Petschenig sees *De grat.* I. 13 as dependent upon *Conl.* XIII, 10; the other instances are found in epistles and sermons.

[74]*Patristische Analecten* (Vienna, 1892), 96-97, cited in Weigel, *Faustus*, 33. He adds *De grat.* I. 3. 16, 16ff., to be compared with *Contra Nest.* VII. 6. 361, 21ff.

[75]"Libero arbitrio e grazia," 267ff. Reference is to human possession of a good will or the seeds (*semina*) thereof. Cf. infra.

similarities between Cassian and Faustus in their use of the book of Jonah.[76] Here we shall simply review and evaluate these instances of dependence.

In I. 13 we find Faustus introducing a series of biblical citations alternately showing the weakness and the capability of the human will: "If you would apply your mind well, you would know clearly and fully how throughout the pages of Holy Scripture the power of grace is asserted in one place and the assent of human frailty in another."[77] Cassian had adopted exactly this mode of biblical argumentation in *Conlatio* XIII, 10,[78] though using a different set of biblical texts. There is no literary dependence, though one can easily speak of a shared approach to biblical exegesis.[79]

This same similarity of perspective extends to the doctrine of grace, about which Faustus expresses his moderation by quoting a "Greek saying" (*Graeca sententia*): "excesses are inconsistencies" (*nimietates inquit, inaequalitates sunt*).[80] In quoting this "saying," Faustus shares not only Cassian's outlook but, in a slightly changed way, his words. In *Conlatio* II, 16, 1, warning against extremes and in favor of the virtuous middle, Cassian wrote: "For the old saying is ἀκρότητες ἰσότητες, that is, excesses are

---

[76]*Le livre de Jonas*, 509ff.

[77]I. 13. 44, 21-23: "Si bene intendas animum, aperte copiosque cognoscis, quomodo per sanctarum paginas scripturarum nunc asseratur gratiae virtus, nunc humanae voluntatis adsensus."

[78]SC 54: 160-62. In the same vein, Faustus in II. 12. 91, 2 cites Ps. 69:2 as an example of the need for divine aid, which Cassian did in *Conl.* X, 10.

[79]Simonetti, in "Il *De gratia*," 130, notes the similarity between Faustus and Cassian as over against Augustine's "reductive" method of argumentation.

[80]I. 16. 51, 18-19.

equals" (*nimietates aequales sunt*). [81] Imprecision notwithstanding, one may justly suspect that Cassian lies behind Faustus's use of this proverb.[82]

Faustus illustrates the practice of disguising evil as an apparent good by using, in I. 3, the analogy of those who conceal poisons:

> So also those sorcerers are accustomed to doing, who make lethal poisons sweet and mix them into a potion or some sweet drink, for those who will taste unknowingly of its deceptive sweetness; they hide the deadly bitterness with a false sweetness. The first whiff of the cup excites, but swallowing a taste of the poison suffocates. It is honey that comes up into the lips, but gall that goes down into the guts.[83]

Cassian used the same analogy, in a different context, in his *Contra Nestorium*. Writing against what he regards as a subtle diminution of the incarnation, Cassian likens his opponent to a poisoner:

> This is the custom, they say, of certain makers of poisons: they mix honey with poison in the drinks they concoct, in order to conceal the coming injury with sweetness. When someone is

---

[81]SC 42: 131.

[82]Credit for locating this saying in the *Conlationes* goes to Engelbrecht, who mentions it in his prolegomena to Faustus in CSEL 21.

[83]I. 3. 16, 16-21: "sic etiam malefici facere solent, qui mortiferos herbarum temperant sucos, in condito aut aliquo dulci poculo nescientibus propinaturis gustum mentita suavitate conponunt, virus amaritudinis obscurant fraude dulcedinis. provocat primus odor poculi, sed praefocat inclusus sapor veneni. mel est quod ascendit in labia, fel est quod descendit in viscera."

enamored of the honey's sweetness, he is killed by the poison's power.[84]

While the imagery may have been something of a commonplace,[85] Faustus's use of it in an antiheretical setting contains enough verbal similarities to suggest that he was acquainted with Cassian's treatise.

Tibiletti's recent suggestion of Faustus's dependence on Cassian has focused on an element of Faustus's anthropology: the notion, Stoic in its origin, of *semina virtutum*, that is, innate potentialities of goodness in the human being. At the beginning of I. 12 Faustus asserts that Scripture, with its frequent exhortations to willing obedience, "evidently ascribes to man the implanted seeds of a good will."[86] The use of the term *semina* here gives Tibiletti reason to link Faustus's formulation to the Stoic doctrine of *logoi spermatikoi* and then to ask where Faustus might have had access to such ideas.[87] He concludes that Cassian, who was connected to Stoic thought through Evagrius Ponticus, is the most likely source.[88] As evidence of

---

[84]*Contra Nestorium* VII. 6 (CSEL 17: 361, 20-23): "veneficorum quorundam, ut aiunt, haec consuetudo est, ut in poculis quae conficiunt venenis mella permisceant, ut dulcibus nocitura celentur, et dum quis mellis dulcedine capitur veneni peste perimatur."

[85]This image has a very old pedigree. Ignatius of Antioch, for example, warned of heretics who mingled poison with Jesus Christ, as if offering a lethal drug in a cup of honeyed wine; *Ep. ad Trall.* 6.

[86]I. 12. 40, 11-12: "insita homini bonae semina voluntatis . . ." He goes on to cite Sir. 15:16, Prov. 3:11, 29, Ps. 31:9, Prov. 6:20 and 5:2, and Ps. 35:4.

[87]"Libero arbitrio e grazia," 267f.

[88]Ibid., 282-83. He does not entirely rule out Tertullian, but finds Cassian more likely, because more proximate. He also notes, as we have, Faustus's prior dependence on Cassian's doctrine of the soul.

Cassian's possible role as inspirer of Faustus, Tibiletti points to *Conlatio*
XIII, 12, in which he speaks of "virtutum semina beneficio creatoris
inserta."[89] Tibiletti's contention is possible, even probable, but not proved.
He certainly shows, or rather underscores, the fact that Faustus and Cassian
partake of a common anthropology that values the created potentialities of the
human being.[90]

Duval's fine study of the sources and influence of Jerome's
commentary on Jonah has shed light on another possible instance of
Cassian's influence upon Faustus. He calls attention to Faustus's use of the
Ninevites in II. 12 as a demonstration both of pagan knowledge of God and as
an argument against determinism. In the case of the Ninevites, Faustus says,
God pronounces an ostensibly immutable judgment upon them but relents in
the face of their repentance, thus showing that the human will is not
overridden by divine necessity: "The merciful heavenly judge is willing to
change the decrees of his plan by a holy lie, if the guilty should hasten to
bring the medicine into play against sin."[91] Cassian invokes the Ninevites
in *Conlatio* XVII, 25, as part of a long line of examples arguing against the
absoluteness of divine determinations. Having said in reference to Isaiah
38:5-6 that "for reasons of his mercy and holiness the Lord prefers to annul
his word,"[92] Cassian turns to the Ninevites as a further illustration of his

---

[89]SC 54: 166.

[90]Besides his single use of *semina bonae voluntatis*, Faustus signifies
the presence of innate good will with terms like *insitum* or *inditum* (I. 10. 34, 4;
II. 8. 76, 9; I. 8. 25, 20f.), *insinuare* (II. 6. 74, 30), *inserere* (I. 9. 29, 26; II. 9.
78, 29), *inesse facultatem* (I. 10. 32, 19). Tibiletti also draws attention to similar
views in Pelagius, *Ep. ad Demetriadem* 3 (PL 30: 17C-18D).

[91]II. 12. 91, 6-8: "optat iudex misericors caelestis decreta consilii pio
inmutare mendacio, si reus medicinam festinet adhibere peccato."

[92]SC 54: 277: ". . . quo misericordiae ac pietatis intuitu mavult dominus
suum cassare sermonem . . . "

point. The penitence and fasting of the Ninevites turns aside the menacing, absolute sentence of God; in view of the conversion (*conversio*) of the city, God threatened its overthrow (*subversio*).[93] Faustus certainly is, as Duval says, reproducing Cassian's teaching. It is, however, open to question whether he is directly dependent on Cassian here. It would seem not, despite the fact that they clearly employ the book of Jonah in the same manner.

Despite the obvious affinities between the thought and the exegesis of Cassian and Faustus, the case for any direct dependence in the *De gratia* is not conclusively proved. Undoubtedly the two share the same perspective and sensibilities on the rapport between divine grace and human free will, and Faustus certainly was an admirer of Cassian and made extensive use of his work. But in this treatise one hears echoes and hints of Cassian without verbatim borrowings, with the possible exception of the "Greek saying" in I. 3. As was the case with the use of Augustine, it would seem that Faustus has assimilated many of the concerns of Cassian; indeed, because Faustus too is a product of the Gallic monastic culture, he may have done so all the more readily. The presence of Cassian in the treatise is, at any rate, somewhat less evident than that of Augustine.

Origen-Rufinus

Carl Weyman, in an 1895 article, noted that the sole Greek source to be found in Faustus of Riez was Origen's *De principiis* in Rufinus's Latin translation.[94] Weyman did not pursue the matter at length but offered in

---

[93]Ibid. Duval, *Le livre de Jonas,* 510, points out the similarity between this play on words and those found in Paulinus of Nola, Gaudentius of Brescia, and again in Augustine.

[94]"Zu Herondas V, 14," 184f.

support of his point the parallel between *De gratia* II. 1. 59, 10ff. and a passage from *De principiis* III. 1. 11. Speaking of the language of God's having "hardened" Pharaoh, Faustus writes: "In the same way we sometimes, in common conversation, adopt this manner of speaking. We may, for example, charge stubborn servants with our own mildness, saying: 'I have made you worse with my patience; I have nourished your malice and pride by my remission; I have made you stubborn by my indulgence; by my indifference I have stirred up your heart to be hardened against me.'"[95] In *De principiis* III. 1. 11 we find the following:

> I think that it would not seem absurd to explain the turn and figure of speech which was written about hardening, even from our common custom. For frequently, kind masters are prone to say to their servants who have grown more insolent and wicked through the master's great patience and indulgence: "I have made you so; I have ruined you; my patience has made you worse; I am the cause of your hard and worthless character, I who do not immediately punish you for each fault with what you deserve for your sins."[96]

---

[95]II. 1. 59, 10-16: "sic interdum familiariter etiam apud homines genus huius elocutionis adsumimus, sic interdum contumacibus famulis exprobamus mansuetudinem nostram ita dicentes: ego patientia mea pessimum <te> feci, ego remissione mea malitiam tuam superbiamque nutrivi, ego te contumacem indulgentia mea reddidi, ego dissimulatione mea cor tuum, ut contra me obduraretur, animavi."

[96]GCS 22: 213: "Tropum vero vel figuram sermonis eius, qui scriptus est de induratione, etiam ex communi consuetudine exponere, puto quod non videatur absurdum. Frequenter enim benigniores quique domini ad eos servos, qui per multam patientiam et mansuetudinem dominorum insolentiores improbioresque fiunt, dicere solent: Ego te talem feci, ego te perdidi, mea te patientia pessimum fecit, ego tibi causa huius tam durae et pessimae mentis existo, qui te non statim per singulas culpas punio pro merito delictorum."

Again, as we are accustomed to seeing in the *De gratia*, the lineage is clear even if the correspondence is not precise. It is difficult to doubt that Faustus had *De principiis* in mind when explaining the hardening of Pharaoh.

More recently, Simonetti has drawn attention to two more aspects of Faustus's treatment of the hardening of Pharaoh that may have been drawn from Origen-Rufinus.[97] First, Faustus attempts in II. 1 to explain the hardening by referring to Heb. 6:7f., the example of rain which falls on the earth and produces diverse effects according to the suitability of the land: "Notice that the earth, under the very same rain, here brings forth thorns and thistles, and there yields fruits suitable for a blessing. In the same way when God's mercy waits and is sparing, the one who obeys is changed for the better, while the impenitent is hardened."[98] In *De principiis* III. 1. 10 we find the same passage of Hebrews used to explain Pharaoh's situation; the summary employs similar words: "yet by the very same operation of the rains, that land which is cultivated brings forth useful fruits with a blessing to its diligent and useful cultivators, while that which has hardened by idleness of its cultivators brings forth thorns and thistles."[99] Clearly Faustus has at least, to use Simonetti's term, drawn inspiration from Origen-Rufinus here, as well in *De gratia* II. 5. 68, where, as in *De principiis* III. 1. 14,

---

[97]"Il *De gratia*," 134-35.

[98]II. 1. 61, 1-5: "agnosce terram sub uno eodemque imbre nunc spinas et tribulos germinantem, nunc fructus benedictionibus idoneos proferentem. eodem modo dum misericordia dei expectat et parcit, emendatur oboediens, obduratur inpaenitens."

[99]GCS 22: 211: ". . . sed uno eodemque opere pluviae ea quidem terra, quae culta est, diligentibus utilibusque cultoribus cum benedictione fructus utiles proferat, ea vero, quae cultorum desidia obdurit, spinas ac tribulos germinet."

Pharoah is compared to the rocky ground upon which seeds fall without finding root (cf. Mt. 13:5-6).

One more substantial instance could be cited. Simonetti has signaled Faustus's use in I. 11 of 2 Tim. 2:20f. as a counterbalance to predestinarian use of Rom. 9:21 and has identified the same scriptural argument in *De principiis* III. 1. 21.[100] The similarity in fact extends beyond simply the Scripture passages adduced. Faustus takes up the same line of argument. Explaining Paul's words in Rom. 9:21 about making "one vessel of honor, another of dishonor," Faustus offers this analysis: "Here he has suppressed in his concluding statement the preceding causes by which a person may be changed into either honor or dishonor. For when a person by grace has begun to be a vessel of honor, he must be especially watchful, that the honor he has received may be kept safe with divine cooperation."[101] Similarly in *De principiis* we read, after a citation of 2 Tim. 2:20: "And so one concludes from this that the cause of each person's deeds first precedes, and each is made a vessel of honor or of dishonor by God according to his merits. Each vessel, then, formed by the creator either for honor or for dishonor, has provided for the maker, from itself, the causes and occasions."[102] Soon thereafter Rufinus uses the locution "ex praecedentibus causis." The line of argument is the same. But while Origen extends the

---

[100]"Il *De gratia*," 134.

[101]I. 11. 36, 18-22: "hoc loco praecedentes causas, quibus vel in honorem vel in contumeliam homo transeat, conclusa elocutione suppressit. nam cum homo per gratiam esse coeperit vas honoris, invigilandum est, ut acceptus honor divina cooperatione servetur . . ."

[102]*De princ.* III. 1. 21 (GCS 22: 238): "Itaque concluditur ex hoc quia prius gestorum uniuscuiusque causa praecedit, et pro meritis suis unusquisque a deo vel honoris vas efficitur vel contumeliae. Unumquodque igitur vas ut vel ad honorem a creatore formetur vel ad contumeliam, ex se ipso causas et occasiones praestetit conditori."

"preceding causes" to include the prior life of the human soul, Faustus is content to limit them to the earthly life in pursuit of virtue.

Several other themes from the *De principiis* have echoes in the *De gratia*: the notion that only senseless things have their cause of motion from without,[103] the need to uphold simultaneously God's justice and mercy,[104] the necessity of labor, zeal, and toil to obtain a salvation which is accredited to God,[105] and the idea of the *similitudo Dei* as something acquired by diligent moral effort.[106] None of these themes arises in such a way as to prove a direct dependence, but taken together they point to the broad affinity between Faustus's theology and that of the *De principiis*. On the whole, the evidence suggests that Faustus was familiar with at least book three of Rufinus's "translation."[107]

Hilary of Poitiers

In view of their massive influence on the theology of the Latin West, the use of Hilary of Poitiers's works in the *De gratia* is not surprising. Indeed, the eastward-looking motifs which arise in Faustus through his use of Cassian and Origen-Rufinus lead one to look for signs of Hilary, since he

---

[103]*De princ.* III. 1. 2; *De grat.* I. 16. 52.

[104]*De princ.* III. 9-10; *De grat.* II. 4.

[105]*De princ.* III. 1. 19; *De grat.* passim.

[106]*De princ.* III. 6. 1; *De grat.* II. 9. 79, 5-6, 28-29.

[107]We know of the availability and popularity of this work in Gaul from a letter of Sidonius Apollinaris (*Ep.* XI). Writing to a certain Donidius, he recounts a journey with friends during which he discovered a library with well-cataloged books. The women found books of piety, the men works of Latin eloquence: Augustine, Varro, Horace, Prudentius, and above all Rufinus's translation of Origen, which was greatly enjoyed by Sidonius's friends. Cf. Latouche, "De la Gaule romaine à la Gaule franque," 386f.

was a vital conduit for the flow of Greek theology into the West. We again
have Tibiletti to thank for beginning to discover several possible instances of
Hilary's influence in the *De gratia*.[108]   Tibiletti observes that a
characteristically "eastern" conception of grace and nature subsisting in a
continuous and harmonic relationship, a conception found, inter alios, in
Gregory of Nyssa, Evagrius, and John Chrysostom, may also be found in the
soteriology of Hilary of Poitiers. To substantiate the point, Tibiletti points
to a number of Hilarian texts that affirm the importance of created human
capabilities in achieving salvation.[109]   He then alludes to the work of A.
Peñamaria, who has shown that Hilary's teaching on grace is irreconcilable
with Augustine's because it refuses to make the counterpositions between
merit and grace or grace and nature which have characterized much of western
theology.[110]   Hilary is an example, then, of someone who, apart from any
Pelagian influence, has produced a soteriology that on some points is in-
commensurate with that of Augustine. This conclusion leads Tibiletti to
compare certain texts of Hilary with the *De gratia*.

This comparative study yields several coincidences of thought and
terminology that could easily lead one to think of Hilary as a source for
Faustus. Tibiletti indicates four loci in Hilary's works that parallel the *De
gratia*. Of these, only one seems close enough to merit consideration as a
direct source. In I. 9 Faustus argues for the universal availability of salvation
with these words: "The possibility of taking hold of salvation is as a kind of

---

[108]"Fausto di Riez," 567-87.

[109]Ibid., 569. He cites *Tract. in Ps. 118* 14, 20; 5, 12; 16, 10; 13, 12;
De Trin. I, 37, *Tract. myster.* I, 26.

[110]Ibid., 570-71. Reference is to Peñamaria, "Libertad, mérito y gracia
en la Soterología de Hilario de Poitiers," 234-50.

to draw from."[111] In like fashion, Hilary, in the *Tractatus mysteriorum* I,
26, writes: "Access to salvation lies open to all."[112] This is the closest
Tibiletti comes to finding an exact correspondence between Faustus and
Hilary, though the other six passages cited show marked similarities of
thought, particularly regarding the need and responsibility for human effort in
the economy of salvation.[113] In addition to passages in the *De gratia* proper
cited by Tibiletti, one might take note of a passage in Faustus's prefatory
letter in which, having invoked examples of dutiful obedience, he concludes
that "it is fitting that grace ... should be connected with inseparable
service."[114] This sentiment was expressed by Hilary in similar terms:
"God's will has connected the zeal of human devotion to God's gifts."[115]

As Tibiletti admits, the case for Faustus's direct use of Hilary is not
conclusive, though it does show that they drew from a common current of
thought and, further, that a source other than Pelagius can explain non-
Augustinian elements in Faustus's doctrine of grace.[116] Still, it would be
difficult to imagine that Faustus did not have some contact with the writings

---

[111]I. 9. 30, 10-13: "aditus capessendae salutis quasi fons quidam in
medium mundi huius expositus et in commune concessus ad hauriendum universis
patet."

[112]SC 19: 120: "Omnibus enim patet aditus ad salutem ... "

[113]Tibiletti, "Fausto di Riez," 571-72. The other passages of Hilary
cited, and Tibiletti's parallels in the *De grat.*, are as follows: *Tract. in Ps. 118*
[CSEL]: 406-7 (*De grat.* I. 1. 8; I. 10. 35, 29); *De Trin.* II, 35 (I. 9. 30); *Tract. in
Ps. 118*: 406 (II. 12. 90-91; I. 6. 22).

[114]Prol. 4, 6-7: "ita oportet gratia ... inseparabili servitute conexa
sit."

[115]*Tract. in Ps. 118* [CSEL 22]: 406-7: "dei muneribus voluntas Dei
humanae devotionis studia connexuit."

[116]"Fausto di Riez," 572.

of Hilary, and Tibiletti's investigation suggests at least the likelihood of such acquaintance. Given Faustus's hesitance to quote sources exactly, one may well wonder whether evidence of a precise concordance with Hilary could be expected. Conservatively, we may say that Faustus's soteriology shares something of Hilary's perspective.

Other Sources

Few other sources suggest themselves at this stage of knowledge of the *De gratia*. Certain themes in Tertullian having to do with the innate goodness of the human soul have been alluded to by Tibiletti,[117] but these are the same christianized Stoic themes to be found in Cassian, a more proximate and likely source. Duval has mentioned that Faustus's use of the Ninevites to demonstrate pagan knowledge of God repeats that of Clement of Alexandria, yet again Faustus's source, if he had a source at all, was probably Cassian.[118] We have noted in chapter 2 a possible echo of Prudentius's *Psychomachia*. Future philological labors may uncover other Christian sources, but Faustus's inexact and allusive use of even his most obvious sources will make such study quite difficult.

When one moves away from Christian writers to the realm of pagan letters, the results are exceedingly sparse. While many Christian writers of Faustus's epoch evidently showed the influence of classical Latin

---

[117]"La salvezza umana," 378, n. 35. In reference to the *insita homini bonae semina voluntatis* of *De grat.* I. 12, he cites Tertullian, *De anima* 41, 3 (Waszink, p. 57): "nulla [anima] sine boni semine." One could also point to Faustus's use of *sanitas* to describe the soul's original goodness, as in Tertullian, *Apol.* 17, 5: "sanitatem suam [i.e., animae] patitur."

[118]"Le livre de Jonas," 510. Reference is to Clement of Alexandria, *Protreptikos* X, 99, 3-4.

literature,[119] Faustus does not. One could, of course, point to the trace of Vergil in Faustus's use of the Scylla-Charybdis metaphor in I. 1. 17, but surely this was a commonplace. Engelbrecht has opined that the monastery of Lérins, and not the secular rhetorical school, supplied Faustus's rhetorical formation.[120]

Whether Faustus knew the writers of classical antiquity is an exceedingly difficult question to answer. We have mentioned in chapter 1 the almost obligatory attitude of scorn toward pagan learning that prevailed in the environs of Lérins. E. Hårleman stresses this point when noting Faustus's lack of references to Greek philosophy: Faustus may have had every reason to conceal his classical heritage.[121] Whatever his acquaintance with pagan literature and philosophy may have been, he certainly does not employ it in any obvious way in the *De gratia*.[122]

*   *   *

The sources employed by Faustus in the *De gratia* are the Holy Scriptures in a Vulgate version, Augustine, Cassian, Origen-Rufinus, and,

---

[119]Cf. Hårleman, "La litterature gallo-romaine," 165. Lactantius, the "Christian Cicero," may have been instrumental on this score. Salvian of Marseilles shows Ciceronian influence; Claudianus Mamaertus knew Vergil, Sallustius, Varro, and others. Alcimus Avitus of Vienne and Ennodius of Pavia made extensive use of Vergil. Cf. Ennodius, *Carmina* (CSEL 6: 507-608); Avitus, *Poematum libri VI* (MGH, AA VI: 203-94).

[120]CSEL 21: xxxiii. Weigel, *Faustus of Riez*, 16, seconds this opinion.

[121]"La littérature gallo-romaine," 160.

[122]The lack of any clear philosophical framework in the De gratia makes all the more curious the flowery evaluation of Faustus's philosophical acumen given by Sidonius Apollinaris, *Ep*. IX, 9 (PL 58: 625). Most probably the explanation lies in Sidonius's tendency toward rhetorical excess.

perhaps, Hilary of Poitiers. The author of the *De gratia* uses Scripture in a manner concordant with the overall rhetorical strategy of the treatise, namely, to pursue a balanced path between theological extremes. He presents himself on this score as the hermeneutical ally of Augustine. While never directly opposing a biblical interpretation of Augustine, Faustus frequently is found counterbalancing predestinarian interpretations which could at least claim some precedent in Augustine.

Augustine's presence pervades the work, despite his being cited only twice. One finds, perhaps surprisingly, that Augustine is used positively in the *De gratia*. Far from being a mere foil, he is the inspirer of Faustus's doctrines of sin and concupiscence. Faustus seems to have assimilated Augustine's anti-Pelagian concerns for the necessity and priority of divine grace and to have incorporated them into the treatise. Yet in doing so he is not a slavish copier of Augustine in the mold of Prosper.

Faustus has also clearly drawn deeply from the world of thought shared by Cassian, Origen, and Hilary. This world, monastic in its motive concerns and Greek in its anthropological affirmations, asserts itself continually in Faustus's insistence on the ongoing human capacity to will, to work, and to obey. Sometimes consciously and perhaps sometimes unconsciously, Faustus reproduces the thought and the words of these predecessors, whose concerns coincide in many ways with the Lerinian ethos which formed Faustus.

The sources of the *De gratia*, then, all come from the Latin Christian literature of the West, but they manifest the diverse theological currents that existed within that linguistic unity. In composing the materials which took shape in the doctrinal battle against Lucidus and came to comprise the *De gratia*, Faustus had before him the task of steering a middle course through these currents, some of which could flow in very different directions. If there are inconsistencies or difficulties in the treatise, perhaps their cause lies in the inherent difficulty of such a task.

CHAPTER FOUR
THE DOCTRINE OF THE *DE GRATIA*

Two assertions are commonly made about the treatise *De gratia*. The first states that it is a polemical work; the second finds it to be an attempted compromise position between the Pelagian assertion of human capabilities and the Augustinian stress upon the priority of grace.[1] Both of these assertions contain truth, although as we have seen, the treatise is more accurately seen as a redaction of polemical material, and Faustus's *via regia* is a matter of conviction rather than compromise. But if a common depiction of the *De gratia* would suggest that its content arises solely from the clash between opposites, this is misleading. The previous chapter has shown that Faustus was a reader of theological literature and a perceptive interpreter of Scripture. He was informed by a positive doctrinal stance that took shape quite apart from the immediate concerns of the polemical battle against Lucidus. The positive doctrine of Faustus finds frequent, if scattered, expression in the treatise.

The task of the present chapter will be to set forth Faustus's teaching thematically, on its own strength. If the overall scope of this study

---

[1]Weigel, *Faustus of Riez,* 104; Koch, *Der heilige Faustus,* 19 et passim; Amann, "Semipélagiens," 1834.

aims to help us understand Gaul's reception of Augustinianism, this section will fulfill the task of illustrating the doctrinal configuration of one of the receptors. We will consider Faustus's doctrine under the broad categories of creation, sin, and redemption.

Creator God and Grace in Creation

The foundation of Faustus's thought in the *De gratia* consists of a theological anthropology derived from God's relationship to humankind in and through creation. Faustus's insistence on doing justice to God under the aspects both of creator and of redeemer stems from his conviction that overzealous predestinarians have subordinated the order of creation to that of redemption or even ignored the order of creation entirely. By contrast, the bishop of Riez reasserts with some force a picture of a creator God whose power is never capricious or abstract but always tempered by a fundamental benevolence toward the creature. This benevolence manifests itself as grace from the very outset, and this initial grace, constitutive of human existence, can never be wholly frustrated. Anthropologically, the *prima gratia* issues forth in a human being in the image of God, a human being endowed with reason and intellect and therefore with a realm of freedom, both of choice and of action. The fact of God's having created such an independent dimension means that one can never simply speak of necessity or predetermination operating in the world. One must consider, then, Faustus's portrayal of God, his account of creation, and his treatment of the reciprocal consequences of creation in delimiting certain divine attributes.

God the Creator

While the *De gratia* is not primarily a treatise about God, its assertions in the realm of theological anthropology also make statements about the nature and character of God. Such statements are few, but they serve as an important background for the development of Faustus's doctrine. As has been suggested above, one can see the treatise to a great extent as a kind of apologia for the order of creation as the good work of God; its affirmations about the creator are thus foundations for the development of Faustus's theology.

The first and most evident aspect of Faustus's portrayal of God is the steadfast refusal to assign any agency to the creator in the matter of human rebellion. On the contrary, God is the source of unvarying benevolence and philanthropy. God's mercy may be delayed for a time, but it is never withheld. In the matter of an alleged divine "hardening" of human hearts, "Should the Christian complain that God is cruel, when even the impious confesses that God is holy? Therefore this heavenly dispensation of mercy brings about in human beings what an unexpected downpour of rain brings about in the earth . . . . Notice that the earth, under the very same rain, here brings forth thorns and thistles, and there yields fruits suitable for blessing."[2] Whatever ill effects might arise, therefore, in the world order do not have their cause in the creator's intention. God is ever philanthropic, never desiring the death even of the ungodly.

The divine power, *potestas*, thus cannot be seen as arbitrary or utterly without limit. Faustus portrays the divine being as constrained or, better, self-constraining, in the creation and ordering of the cosmos. For example, human affairs are not subject to the caprice of an impetuous creator but are ordered by divine equity: "If God, as impiety blasphemes, arranges the human state not by equity but by power, then one who has knocked

---

[2]II. 1. 60, 18-61, 3: "Inmitem deum Christianus esse conqueritur, quem pium etiam impius confitetur? Hoc ergo agit in hominibus caelestis misericordiae dispensatio, quod in terris pluviae supervenientis infusio. . . agnosce terram sub uno eodemque imbre nunc spinas et tribulos germinantem, nunc fructus benedictionibus idoneos proferentem."

might be shut out, and one who has not sought might be drawn in. And so he will seem to have been neither merciful toward the saved . . . nor . . . just toward the lost."[3] Faustus really argues, then, against a species of voluntarism, saying that the human notion of equity describes a quality that obtains even in the realm of divinity and that is not subject to divine caprice or frequent exceptions.

Further insight into Faustus's conception of God is supplied by the remarkable dialogue among the four virtues in II. 12. In this imaginative passage the author depicts the presence of four virtues—*Potentia, Bonitas, Sapientia,* and *Iustitia*—in the intradivine counsel as God contemplated creating the human race. Each of the four voices her concerns in creating humankind, such that the particular interest of each virtue must give account to the others. Justice cannot be sacrificed to goodness, nor goodness to wisdom, and so on. Only in the balanced result of their dialogue do they express the divine mind. To illustrate:

> *Potentia* may say, "Let us make, after the kingdom of heaven, in the second rank a marvelous creature, lest things that are first in possession of our dominion should appear to be last. Let us complete that splendid scheme of the world so that we may make man in it and appoint him over it, through whom the world may be ordered, possessed, and adorned." *Bonitas* would say, "It is not right that only the heavens should enjoy our benefits. Let us also make man on the earth, toward whom we may exercise the abundance of

---

[3]II. 4. 65, 15-20: "Si hominis statum deus, sicut blasphemat impietas, non aequitate sed potestate disponit, ille fortassis, qui pulsavit, excluditur et ille, qui non quaesivit, adtrahitur. ac sic nec circa salvatos misericors fuisse videbitur, nec circa perditos . . . iustus."

our grace, toward whom we may extend the gifts of benevolence, in whom we may deepen the riches of his inborn piety."[4]

The discussion goes on at length, but the theological point is made: God the creator is bound, constitutionally, not to express any of these virtues or attributes to the exclusion of another in the creation of the human race. Any portrait of a God who could exercise power at the expense of goodness or justice, and so on, would be a flawed and excessive representation. The sharp polemical edge of such a perspective over against rigid predestinarianism is obvious. But we should note, too, the positive force of Faustus's presentation, for it manifests his tendency toward the golden mean, his *via regia*, with its integrative rather than exclusive method. God is, indeed, a *moderator* who exercises judgment, not a tyrant who issues absolute decrees.[5]

A few important statements about God arise in *De gratia* II. 9, a chapter to which extended attention will be given later. First, Faustus has an explicitly trinitarian theology. He contrasts, for example, trinitarian sonship with adoptive filiation in his discussion of *imago* and *similitudo*: ". . . in man, to whom the reality of grace, not of nature, was handed on by God in

---

[4]II. 12. 93, 8-17: "potentia dicat: faciamus post caeli reglum in secundis mirabilem creaturam, ne in imperii nostri possessione, quae prima sunt, haec etiam videantur extrema. istam speciosam mundi machinam consummemus, ut in ea hominem faciamus, et praeficiamus, per quem mundus ordinetur, possideatur, ornetur. bonitas dicat: fas non est, ut sola beneficiis nostris caelestia perfruantur. faciamus et in terra hominem, circa quem abundantiam gratiae nostrae exerceamus, circa quem benivolentiae munera dilatemus, in quem pietatis ingenitae divitias profundamus."

[5]II. 6. 71, 16ff. Commenting on Paul's use of Jacob and Esau in Rom. 9: 9, Faustus notes: "in his verbis hoc vult intellegi gentiliciae persuasionis impietas, quod deus absque ullo inter malum et bonum moderatoris examine non ordine regentis, sed iure dominantis illum affectu dignum reddat, hunc odio . . . "

the very likeness, *image* would rather designate something received from one who is prior and superior, and *likeness* is better seen as conferred from the truth that the Father rightly communicates to his Son by nature."[6] Within his trinitarian framework Faustus emphasizes the fundamental unity of the divine nature. He repeats a tidy formula—"subtilis, simplex, sincerus"—to describe God as being identical with the divine perfections:

> Therefore it is said of God: subtle, simple, sincere. *Simple* certainly means that nothing extrinsic is added to him, nothing has been granted from elsewhere, but in him power is essence and substance. And so God is what he possesses. Man, unless he receives these gifts, does not possess them. So while God is both just and justice, merciful and mercy, holy and holiness, man can be just but not justice; merciful, but not mercy; holy, but not holiness; . . . what is grace in man is nature in God.[7]

Conferred upon human beings is the image of the shared divinity of the three divine persons, for "whatever the Trinity bestows in common upon man is derived from the likeness of the deity . . . When, therefore, this image

---

[6]II. 9. 77, 21-25: ". . . in homine, cui in ipsa similitudine a deo gratiae res traditur, non naturae, imago hoc potius nuncupetur, quod a priore et superiore suscipitur, et de veritate similitudo fuisse conlata plenius indicetur, quam tamen cum filio naturali pater iure communicat."

[7]II. 9. 79, 6-16: "et propterea de deo dicitur: subtilis, simplex, sincerus. simplex utique, quia nihil illi extrinsecus adiectitium, nihil aliunde conlatum, sed in illo virtus, essentia atque substantia est. ac sic deus quod habet est, homo vero haec dona, nisi acceperit, non habet. cum ergo deus iustus ac iustitia, misericors et misericordia, pius et pietas sit, homo iustus esse potest, iustitia esse non potest, misericors esse potest, misericordia esse non potest, pius esse potest, pietas esse non potest . . . et in homine gratia est, quod in deo natura est."

is conferred by the Father, Son, and Holy Spirit, undoubtedly the one divinity of the three persons grants the dignity of its image to the first man."[8] So, taking up a line of thought he may well have learned through Augustine, though also from the polemical battle against Arianism, Faustus gives voice to a doctrine of the Trinity rooted in the idea of the one shared divine essence.

In sum, the most striking aspects of Faustus's conception of God are its moderation and its fundamentally anthropological focus. God is not abstractly free to order the world apart from the mitigating forces of equity, justice, and goodness. On the contrary, divine philanthropy and benevolence virtually insure that God rules as a wise governor, never rashly or excessively exercising justice at the expense of mercy or vice versa. Faustus has taken up a doctrine of God that is, so far as we can tell, unexceptional and orthodox, not incompatible with the trinitarian teaching of Hilary of Poitiers or Augustine. But Faustus's addition of an element of divine accomodation or self-limitation runs counter to the portrayal implied by a hyper-Augustinian predestinarianism with its stress on the absolute determinations of the divine will.

Grace in the Human Constitution

The doctrine of God proper is, then, not a thematic focal point in the *De gratia*; it arises rather as the background of a theological anthropology. At the center of that anthropology lies Faustus's positive account of the endowments that inhere in human beings by virtue of their having been created by God. Faustus discusses these gifts or capacities in several places

---

[8] II. 9. 78, 12-13, 22-25: "ideoque ex deitatis similitudine derivatur, quidquid homini trinitas in commune largitur . . . cum ergo imago haec a patre et filio et sancto spiritu conderatur, suae absque dubio trium personarum una divinitas primo homini suae imaginis tribuit dignitatem."

in the treatise, most extensively in II. 9-10. The language he employs to describe them varies, but his treatment tends to focus on two main aspects of created human capabilities: (1) their relation to the image and likeness of God, and (2) their gratuity. Indeed, Faustus speaks, albeit in a circumscribed fashion, of these capabilities as grace.

The first invocation of the *imago Dei* as an anthropological category occurs in I. 1, and is directed against Pelagius's putative statement that Adam was created mortal. Against this Faustus writes: "What else could one understand, when it says that man was created in God's image, but the mark of perpetuity? Indeed you know not only that the perpetuity of the soul is not lost, but also that the perpetuity of the body is restored by virtue of the resurrection. Therefore you should not doubt that immortality was given to man prior to sin, as you see it being restored after his fall."[9] So a primary referent for creation in God's image is the perpetuity or immortality of the soul, which cannot be lost. The human soul's perennial existence is the mark (*insigne*) of God's perpetuity. Faustus seems to assume an original corporeal eternity for the human being; he implies as much by saying that perpetuity of the body is "restored" (*reddi*) by the resurrection.

Immortality, however, does not exhaust the list of creational endowments inherent in the human being. In I. 7, answering the opinion that free choice of the will has been removed, Faustus declares: "One who asserts this perverse argument regards the human being—one who is rich with understanding, endowed with reason, and decorated with the honor of the

---

[9]I. 1. 10, 3-8: "Quid vero aliud intellegendum est etiam in ipsa, qua homo conditus est, dei imagine nisi perennitatis insigne? quam perennitatem non solum animae non ademptam, sed etiam corpori agnoscis resurrectionis virtute reparatam. quapropter inmortalitatem homini conmissam non dubites ante culpam, quam reddi perspicis etiam post ruinam."

divine image—as comparable to brute animals and dull beasts."[10] Possession of the faculties of intellect and reason, which are also associated with, but not identical to, the divine image, separates the human being from the rest of creation. Whereas, continues the author, it is the nature of senseless beasts and of base matter to be moved about by another without any exercise of choice or reason, human beings by their very constitution must make willful choices in order to pursue either virtue or vice.[11] While Faustus is somewhat inexact here, it would seem that freedom to will and to act constitutes another facet of the divine image.

By making the human will analogous to the obvious physical capabilities of bodily members, Faustus reiterates in I. 9 how fundamental the will is to theological anthropology:

So God, who is creator both of the exterior and of the interior person, just as he arranged by his power the members of the human body, so he, by his ordination, permits a person to act and dispense the ministry and use of the members. Just as he formed each person's right hand yet placed it under human control—so that one can extend it to what he or she wishes and apply it to diverse deeds—in like fashion God inserted, inspired, inpoured the sense of reason and the will's power of choice into every soul yet relinquished

---

[10]I. 7. 23, 4-7: "Huius inprobae persuasionis assertor hominem intellectu locupletatum, ratione praeditum, divinae imaginis honore decoratum brutis animantibus et iumentis insipientibus aestimat comparandum. . . "

[11]I. 7. 23, 8-24, 16.

the role of moderating and exercising it to the hand of human counsel and committed its duties to human judgment and dominion.[12]

The granting to all of intellect and will in freedom entails the ability to choose to lead a life of righteousness, leading to salvation. This means for Faustus that the pursuit of righteousness, and therefore access to human salvation, is a general creational gift: "Righteousness in man is not, therefore, a personal, but a general and public, gift of God. The possibility of taking hold of salvation is as a kind of fountain set in the midst of this world, given in common for all to draw from, so that one who neglects to do so stands justly accused before the giver."[13] As a polemical weapon, such a positive evaluation of the salvific potency of the created human will strikes at the heart of the predestinarian notion of a *numerus clausus* to whom salvation is confined. But its usefulness in this regard should not obscure its positive weight, which is to exalt God precisely as a munificent creator who has from the first placed the *fons salutis* in our midst. Faustus, commenting on Rom. 6:16, remarks that the Pauline exhortation shows the presence of a

---

[12]I. 9. 29, 20-29: "itaque conditor utriusque, id est exterioris et interioris hominis deus, sicut potentia sua corporis humani membra disposuit, ita ordinatione sua ministerium usumque membrorum homini agere ac dispensare permisit. et sicut dexteram in omni homine ipse formavit, sed in potestate hominis posuit, ut eam quo vellet extenderet et ad diversa opera conferret, pari modo sensum rationis et arbitrium voluntatis in unamquamque animam inseruit inspiravit infundit, sed eam in manu humani consilii moderandam et exercendam reliquit eiusque officia iuri hominis dominioque conmisit . . . "

[13]I. 9. 30, 9-13: "iustitia ergo in homine non personale, sed generale et publicum dei munus est. aditus capessendae salutis quasi fons quidam in medium mundi huius expositus et in commune concessus ad hauriendum universis patet, ut largitori merito reus sit, qui haurire neglexerit."

good will in human beings, "which, when we show it forth, we proclaim the ordination and wonderful disposition of the creator to man."[14]

This brief passage also affords an example of the presence of a characteristically eastern way of explaining the economy of salvation. We have already shown the similarity between this passage and the thought of Hilary of Poitiers, an important western interpreter of the Christian East.[15] J. Patout Burns has, in broad terms, spoken of a tradition of Greek thought, developed from Justin Martyr through Origen and Gregory of Nyssa, that stresses the general availability of the means of salvation, the universal work of Christ, and the fullness of Christ's presence in the Church. Against this he has set a Latin orientation that runs counter to such universalizing tendencies and stresses the exclusive role of participation in the Church for salvation, with little attention to one's created potentialities.[16] Burns's typology is helpful here, if only to show that Faustus stands in the line of those Greek thinkers who would not see a radical disjunction between the question of salvation and that of created human capacities.

With the granting of a will in creation comes a realm of freedom for the human person, and God does not intrude upon it. Asserting that the will is essentially good, Faustus seems to suggest its fundamental orientation toward choosing the good. He speaks of this orientation in some places as a potentiality, invoking the notion of "seeds of a good will implanted in man" (*insita homini bonae semina voluntatis*)[17] which are, as it were, coaxed into

---

[14]I. 10. 32, 20-22: "quam cum praeferimus, aperte ordinationem atque mirabilem dispositionem sui praedicamus auctoris . . . "

[15]See above, p. 151.

[16]"The Economy of Salvation," 599ff. In developing the contrast Burns uses Augustine and Gregory of Nyssa as his exemplars.

[17]I. 12. 40, 11-12.

growth by biblical exhortation. Though some people may be unwilling to do good and heedless of exhortation, the ability or potentiality to choose the good is always present. The failure to make actual the will's capacity to obey, that is, the neglect of God's gift, is the criterion by which a person is judged. Guilt can only obtain, after all, when one has freedom to choose. Thus a predeterminist scheme, wherein a fatal necessity overrides the prerogatives of human choice, is an affront both to the dignity of human capabilities and to divine justice.

In II. 2, in the context of his argument concerning foreknowledge and predestination, Faustus again simultaneously asserts the created goodness of the human will and its potential to turn toward either good or evil. The speech that the author places in the mouth of divine Providence affirms that the human being has been created good because of divine justice yet can become evil as a result of following after a sinning will. Faustus never goes so far as to assert that the will itself could be evil; it remains a good gift of the creator. A person can incur guilt, however, by his or her own willful consent to evil: "Whenever not compulsion but consent to sin is the cause for complaint, then not the creator but the sinner is guilty."[18] A kind of theodicy is therefore built into the question of the created status of the human will: to suggest that one's will could be configured so as to lead one into sin is to blaspheme by making God the cause of sin. If the creational gift of free power of choice is, as Faustus claims, partially constitutive of authentic human existence, then there can be no real human being who is not endowed with this gift. Possessed of it, one is free, with no hint of compulsion, to

---

[18]II. 2. 62, 2-4: "ubi non conpulsio, sed consensio peccandi deprehenditur in querella, non auctor, sed praevaricator in culpa est."

choose between one's basic orientation toward the good and the enticements of evil.

The capacities and endowments given to humankind in creation include more than mere freedom of choice and the potential for goodness. Closely linked with the human sphere of freedom is an inward datum that Faustus describes as a law written on the inner parts. This inward law, which he also calls the law of nature (*lex naturae*), is of such import that he refers to it as the "first grace of God" (*prima dei gratia*). By following this law, that is, by making proper use of the first or primal grace, many have attained to the salvation wrought by Christ. Thus Faustus introduces his discussion of the Old Testament righteous: "Since people have been endowed with the image and likeness of God, so that many will be worthy to be called children of God, it would be appropriate for us to make plain with a few examples how many there are who, prior to the law of the letter, by following the law of nature, which is, as we have said, the first grace of God, will enter the doorway of salvation, being led by Christ to the very inner chamber of life."[19] So, while keeping before himself the saving role of Christ, Faustus asserts that the *prima gratia,* here understood as the natural law, is salvifically efficacious in a way that complements or accords with Christ's work.

The human response, the *affectus* of the will in obedience to this inward law, is faith. So within the subjectivity of each human being, God has created a positive relationship of faith as the place of the will's response to the innate law. Faustus's comments on Abel in II. 8 make this point explicit, and introduce a more detailed discussion of the image of God:

---

[19]II. 9. 79, 30-80, 4:   ". . . cum homines ita fuerint imagine et similitudine <dei praediti, ut multi etiam filii> dei meruerint nuncupari, vel paucis adhuc exemplis praestringere nos oportet, quanti ante legem litterae erudiente lege naturae, quae prima, ut diximus, dei gratia est, vestibula salutis intraverint per Christum ad ipsa vitae penetralia perducendi."

But Abel, too, was worthy to be pleasing in the divine sight through an innate good given generally by God, that is, through the affection of his own will. This man, therefore, to whom the perfection of an immaculate life gave the title of "just": by what instruction would he have been a follower of righteousness, unless a law written on his inward parts had taught him? Or whence would he have known to choose offerings . . . that would please God . . . unless faith, which made him a lover of virtues, had inspired him. . . ? And you regard as having nothing of his own by God's ordination the one to whose devotion God gave testimony? Do you see that the good of belief is not a new privilege but an old one, and that in the very beginning of the world's establishment the human mind was endowed by the most high author not only with intellect and reason, but also with faith? Indeed, he gave a knowledge of himself to the soul already at that time, when he deigned to commit his image to it.[20]

Though he does not say it in so many words, the author of these words is absolutely refusing to acknowledge the existence of what one might call a "purely natural" human being. Much of what can be predicated of a

---

[20] II. 8. 76, 8-25: "sed et Abel divinis placere conspectibus per insitum a deo generaliter bonum, id est per propriae meruit voluntatis affectum. hic ergo, cui cognomen iusti inmaculatae vitae perfectio dedit, quo erudiente iustitiae sectator existeret, nisi eum lex visceribus inscripta docuisset? aut unde placituras deo hostias . . . scisset eligere, nisi fides, quae eum amatorem virtutum fecerat, inspirasset . . . ? et tu nihil eum ordinatione dei habere iudicas proprium, cuius devotioni deus perhibet testimonium? vides bonum credulitatis non novellum esse privilegium, sed vetustum, et inter ipsa mundi coalescentis exordia mentem hominis sicut intellectu atque ratione ita etiam fide a summo auctore dotatam? itaque iam tum dedit animae notitiam suam, quando ei committere dignatus est imaginem suam." On the notion of faith as a creational gift, cf. also I. 16. 49, 5.

Christian, including his or her possession of faith, can in fact be extended to all people by dint of their being objects of the creator's primal intention.[21] The category of image of God, treated in detail in II. 9, thus becomes the basic anthropological referent in describing the gifts given in creation.

As noted in chapter 2 of the present study, Faustus's treatment of the *imago Dei* is directed against a curiously christologized interpretation of Gen. 1:26, wherein the "image" after which the first man was formed was that of Christ. Leaving aside the question of that view's origin, one should note that its main error for Faustus lay in its excessive valuation of the order of redemption over that of creation, of the late age of the world at the incarnation over the primal age of creation. Indeed, Faustus's imagined opponent regards the connection of the image of God to the original grant of free will to be an irrelevance.[22] Faustus's response demonstrates not only the continuing significance but the centrality and indispensability of creation *ad imaginem Dei* as the primal, even primary, manifestation of divine grace.

---

[21]Carlo Tibiletti, in "Libero arbitrio e grazia," has underscored the sensational nature of such an affirmation vis-à-vis St. Augustine's thought. Far from seeing faith as being granted with the law of nature, Augustine in his anti-Pelagian works saw it as a special gift derived from the grace of Christ. For example, in *De praed. sanct.* 11, 22 we read: "Et in suis incrementis et in suis initiis Dei donum est fides." Weigel, in "Il concepto de la fe," 40ff., puzzles over whether faith for Faustus is in the final analysis a divine gift or somehow natural. While Weigel ascribes the difficulty to Faustus's polemical rather than systematic presentation, the real difficulty is that "nature" and "grace" are apparently not mutually exclusive categories in the *De gratia.* Koch, in *Der heilige Faustus,* 94ff. suggests that the Old Testament righteous, as recipients of a special revelation, should not be regarded on the same level as pagans; his argument is unconvincing, however, since Faustus in II. 11-12 extends the reach of his treatment to include those like the Ninevites who are not among the recipients of a special revelation.

[22]II. 9. 76, 28-77, 2: "Sed dicis: quid mihi ad libertatem arbitrii iungis imaginem dei, cum ille eximius conditor futurus secuturis saeculis et redemptor ad illam magis imaginem fecerit hominem, quam per virginem erat adsumpturus ex homine?"

Faustus makes note of some of the unworthy implications of the opposing view. Among them is the impropriety of anticipating redemption from sin during the time of innocence. Faustus then goes on to link the creation of Adam both with grace and with adoptive kinship:

> Thus, it was not fitting that he [Adam] be completed or perfected to the image of him through whom what was lost had to be repaired, lest under the name of the coming physician the ruin of the fall should be predicted in the very time of blessed origins. It is therefore more reasonable that in humankind, to whom the reality of grace, not of nature, is handed on by God in the very likeness, *image* should rather be called what is received from one who is higher and superior, and *likeness* is better understood as conferred from the truth that the Father rightly communicates with his Son by nature.[23]

So in the creation of the human race one has to do neither with a nature that awaits an augmentation from without, nor with a mere adumbration of a later outpouring of divine aid, but with the *res gratiae*, the very reality of grace. To partake of this grace is to share in a kind of adoptive filial relationship, given gratuitously by God. To be in the divine image is to receive grace.

While existence in the image of God, with its attendant capacities of reason, perpetuity, intellect, and free choice, constitutes human life and is

---

[23] II. 9. 77, 17-25: "consequens itaque non erat consummatum atque perfectum ad imaginem illius fieri, per quem necesse erat perditum reparari, ne sub nomine venturi medici in ipso tempore felicis exordii subplantandi videretur ruina praedici. id ergo rationi magis congruit, ut in homine, cui in ipsa similitudine a deo gratiae res traditur, non naturae, imago hoc potius nuncupetur, quod a priore et superiore suscipitur, et de veritate similitudo fuisse conlata plenius iudicetur, quam tamen cum filio naturali pater iure communicat."

therefore indelible, one's share in the likeness of God, the *similitudo*, may increase or decrease according to one's pursuit of virtue. Here we gain some insight into the will's status as both (1) good and (2) capable of good and evil. Seen under the aspect of the image of God, the human will as the capacity to choose is always a *bonum*. It can neither become evil nor be irreversibly turned toward evil, since by definition it is a good gift of God and free in its choice. Seen, however, under the aspect of the divine likeness, the moral resemblance to God, the will can, as a consequence of its choices, lead one toward either good or evil, virtue or vice: "It is from the image of God that one understands, that one knows what is right, that one discriminates between evil and good by the scrutiny of one's judgment. Since God is goodness, mercy, patience, and justice, the more one is found to be more just or patient, so much closer one is proved to be like God, whose likeness is possessed not in appearances, but in virtues."[24]

The image of God functions as a summary term for the whole complex of capacities and aptitudes consequent upon the creation of humankind. Again, though, one should be cautioned against supposing that Faustus wishes to explicate a doctrine of human nature or of natural capabilities. On the contrary, Faustus emphasizes, especially in II. 9, the divine origin and gratuity of these endowments. He does not limit his use of the term *prima gratia* to the law of nature but applies it more broadly to the positive qualities implanted in the human being, including the freedom of the will: "You will hardly doubt that the freedom of his own will, albeit

---

[24]II. 9. 78, 30-79, 6: "de imagine dei est, quod intellegit, quod rectum sapit, quod inter malum et bonum iudicio examinante discriminat. et cum deus bonitas misericordia, patientia atque iustitia sit, quanto quisque magis iustus ac patiens invenitur, tanto magis deo similis adprobatur, cuius utique similitudo non in vultibus, sed in virtutibus possidetur." Also, the voice of Divine Providence in II. 2. 62, 1-2 describes a person as becoming evil by following after "the iniquity of your will."

attenuated, belongs to man, if you give attention to the first grace by which he was honored by God. Man therefore is called the image of God because truth kindly and graciously implanted justice in him; and reason, wisdom; and perpetuity, eternity."[25] From this focus on the gratuitous character of the human constitution, one sees that for Faustus, human nature itself, inasmuch as it was made in God's image, is grounded in the *prima gratia*. This is true not only in the case of prelapsarian or original justice, which Faustus certainly affirms in his depiction of the original Edenic condition, but also, and most importantly, in the many cases he cites of people who after the fall are able to achieve righteousness and salvation on the strength of the innate human capacities.[26]

Can one distinguish between "nature" and "grace" in Faustus's theological anthropology? How Faustus treats this distinction shows itself in two closely connected passages in II. 9. In the first, to which we have alluded above, the author describes God as "subtilis, simplex, sincerus" and goes on to speak of God as self-subsisting. The human being, with regard to attributes like justice, mercy, and holiness, "does not possess these things naturally, but as gifts."[27] Possession of such virtues *naturaliter* can be predicated only of God, for God alone lacks contingency and dependence. As

---

[25]II. 9. 78, 26-30: ". . . inesse homini licet adtenuatam voluntatis propriae libertatem minime dubitabis, si primam gratiam, qua a deo est honoratus, inspexeris. imago dei homo dicitur, quia ei indulgenter ac dignanter inseruit veritas iustitiam, ratio sapientiam, perennitas aeternitatem."

[26]As noted by A. Michel in "Justice originelle," *Dictionnaire de Théologie Catholique* VIII/2: 2021, all patristic writers agree on the array of gifts given to humankind in creation: immortality, integrity, knowledge, etc. The theological problem concerns the relation of these gifts to human nature as it has continued after the fall, namely, whether they were superadded to human nature and could therefore be stripped from it by sin. Faustus's position is that those original gifts which comprise the image of God perdure.

[27]II. 9. 79, 14: "non naturaliter habet ista, sed largiter."

Faustus continues: "For instance, God is gold, while humankind can be seen as a gilt vessel; that which is grace in the human is nature in God, and something created in the one is increate in the other. Thus for this reason humankind's twofold status becomes the more apparent, into whom these things are implanted in such a way that they may frequently be separated and removed."[28] Some aspects of one's inner life, such as the virtues, are not, as such, constitutive of human existence. One could imagine life going on, albeit not ideally, without them, and in fact they are often lacking. Those gifts, however, that are aspects of the *imago Dei* perdure despite any onslaught of sin. At the most fundamental level, the psychic life of the human being is maintained by the indelible presence of the first grace given in creation:

> They err, therefore, who regard justice and the other virtues as the substance of the soul, without which it could subsist anyway by the vital power in its nature, without which even the devil is seen to remain in his nature. These virtues are manifestly shown to have been added when they are stripped away by the intervention of sins. Only the power of choice and immortality (which is even implanted in evil people) are not removed, although the dignity and blessedness of immortality can be removed. Insofar as it pertains to freedom of choice and immortality, then, even evil people can possess the

---

[28]II. 9. 79, 14-19: "verbi gratia ille aurum est, homo vero deauratum vas videri potest, et in homine gratia est, quod in deo natura est, et in hoc creatum est, quod in illo probatur ingenitum. et ideo iuxta hanc rationem magis duplex status hominis apparet, cui haec ita inseruntur, ut separentur saepius et auferantur."

image of God, though tarnished by them and in them, but only the good can possess the likeness.[29]

As regards anthropology, then, one is better advised to speak of levels or gradations of primal grace rather than of a strict dichotomy between grace and nature. Even when stripped of all apparent virtue by sin, the soul continues, not on the strength of a natural potency but by virtue of the freedom and perpetuity that are graciously given in creation as the *imago Dei*. Therefore the irreducible core of what it means to be human—the datum of human nature, as it were—is grace in its primal manifestation, grace consisting of the free will and immortality associated with the image of God.

At the next level, also an aspect of the *prima gratia*, lies the innate sense or capacity for discerning and following the law of nature. This is the moral sense by which one pursues the virtues and becomes worthy to be called a child of God.   While as an innate element of the human makeup it shares the indelible character of those gifts associated with the *imago*, it may or may not call forth an obedient response of will and intellect. Faustus cites the obedience of Abel and Enoch: "How would [Abel] have been able to reject the profane undertakings of his brother and to choose better ones, unless intellect and reason had directed him in the proper path . . . How would Enoch have been able to walk with God and to be pleasing to God, unless a law infused in his inward parts, by a hidden guidance, illumined him so much that because he knew nothing earthly, he was seized away, being

---

[29] II. 9. 79, 20-29: "Errant ergo, qui iustitiam reliquasque virtutes animae putant esse substantiam, sine quibus utcumque potest vitali in natura sua vigore subsistere, sine quibus et diabolus in natura sua manere dinoscitur. manifeste enim inveniuntur adposita dum culpis intervenientibus exuuntur. solum vero arbitrium et inmortalitas, quae etiam malis insita est, non aufertur, licet dignitas et beatitudo inmortalitatis possit auferri. quantum ergo ad libertatem arbitrii et inmortalitatem pertinet, imaginem dei licet a se et in se decoloratam etiam mali habere possunt, similitudinem nisi boni habere non possunt."

wondrously taken up from the earth by God?"[30] The example of Enoch also demonstrates that faith is intimately connected with, perhaps identical to, the capacity for obeying the inner law: "The one who exceeded all others in the merit of faith in the first age of the world taught that that very faith had been passed on to him with the law of nature."[31]   Since the Epistle to the Hebrews (11:5-6), which mentions Enoch, asserts that faith is necessary to please God, the role of faith in Enoch's following the law of nature can hardly be denied.

So the aspect of the *prima gratia* entailing a natural law, and the corresponding faith, depends upon one's exercise of the capacities of intellect and choice to make faith actual. Faustus says of Noah that he "adorned the general gifts of faith with the special zeal in himself."[32] The written law of Moses had to be given precisely because the law of nature had been, if not obliterated, rendered impotent by human neglect: "The heavenly dispensation undoubtedly would not have granted the written law unless sin, having flowed along to the point of the flood's wrath, had obstructed the law of nature."[33] The Mosaic law, ostensibly first, is in fact the second. The primary law of

---

[30]II. 9. 80, 6-8, 14-18: ". . . unde profana fratris instituta respuere, unde meliora potuisset eligere, nisi eum in viam rectam intellectus et ratio direxisset, . . . unde Enoch cum deo ambulare vel deo placere potuisset, nisi eum lex visceribus infusa secreto magisterio inluminassat in tantum, ut nihil terrenum sapiens mirabiliter a terra deo adsumente raperetur?"

[31]II. 9. 80, 18-20: "qui dum fidei merito in prima saeculi illius aetate ceteros antecellit, fidem ipsam cum lege naturae sibi traditam fuisse perdocuit. . . "

[32]II. 9. 81, 6-7: ". . . generalia fidei dona speciali in se studio . . . excoluit."

[33]II. 9. 81, 14-17: "legem itaque litterae absque dubio caelestis dispensatio non dedisset, nisi legem naturae interpellaset usque ad iram diluvii perducta transgressio."

nature, a vestige of creational grace, is available to all human beings, and the Noahic flood was but a general judgment upon their neglect of it.

To what extent does this law of nature continue to be effective in the human race? That is, given that it was rendered virtually impotent prior to the giving of the written law, can one still regard the natural law as relevant to the human condition? Or, put differently, Does the very presence of the law of nature within the creature depend entirely upon human apprehension and obedience? Faustus spends nearly the entire last three chapters of his treatise addressing this aspect of creational grace. Most of his treatment will be discussed in later sections of the present chapter, but we may here summarize its controlling notion.

Put succinctly, Faustus regards the law of nature as a vestigial, but still functional, remainder of the original endowment. After somewhat clumsily citing Augustine in support of the notion of the law of nature, Faustus continues: "Further, no one's sin is so contrary to nature as to blot out the last vestiges of nature. For it is because of this that even the ungodly think about eternal matters, and make praiseworthy laws even in the present world, and properly restrain and properly condemn many matters of human conduct. By what rules, in the end, do they judge these things if not by the natural rules, in which they see the way one should live, even if they themselves might not live this way?" [34] Immediately one is struck by Faustus's phrase "vestiges of nature," since he has placed such stress upon the gratuity of human endowments. On the one hand, this may be simply an

---

[34] II. 9. 81, 24-30: "item nullius quippe vitium ita contra naturam est, ut naturae deleat etiam extrema vestigia. nam hinc est, quod etiam impii cogitant aeterna ac praedicanda etiam in praesenti saeculo iura constituunt et multa recte reprehendunt recteque laudant in hominum moribus. quibus ea tandem regulis iudicant nisi naturalibus, in quibus vident, quem ad modum quisque vivere debeat, etiam si nec ipsi eodem modo vivant?"

imprecision of vocabulary. On the other hand, and more probably, *natura* refers here not to an abstract human nature, but to the created order in which is implanted the natural law. In either case, the force of the law of nature as an impetus toward a virtuous mode of life has not been obliterated; that law may be discerned and to a degree be obeyed, even beyond the pale of Christian or religious life. This important question of the extent of grace will be taken up in detail in a subsequent section .

To summarize, Faustus's doctrine of the gratuitously given image and likeness of God, which is to say his fundamental theological anthropology, takes its beginning from the notion that the entire complex of capacities and orientations that separate the human being from the broader creation may in a sense be designated as grace. He has no interest in a purely natural anthropology. This primal grace finds expression at different, interrelated levels. Most fundamentally, the granting of the image of God encompasses the immortality of the soul and is closely connected with the capacities of intellect, reason, and free choice of the will. Such things cannot be removed, for they constitute human life. The will,[35] with an innate or seminal potential for good, can also turn toward evil but cannot lose its essential freedom. Human righteousness, or at least access thereto, is granted to all, and so all have equal opportunity for salvation.

Certain benefits of one's positive constitution, however, can be forfeited, even if its most basic gifts cannot. An inward law is granted but can be obeyed or disobeyed according to the affect or response of the will in faith. Faith, then, is among the primary gifts of divine grace in creation but must be exercised volitionally. One's moral resemblance to God, the

---

[35]*Voluntas* and *arbitrium* seem to be used interchangeably in the *De gratia*.

likeness, can, while an aspect of the creator's grace, be possessed in varying degrees and apparently can be lost altogether, for it is a potentiality that must be made actual through willing obedience. Yet even the evil and godless, denuded both of virtue and of religion, continue to possess immortality, freedom of the will, and some discernment of the law of nature. Such are the anthropological presuppositions of Faustus's theology.

Divine Foreknowledge and Predestination

Not surprisingly, the immense realm of freedom, intellect, and self-determination that the first divine grace accorded to humankind in creation limits the amount of direct control that God exercises over human affairs. Because the question of predestination is a central point of argument in the polemical setting of the *De gratia*, one finds the treatise shot through with references to it. Two chapters, however, II. 2-3, comprise Faustus's most direct and focused treatment of foreknowledge and predestination. In examining them we shall see this discussion as the direct consequence of his theological anthropology.

"People misunderstand God's foreknowledge and predestination," Faustus begins in II. 2, "when they presuppose that the cause of human actions arises therefrom."[36] The reason for his assertion is that the human being, as created in the image of God, cannot be foreknown in the same manner as can the rest of creation:

---

[36]II. 2. 61, 9-10: "Praescientiam et praedestinationem dei male intellegunt astruentes, quod inde humanorum actuum causa nascatur."

One does not set about to do something because the authority of the foreknower might be about to compel him or her. Rather, the freedom and the will of the one foreknown impose a quality upon the foreknowing God. So the cause of sin is not imposed upon a person by a harshness of foresight; instead, the order of foreknowledge arises from the rewards deserved by people. So general foreknowledge, which lies before God and concerns the state of the whole world, arises from power. But as to the state of human beings, the qualities and kinds of foreknowing depend on a consideration of human actions.[37]

Because, then, the human being possesses a sphere of freedom and the capacity of willing, he or she is, as it were, a singular case within the general divine foreknowledge of the course of the world. By virtue of the very constitution of humankind—the primal divine grace—a clear limit has been placed upon the scope of divine foreknowledge. Whereas general foreknowledge may be a more or less pure exercise of divine power, implying, it would seem, divine causation in the course of the world, foreknowledge of human behavior does not and cannot involve direct divine causation of free human acts. God has created a world in which the free creature, though foreknown, is in no way compelled.

This state of affairs means, therefore, that God cannot be blamed for sin. To an imagined interlocutor who accuses God on this score, Faustus

---

[37]II. 2. 61, 12-20: "non propterea homo quodcumque facturus est, quia cum coactura sit praescientis auctoritas, sed magis deo praesciendi ingerit qualitatem libertas praesciti hominis ac voluntas. ergo non de violentia praevidendi inponitur homini causa peccandi, sed magis de consecuturis hominum meritis ordo exoritur praenoscendi. generalis itaque praescientia, quae de statu mundi totius apud deum manet, de potentia nascitur, sed circa statum hominis qualitates et species praenoscendi de humani actus inspectione mutuatur."

answers: "That God wills is one thing; that God permits is another. Thus God wills good, permits evil, and foreknows both. He aids righteous pursuits by his goodness; he allows unrighteous pursuits for the sake of freedom of choice. That he gives grace is his affair; that he foreknows an offense is yours."[38] The divine will is not abstractly omnipotent; in God's freedom as creator, for the sake of the created human free will, God allows actions contrary to the divine will. At the same time, the human being has always at his or her disposal the wherewithal for pursuing virtue. Foreknowledge follows upon the free decision of the human will. Even an apparently predetermined necessity, such as the prophesied death of King Hezekiah, can be turned aside by human action, in this instance by humble prayer: "Prayer puts a stop to the oracle; entreaty loosens the constraint; complete faith in what was said overcomes its truth; the utter weakness of a weeping man conquers the inevitable cause of a threatened death. Human frailty humbles itself and the divine purpose suffers a certain violence."[39]

Faustus distinguishes between foreknowledge and predestination in II. 3; his distinction, however, is not at all to be identified with a passive versus an active exercise of power.[40] Rather, foreknowledge is to be

---

[38]II. 2. 61, 23-26: "aliud est, quod vult deus, aliud est, quod permittit deus. vult itaque bonum et permittit malum, praescit utrumque. iusta bonitate adiuvat, iniusta pro arbitrii libertate permittit. de suo est, quod dat gratiam, de tuo, quod praenoscit offensam."

[39]II. 2. 62, 28-63, 2: "oratio interdicit oraculo, resolvit deprecatio definitionem, fides plena dicti superat veritatem, inevitabilem denuntiatae mortis causam extrema vincit deflentis infirmitas. humiliat se fragilitas humana et vim quandam patitur divina sententia."

[40]Augustine, too, generally kept the two concepts distinct. In *De natura et origine animae* I. vii. 7, for example, he speaks of foreknowledge as foreknowing, but not making, sinners who are to be healed. Predestination, on the other hand, refers to God's granting of the necessary salvific gifts to the elect; cf. *De praed. sanct.*, passim. Pelagius, commenting upon Rom. 8:29, made the two concepts identical (cf. Pelagius, *Expositions*, 194). A. J. Smith, in "Latin

understood as God's knowledge in advance of the freely chosen actions of human beings. Predestination, on the other hand, is simply the operation of divine justice in allotting reward or punishment for the behavior of the person. Such behavior is foreknown, of course, but is not compelled. Faustus illustrates by citing the case of the martyrdom of the Holy Innocents: the evil of their murder was foreknown; the glory of those slain was predestined.[41]

The force of such a position over against predestinarianism shows itself in I. 12. Here Faustus notes that a "heretic" teaches predestination or predeterminism by arguing from Rom. 9:15, "I will be merciful to whom I wish and will show mercy to whom I have mercy." If divine justice is to be respected, says Faustus, one should understand the object of divine mercy here as "the one whom I know to be just, whose ready faith I see, whom I will have known to be obedient to my precepts, whom I will have proven a doer of my will."[42] So the force of foreknowledge serves but to recognize the future human exercise of faith, while predestination ordains the proper reward of divine favor for that faith.

The case of Jacob and Esau further illustrates the function of the two divine powers. Paul's assertion in Rom. 9:9 that Jacob was preferred to Esau in the womb "when they had not yet done any sort of good or evil" had become a kind of locus classicus for the predestinarian position.[43] Faustus,

---

Sources," 201f., has found instances of a view like that of Pelagius also in Ambrosiaster and elsewhere in Augustine.

[41]II. 3. 65, 4-10.

[42]I. 12. 43, 14-17: ". . . cui iustum esse cognovero, cuius promptam fidem videro, quem praeceptis meis oboedire perspexero, quem meam facere probavero voluntatem."

[43]Beginning with his *De diversis quaestionibus ad Simplicianum*, Augustine had used this passage to argue for the utter priority of divine initiative

however, regarding Jacob and Esau as types of the Jews and the gentiles, sees
the Scriptures teaching God's foreknowledge of the faith of the gentiles and
subsequent reward of that faith. Faustus responds directly to the opposition:

> But you say "'when they had not yet done any sort of good or evil"
> means they are already assigned to predetermined parties. Yet what
> is remarkable if he foresees the actions of those whose end he
> foretells, and thus, as it is agreed that the course of their life is to be
> disposed by their own choice of will, so according to God's power
> they are foreknown, and according to justice they are foreordained?
> All of this is predicted of them, not prefixed.[44]

Again, foreknowledge is a function of divine power; predestination, of
justice.

Faustus's doctrine of foreknowledge and predestination is thus a
function of his theological anthropology.   The initial outpouring of grace
upon the human creature is of such importance that God places a limitation
upon God's own power rather than intrude upon the capacities and
prerogatives given. As we shall now come to see, not even the reality of
human sin can delete these original gifts.

---

to human merits, and that the relative merits of the two brothers had nothing to do
with God's decision. The same position finds expression in *Ep*. 194. 39, *Contra
duas epistulas Pelagianorum* 2. 15, and elsewhere. Long before, Rom 9:9 had
evidently been used by the predestinarians against whom Origen wrote in *De
Princ*. III.

[44]II. 6. 74, 9-14: "Sed dicis: cum adhuc non egissent aliquid boni aut
mali, iam praefinitis partibus deputantur. quid mirum si, quorum actus praevidit,
eorum exitus praesignavit, et ideo, sicut eos cursum vivendi pro arbitrio proprio
disposituros esse constabat, ita pro dei potentia praenoscuntur, pro institia
praeordinantur? hoc totum de eis praedicitur, non praefinitur."

Human Sin: Essence, Consequences, Transmission

The time of origins—creation of the human race in God's image—dominates Faustus's theological enterprise, as we have seen. His positive evaluation of the human capacity to will and to act raises the immediate question whether, or to what extent, Faustus has taken seriously the consequences of sin, both for individuals and for the human race as a whole. This question will occupy the present section of the study. In brief, one can say that Faustus has inherited and has developed in the *De gratia* a clear doctrine of sin that is derived in many of its particulars from Augustine. At the same time, the bishop of Riez refuses to follow Augustine's pessimistic estimate of human capabilities after the fall. We will here consider Faustus's hamartiology by examining first his treatment of the fall and its consequences and then his doctrine of the transmission of Adamic sin to the human race.

The Fall and its Consequences

The first parents, as we have noted, participated in a real measure of grace, namely, in the primal constitutive grace by which the human being was made after God's image and likeness. At the most fundamental level, possession of this grace meant the eternity of the soul and the free choice of the will. In the will's freedom lay the possibility of giving consent to evil, and precisely in this consent rests the essence of human sin:

We see . . . that the consent of the human mind is able to move toward both the good part and the opposite . . . Clearly, one to whom victory is promised if he chooses the good is not constrained by a necessity of evil. The law of his origin does not draw onto the wrong path the one whom the creator has placed at a crossroad. So to one to whom a will is given so that he can conquer evil, should he perchance yield to his enemy, he has lacked the desire to struggle and will not fail to obtain the result.[45]

The special offense of sin is its contempt of God in spurning or abusing the divine gifts. A human being falls willingly into error and therefore does not reap the consequences of sin as though he or she were abandoned, "but as an ingrate who has withdrawn from the outpouring of mercy."[46] Sin incurs guilt only because it is chosen in this way, in deliberate rejection of the capacity for perceiving and obeying the truth. Just as the will is granted in order that one choose the good, the faculty of intellect bears the ability to know God's will through the created order: "Thus he [Paul] condemns first for having abused their intellect those impious whose unrighteousness he accuses for their contempt of divinity."[47]

Such is the basic character of sin in general. The singular force of Adam and Eve's sin was not to be found merely in its position as the temporally first instance of human sin, but in its intent: to be as gods. Their rebellion reached beyond the point of spurning the creator's gifts; it was an act of lèse-majesté. Faustus comments on Gen. 2:17:

---

[45]I. 12. 41, 9-10, 18-23: "Videmus ergo et in bonam et in contrariam partem posse humanae mentis transire consensum . . . aperte mali necessitate non premitur, cui victoria de boni electione promittitur. non enim in devia lex originis trahit, quem auctor in bivio conlocavit, ac sic, cui voluntas indita est, ut vincere malum possit, si forte adversario suo cessit, animus ei pugnandi defuit, eventus non defuit obtinendi."

[46]I. 12. 42, 15-16: ". . . qui se ingerenti misericordiae subtraxit ingratus . . . "

[47]II. 9. 82, 23-25: "impios ergo et de intellectu, quod abusi sunt, damnat, quorum iniustitiam in contemptum divinitatis accusat."

The one cast down envied him his immortality and thus introduced the cause of death by saying, "In the day you eat of this tree, your eyes will be opened, and you will be as gods." Now if he had said only "When you eat, you will have your fill of the food's sweetness," the transgression would have attained only to the level of the seduction of fleshly desire. But when he set forth the goal of this sin by saying "you will be as gods," the sin of greed gave way to the desire for divinity and to treason against majesty. And so they became as gods deprived of the gift of heavenly grace, thrown down from the pinnacle of their blessed station. Thus the clever serpent, who was cast down from heaven for the evil of pride, devised for himself, from his own fall and descent, tricks for tripping man. As he cut him down, so he took him captive.[48]

A crime of such a kind as our first parents', then, does not simply merit the punishment due a lapse into carnal pleasure, but rather effects a fundamentally changed orientation toward God, in that it imitates the evil pride that brought on the devil's fall.

Faustus's primary interest in Adam's sin lies neither in its essence nor in its motive forces, but in its consequences. These consequences are, first, the introduction of bodily death into the human race and, second, the

---

[48]I. 1. 9, 21-10, 2: ". . . ei inmortalitatem deiectus invidit, ideo causam mortis ingessit dicendo: in quacumque die comederitis de ligno hoc, aperientur oculi vestri et evitis sicut dii. si hoc tantum dixisset: cum manducaveritis, satietatem de cibi suavitate capietis, usque ad consupiscentiae carnalis inlecebram transgressio pervenisset. cum vero hanc praevaricationis proposuerit finem dicendo: eritis sicut dii, edacitatis culpa usque ad divinitatis ambitum et usque ad crimen maiestatis accesit. facti sunt ergo sicut dii dono gratiae caelestis exuti et de beatae stationis culmine proturbati, ac sic callidus serpens pro superbiae malo eiectus e caelo machinas sibi ad hominem subruendum de casu proprio lapsuque disposuit et, quomodo cecidit, sic decepit."

tarnishing of those primal divine gifts to humanity which Faustus has called the *prima gratia*. The former is of relatively little importance in the *De gratia*, but the latter has central implications in Faustus's argument.

Against Pelagius's putative assertion of a created mortality, Faustus affirms that bodily death is a consequence of human sin. As he puts it in a terse formula: "Humankind is God's work; sin is the devil's work; death is the penalty for sin."[49] The creator's original gift, or at least original intent, was bodily perpetuity. In evidence of this Faustus is content to note the restoration of physical immortality in the resurrection: "Therefore you should not doubt that immortality was given to man prior to sin, as you see it restored even after his fall."[50] Death of the body is an alien evil, not a part of the created human constitution. The immortality of the soul, however, is not, and cannot be, forfeited due to sin, for it is an element of the indelible image of God.

The second and most telling consequence, or set of consequences, for the human race is the corruption or pollution of the original gifts, such that they are impaired in achieving their intended ends. Faustus uses metaphors of impurity to describe this effect. He speaks in one place of how "wickedness, when mixed in, corrupted the goodness of the will and of faith."[51] This corruption of the original human powers manifests itself first and foremost in the enfeeblement (*infirmitas*) of the capacity for free choice of the will. The practice of sin impairs one's free will, primarily by the force of habit.

---

[49] I. 1. 10, 28-29: "homo enim opus dei, peccatum opus diaboli, mors poena peccati."

[50] I. 1. 10, 6-8: "quapropter inmortalitatem homini conmissam non dubites ante culpam, quam reddi perspicis etiam post ruinam."

[51] II. 5. 68, 4-5: "bonum voluntatis et fidei admixta malitia depravavit."

Faustus compares the effects of sin upon the power of choice to those of illness, or of habitual drunkenness, or of sexual indulgence: the allure of indulging in sin exerts a downward pull upon one's faculties. What was once an unimpeded choice must now overcome opposition in order to choose the good:

> A person who, in the primal age, might have been able to walk among the blandishments of carnal sin and retain innocence is now brought back to the way of virtue only after great effort. Just so, the freedom given by God to the human will has lost the flower and vigor of his grace. But the freedom itself has not been lost; so one should not suppose that the divine gifts have been cut off from one, but rather should know that they must be sought again by one with the greatest labor and toil, and through the patronage of assistance.[52]

The will retains its freedom, although this freedom is attenuated.

Consequently, the divine intention that the human will should choose to pursue the path of virtue continues to hold sway after the fall, despite the human propensity to err: "The most holy governor, desiring his creation to be noble even after it had fallen into ruin, commands that it is proper for humankind's will not to be the servant of all passion and concupiscence, but their master ... By no nececessity of sinning is one

---

[52]I. 8, 25, 2-8: ". . . facile prima aetas statum suum retinens calcare potuisset, cum magno luctamine velut contra ardui montis ascensum ad virtutis viam reditur, ita humani arbitrii a deo concessa libertas florem vigoremque gratiae suae perdidit, tamen ipsa non periit, ut divina munera non tam interdicta sibi sentiat, quam cum summo labore ac sudore per adiutorii patrocinium sibi repetenda esse cognoscat."

bound, to whose discretion it has been given to master sin with the liberty of a superior. Yet the fallen soul, which with God's favor can obtain victory from sin, prefers, to God's offense, to be a slave to sin."[53] So after the sin of the first parents, what followed was not the impossiblity, but only the difficulty, of doing actions pleasing to God. Significantly, Faustus's examples of the operation of innate goodness and freedom of the will are not Adam and Eve, but postlapsarian figures: Abel, Enoch, Noah. Adamic sin stains and impedes, but does not obliterate, the operation of the fundamental capabilities of the human will. As the force of habitual sinning impresses itself upon a person, one's will prefers (*mavult*) sin but is not wholly determined toward choosing to sin.

Despite the ability of sin to strip away virtue and to harden the human heart, despite even the "depravity of the will"[54] that is revealed in, and furthered by, repeated sinning, the human being never loses the ability to turn from the path of vice to that of virtue. One can arise to be a "vessel of honor" after having become a "vessel of dishonor": "Whenever, therefore, one strives by one's mind's judgment to be made evil instead of good, or good instead of evil, the will, which is free, a gift of God, is corrected; the power of predestination does not bring it about . . . As many times as a person is converted for the better from an inferior, rejected state with the help of grace, so often is a vessel of honor made from a vessel of dishonor."[55] While one

---

[53]II. 8. 75, 17-76, 5: "Ecce piissimus moderator generosam esse cupiens facturam suam etiam post ruinam inclinatam, licet hominis voluntatem totius passionis et concupiscentiae non famulam iubet esse, sed dominam . . . nulla peccandi necessitate concluditur, cuius discretioni committitur, ut peccato superioris libertate dominetur. degener vero animus, qui cum beneficio dei de peccato potest victoriam consequi, mavult cum offensa dei servus esse peccati."

[54]II. 10. 85, 16-17.

[55]I. 11. 38, 22-39, 3: "Si quando ergo homo ex bono malus vel ex malo bonus effici arbitrio mentis adnititur, voluntas, quae libera est, a deo data

needs the aid of divine grace in a new way because of the damage inflicted by sin—this will be treated in a later section of the present study—the effects of original sin upon the human will are not finally decisive. Adamic sin corrupts the *prima gratia* of free choice in the sense that it has whetted the appetites, thus making easier the lapse into self-perpetuating, habitual sin.

Humankind does not, therefore, stand under a general condemnation by virtue of original sin; it is not a *massa damnationis*, to use Augustine's term. Divine judgment is meted out only in return for one's deeds. Faustus certainly says that "the whole human race has fallen faint from the strike of one serpent's bite,"[56] so the consequences of original sin are real and universal. But one must immediately add that this is said in reference to an infirmity. One can be held fully guilty only in denying the existence of this infirmity by turning away from the one who can heal it. The human condition per se is not liable to judgment after the fall, because even in their weakness the capabilities of will and intellect can be turned toward actions pleasing to God: "How can you then contend that the hardened stain of sin belongs inseparably to our origin and condition, when you know it can be put off and set aside?"[57]

---

corrigitur, non vis praedestinationis operatur . . . et quotiens homo ad meliora deterioribus repudiatis gratia iuvante convertitur, totiens de vase contumeliae vas honoris efficitur."

[56]I. 9. 27, 28-29: ". . . universitas generis humani uno serpentis morsu percussa languebat."

[57]I. 10. 33, 19-21: "quomodo concretam peccati labem inseparabiliter ad originem et conditionem pertinere contendis, quam deponi et exui posse cognoscis?"

Transmission of Adam's Sin

The consequences of Adamic sin—physical death, the weakened power of choice, the clouded intellect, the propensity to err—become universal in humanity by being handed on through procreation. We have demonstrated in chapter 3 Faustus's dependence upon Augustine on this point. In this brief section we shall simply examine the main points of Faustus's own presentation.

The bulk of his discussion of the transmission of original sin arises in the refutation of Pelagian errors early in the treatise (I. 1-2). After speaking of the violence done to humanity's privileged status by the first transgression, Faustus continues, citing Rom. 5:12: "Let us see whether our sad, lamentable condition had its origin in the will of God or in human depravity. Hear what the trumpet of truth resounds: 'Therefore just as through one man sin came into this world and through sin death, so death pervaded all, in whom all have sinned.'"[58] Thus sin and death extend their sway even to infants, and so the Pelagian denial of the need of infant baptism is really a trivialization of the power of original sin and therefore empties redemption of all value.[59]

How, precisely, is sin passed on to infants? Faustus, using Pelagius as a mouthpiece, puts the question into its most troubling formulation: How can two baptized parents, freed from original sin, transmit

---

[58]I. 1. 10, 20-25: "videamus, utrum per voluntatem dei an per hominis pravitatem infelix et deflenda conditio initium sumpserit. audi quid tuba personet veritatis: propterea, inquit, sicut per unum hominem in hunc mundum peccatum intravit et per peccatum mors, ita in omnes homines mors pertransiit, in quo omnes peccaverunt."

[59]I. 1. 11. 2-4.

to their offspring what they themselves did not at all possess?[60] To this question Faustus gives an answer that is somewhat at odds with the broad outlines of his theology expressed elsewhere in the treatise, for it makes a very sharp distinction between grace and nature.[61] He responds first by making a distinction between two births: one transmits sin through the desire of the one who procreates (*ex generantis voluptate*); and the other gives sanctification by virtue of the adoption of the one who regenerates.[62] The two kinds of birth, generation and regeneration, correspond to the distinction between nature and grace. Still speaking of baptized parents, Faustus elaborates:

> Regarding this nature, the Apostle has said "You were children of wrath by nature." They are justly unable to give, as if it were their own, what they themselves have received from above and from without. Pelagius most imprudently believes that the purity of innocence is given to children through their parents. The second birth does not pertain to the role of the parents. He wishes to make God's gift into a human duty, as if one could, by hereditary order, pass on to the human posterity something whose substance is outside the human realm. Undoubtedly original sin is passed on,

---

[60]I. 2. 12, 8-9: "quomodo, inquit, mittunt ad posteros, quod ipsi in se minime habuerunt?"

[61]As observed earlier in the present study, the two anti-Pelagian chapters I. 1-2, and the treatment of concupiscence in particular, are materialy more dependent upon Augustine than is the rest of the treatise. This is hardly surprising, given the subject matter, but it may also explain why in this place Augustine's more rigid nature-grace antithesis has displaced the rather more fluid categories one finds, e.g., in II. 9.

[62]I. 2. 12, 9-12. Cf. Augustine, *De nupt. et conc.* I, 19, 21; II, 34, 58, and *De grat. Chr. et pecc. orig.* II, 40, 45; II, 39, 44.

even from baptized parents, to their children through their fleshly
origin.[63]

Whereas elsewhere in the treatise Faustus has avoided a rigid
distinction between nature and grace, in this context the demarcation is
important. We should not, however, suppose that we have found here a
fundamental inconsistency. His use of *natura* and *humanam substantiam* in
this connection need not refer to a "bare" human nature, somehow denuded of
the divine gifts. We have seen already that for Faustus human existence is
radically bound up with God's granting of image as the initial grace. Nature
should therefore be seen as the concrete reality of human life as originally
constituted by God's gifts and as later lacking something of its created vital-
ity.[64] In the context of this anti-Pelagian polemic, largely taken up from
Augustine, Faustus must necessarily stress human nature's present deficiency
vis-à-vis its restoration by Christ. But this weakened nature, which is passed
on from parent to child, retains the vestiges of its original dignity even as it
bears the scars of sin. In II. 9, after citing Augustine's *De civitate Dei* XII
as evidence of the persistence of creational goodness, Faustus continues:

---

[63]I. 2. 12, 16-25: "de qua natura apostolus dicit: eratis, inquit, natura
filii irae. merito quasi de proprio dare nequeunt, quod de sursum et extrinsecus
acceperunt. inprudentissime per parentes filiis innocentiae puritatem Pelagius
dari credit. ad parentum ministerium nativitas secunda non pertinet. officium vult
esse hominis quod dei munus est, ut velut quodam hereditario ordine per hominum
currat posteritatem quod extra humanam constat esse substantiam. originale autem
peccatum ex parentibus etiam baptizatis per carnis originem ad filios transire non
dubium est . . . "

[64]Faustus's difference from Augustine on this point is a matter of degree.
For the latter, human nature has been so utterly corrupted by sin as to become
virtually a principle of evil. The free will, for example, is sufficient for sinning
but utterly incapable of turning toward good. Hence in *De nat. et grat.* 53: 62
human nature is "vulnerata, sauciata, vexata, perdita . . . " and in 23: 25, "ut in
peccatum iret, sufficit liberum arbitrium, quo se ipse vitiavit; ut autem redeat ad
iustitiam, opus habet medico, quoniam sanus [homo] non est."

"Again, no one's sin is so contrary to nature as to blot out the last vestiges of nature."[65]

Finally, lest he appear to condemn marriage in his denunciation of concupiscence, Faustus stresses the fundamental goodness of marriage as a creational ordinance. His objections, he asserts, are not to matrimony as such, but to the corruption that sin has introduced into it: "As to procreation and concupiscence, whatever the divine precept has established, this I praise; whatever human sin has introduced, this I reprove."[66] As a result of sin, marriage has not lost its essential character, but, as a white garment spotted with a black stain, it has lost its highest dignity. Had not Adam's sin intervened, procreation would have been chaste, free from sinful desire; unfortunately, "just as he lost the privilege of immortality, so he lost the gift of purity."[67]

----

[65]II. 9. 81, 24-15: "item nullius quippe vitium ita contra naturam est, ut naturae deleat etiam extrema vestigia." In the passage from Augustine, mention is made of "malum, quod a parente trahitur, et bonum, quod a creante tribuitur," the verb *trahere* being Augustine's favored term for the transmission of original sin. While this would seem to confirm Faustus's alignment with Augustine as to the transmission of original sin, Friedrich Wörter, in *Zur Dogmengeschichte des Semipelagianismus,* 64, felt that this *malum* did not really signify sin for Faustus, but only a less precise evil. This opinion is echoed by Godet in "Fauste de Riez," 2104. But surely the term could only have been understood by Faustus as referring to original sin. Cf. Tibiletti, "Libero arbitrio e grazia," 261, n. 16. In Wörter's defense, however, one should note that for Faustus original sin does not bear the aspects of universal guilt and liability to punishment as it does for Augustine.

[66]I. 2. 14, 4-6: "inter generationem et concupiscentiam quidquid praeceptio divina constituit, hoc laudo, quidquid humana praevaricatio adiecit, hoc reprobo."

[67]I. 2. 14, 12-13: ". . . sicut inmortalitatis privilegium, ita donum perdidit puritatis." Augustine too reprises this old theme of an original chaste procreation; in *De nupt. et conc.* II, 22, 37 we find: "in paradiso si peccatum non praecessisset, non esset quidem sine utriusque sexus commixtione generatio, sed esset sine confusione commixtio."

Faustus thus sees Adamic sin as passing its consequences—infirmity of the will, physical death, the propensity to fall into the habitual force of sinful desire—to the whole human race through the vehicle of concupiscence in procreation. But the vitiated nature handed on in this way does not seem to constitute automatically a *massa damnationis*; no one is pressed into sin, and thence into perdition, by a fatal necessity of human nature. Rather, the attenuated, vestigial capacities of the *prima gratia* now stand in need of further assistance, which must have a restorative character.

The Grace of Redemption

So far we have examined the *De gratia's* presentation of the primal gifts of free will and perpetuity, which also involved the innate natural law and the capacity to exercise faith. The human being was created in the image and likeness of God; the image is indelible, but the likeness depends upon the willing exercise of one's created capacities in pursuit of virtue and righteousness. By rightly pursuing this course in freedom, the human race would have shared in the divine life in an unhindered way. We have, second, given attention to the origin, consequences, and transmission of sin, which has enfeebled the original human constitution such that it can no longer share fully in both the image and the likeness of God. The initial grace of God, which is to say, the fundamental grounding of human nature in the divine gifts, has been attenuated but not abrogated. The human race therefore needs, not the overcoming or recreation of an utterly perverse nature, but an *adiutorium*, an assistance, for the infirm, but essentially good, powers of human free will. This special aid, which continues the grace of God given in creation, is the grace of redemption.

Continuity of Creation and Redemption

Axiomatic in the *De gratia* is the identity of the one God as both creator and redeemer. The divine munificence manifests itself in both instances, and therefore God's gifts, considered under either aspect, merit the designation *grace*. The original gifts that orient human existence toward God—perpetuity, the free will, and the inner law of nature—do not aim at a fundamentally different end from the grace brought by Christ, which has the character of healing. Faustus certainly distinguishes between the two but sees them as moments or dispensations in the action of the same God. Specifically, both dispensations have as their goal the fashioning of the human being fully in God's image and likeness. One may justly say, with Tibiletti, that salvation history begins with the gifts implanted in the human being by God in creation.[68]

Concerning creation, Faustus writes in reference to the Ninevites in II. 12: "Faith is demonstrated, striving exercised, the disposition made manifest. An inner fire, implanted in man by God and nourished by man with God's grace, does all this in man. So this people shows that God, by the very order of creation, had placed in man the things required for human salvation, and that prior to the redeemer's gifts, the author's gifts had always flourished about the rational creature."[69] But while the requisites for salvation lie naturally, as it were, in the human, they do not suffice to conduct one to full beatitude, owing to the infirmity introduced by sin. So the creational gifts, "having been given by the most high creator through nature,

---

[68]"Libero arbitrio e grazia," 269-70.

[69]II. 12. 90, 18-24: "fides probatur, exercetur ambitus, manifestatur affectus, totumque hoc in homine ignis interior a deo insitus et ab homine cum dei gratia nutritus operatur. ostendit itaque gens illa ea, quae saluti hominis conpetunt, ipsa ordinatione facturae deum intra hominem conlocasse et ante munera redemptoris circa rationabilem creaturam semper auctoris dona viguisse."

were to be confirmed through grace. Through grace, I say, in whose time the
salvation of the past world was to be consummated, because the light neither
of the letter nor of nature brought anything to perfection."[70] The whole
course of creation therefore anticipated its final consummation by redemptive
grace. Put differently, the grace of Christ, which Faustus calls "special"
grace and describes with metaphors of assistance and healing, has always
operated as the principle that brings the gifts of creation to their full
perfection. The line of demarcation between *gratia creatoris* and *gratia
salvatoris* becomes, in this sense, indistinct.[71]

In II. 9 Faustus elaborates on the notion that Christ has been in all
ages the agent of human salvation. Returning to his introduction of the
examples of Abel, Enoch, and Noah, we read: "Since people have been
endowed with the image and likeness of God, so as to be worthy to be called
children of God, it would be appropriate for us to make plain with a few
examples how many there are who, by following the law of nature which is,
as we have said, the first grace of God, prior to the written law, have entered
the doorway of salvation, to be led by Christ to the very inner chamber of
life."[72] A basic agreement or continuity thus exists between the creational

---

[70]II. 12. 90, 24-91, 1: "a conditore quidem summo praestita per
naturam, sed confirmanda per gratiam. per gratiam, inquam, in cuius tempore
praeteritorum salus erat consummanda saeculorum, quia nihil ad perfectum adduxit
lex vel litterae vel naturae."

[71]Koch, in *Der heilige Faustus*, 99-100, remarks: "Denn Faustus
verkennt den spezifischen Unterschied der gratia saluatoris von der gr. creatoris
und verwischt so die Grenze zwischen den Gebieten der Natur und der Gnade."
Tibiletti, in "La salvezza umana," 384, n. 58, criticizes Koch for locating his
analysis in a dogmatically Augustinian, rather than historical, manner.

[72]II. 9. 79, 30-80, 4: "cum homines ita fuerint imagine et similitudine
<dei praediti, ut multi etiam filii> dei meruerint nuncupari, vel paucis adhuc
exemplis praestringere nos oportet, quanti ante legem litterae erudiente lege
naturae, quae prima, ut diximus, dei gratia est, vestibula salutis intraverint per
Christum ad ipsa vitae penetralia perducendi." The bracketed phrase is added from

prima gratia and the grace brought by Christ. Only the latter brings salvation in the sense of conducting humankind to the fullness of life. Christ's redemptive work consists in taking up and assisting the primally good, but infirm, human capacities and orientations and leading them to their ultimate development.

So, for example, faith—Faustus uses *fides* and *credulitas* synonymously—as a creational gift with a kind of latency or potentiality must become active in the human disposition. Faustus speaks of an affect of belief (*credulitatis affectum*) which grows with divine help.[73] The consummation of this assisting process depends upon the grace of Christ, which Faustus also calls special grace (*gratia specialis*) in II. 10, because natural law and precept are insufficient. Faustus's terminology describing this grace tends toward metaphors of assistance rather than of transformation; these metaphors succinctly describe the fundamental relationship between creational and redemptive gifts.[74]

Faustus further elucidates the distinction between the two orders by his juxtaposition of the terms *libertas* and *liberatio* in II. 10. Liberty (*libertas*), or freedom to choose between good and evil, is not a special gift granted only to an elect few; it is a *res naturae*, a constitutive element of the

---

a citation by John Maxentius; cf. Engelbrecht, *Studien über die Schriften des Bischofes von Reii Faustus,* 19.

[73]I. 6. 22, 25-26: ". . . ut credulitatis affectum proficientibus augeat et laborantibus adiutor cotidianus adsistat." Cf. I. 14. 46, 32. See also the dated but important article of J. Chéné, "Que signifiaient *initium fidei* et *affectus credulitatis* pour les semipélagiens?" 566-88.

[74]Koch, in *Der heilige Faustus,* 89, n. 6, helpfully records this terminology: *gratia iuvans* (I. 12), *adiuvans* (I. 1), *cooperans* (I. 11), *comitans* (I. 5), *manus adiuvantis* (I. 10), *auxilium miserantis* (I. 10), *virtus dei adiutoris* (I. 9), *adiutorium dei* (I. 12), *patrocinium adiutorii* (I. 9), *dextera praesidii et adiutorii* (I. 10), *adminicula gratiae* (I. 9), *patrocinium gratiae* (I. 1).

human makeup, common both to good and to evil people. As such, *libertas* is not a decisive or even interesting matter in the economy of salvation. Of more consequence is one's liberation (*liberatio*), that is, the ability to pursue a life of virtue pleasing to God, obediently placing one's infirm capabilities in the service of such a life. For this task a special assistance beyond that of the *prima gratia* is necessary:

> Liberation has to do with the gift of grace and the purpose of a consenting life, but liberty of choice is the reality, not of an added generosity, but of nature. The former is either bestowed or conserved in those who seek, while the latter is conferred even upon those who do not seek. The former is administered to the reborn, the latter to the born. Liberty has to do with the sole work of God, liberation with the service of the human subject. The former is confirmed in good people, the latter is implanted even in evil people.[75]

Liberation is the full realization of those things for which liberty was originally given in creation. The distinction *libertas/liberatio* corresponds almost exactly to that between *imago* and *similitudo* in Faustus's basic anthropological orientation. Just as God's image perdures in all people, and God's likeness attends human existence only to the extent that one applies one's capacities to the pursuit of virtue, so *libertas*—an aspect of the

---

[75]II. 10. 88, 28-89, 3: "liberatio ad donum gratiae et ad propositum consentientis pertinet vitae, libertas vero arbitrii non est res accedentis munificentiae, sed naturae. quaerentibus illa vel tribuitur vel conservatur, etiam non requirentibus ista confertur. illa renascentibus ministratur, ista nascentibus. libertas ad solam dei pertinet operationem, liberatio et ad subditi hominis servitutem. illa bonis confirmata, ista et malis insita est."

image—has not been lost, but reaches its intended end in *liberatio*. Seen in this light, the grace of redemption is none other than a continuation or reiteration of the creation of humankind in the image and likeness of God.

Despite some imprecision in his terminology, Faustus certainly regards as grace all of God's gifts to the human race, whether in creation or in redemption. His use of *nature* relative to creational human endowments cannot be taken to suggest an entirely separate order of nature over against that of grace. Looking forward toward liberation, that is, toward the restoration of the image and likeness of God, Faustus necessarily emphasizes the present deficit of human nature which stands in need of the grace of Christ. The bulk of the *De gratia*, however, for reasons both positive and polemical, looks backward toward creation, emphasizing the continuing relevance of God's image in humankind. Salvation history comprehends both creation and redemption, for in creation "humankind begins that salvation which only the grace of Christ, absolutely necessary, can realize."[76]

By contrast, Augustine had considered it senseless to treat the created human endowments as grace in any salvifically important sense, though he did not entirely spurn the term in describing these gifts. The gifts of nature are common to all, while grace, that is, the grace of Christ, separates the good from those who are in bondage to sin. One might speak of the grace of nature as distinguishing human life from that of brutes, but the decisive distinction—that between those who have faith and those who do not—pertains only to the grace of Christ. Meaningful discussion about grace does not therefore include its creational aspect: "The grace of God, not by which

---

[76]Tibiletti, "La salvezza umana," 384:   "L'uomo comincia quella salvezza che solo la grazia di Cristo, assolutamente necessaria, può realizzare."

one is created, but by which one is restored, is in question."[77] Against just such a view Faustus insists that the identity of the author of both graces implies their inseparability.

As Simonetti has pointed out, Faustus's attempt to hold the two together meets with some difficulties, primary among them being the distinctness of the life of the baptized Christian. If the capacity for belief (*fides, credulitas*) inheres in all people as an aspect of the image of God and has not been obliterated by sin, how, specifically, is one's lot improved by Christian baptism? Faustus affirms and exalts the advantages of redemption in Christ but does not spell them out.[78] But despite such problems, Faustus's thesis of a fundamental continuity between the grace of creation and that of redemption remains clear and prominent:

> But since the same one who is the creator is the restorer, one and the same is blessed with praise in both works, and one and the same is celebrated with glory in both works. Rightly I proclaim a gift in both realities, for I know that I owe the fact of my birth to the one to whom I owe my rebirth. For this reason, then, I shall not deny the creator's gifts because I squandered them, but neither shall I equate the prior gifts with those that followed because in many ways I have had them repaired for the better. I will extol the benefits of the creator, yet immeasurably prefer those of the redeemer.[79]

---

[77]*De nat. et grat.* LIII, 62: "gratia ergo dei, non qua instituatur, sed qua restituatur, quaeratur." Cf. *De praed. sanct.* 5, 10.

[78]Cf. Simonetti, "Il *De gratia*," 143-44.

[79]II. 10. 83, 20-28: "cum vero ipse sit conditor, qui reparator, unus idemque in utriusque operis laude benedicitur, unus idemque in utriusque operis praeconio celebratur. iure itaque utriusque rei munus assero, quia me illi scio debere, quod natus sum, cui debeo, quod renatus sum. et propterea non ideo negabo

Divine and Human Initiative

While broadening the emphasis of the term *grace* beyond the bounds of what Augustine might have deemed proper, Faustus has still maintained the most fundamental anti-Pelagian concern: the absolute necessity of the grace of Christ for human salvation. Having established its necessity, we must now ask about its mode of operation. Specifically, How does one account for the role played by human will and action in the economy of salvation? Is grace truly gratuitous, or does an element of human merit intrude? Is grace prevenient, or does the human will move antecedently toward God? Does grace work internally, transforming the human will, or externally, as a stimulus to one's innate capabilities? Questions of this kind reveal in their very formulation the extent to which Augustinian categories pervade western thinking about divine grace, but they provide a useful framework for exploring the matter at hand.

Human effort and application as the counterpart to divine grace constitutes a recurring theme in the *De gratia*, finding expression in terms like *devotio, studium, labor, sudor, conatus, servitus, oboedientia, officium, servitium, obsequium,* and *industria.* Underlying Faustus's use of such terms is the conviction that predestinationism eliminates the need for Christian activity and encourages an otiose attitude. Against the threat, real or imagined, of such a quiescent Christianity, Faustus wishes to grant supremacy to divine grace without thereby diminishing the role of human co-operation. To make clear his distance from the Pelagian position, he casts grace in the role of *patronus, dominus, imperator,* and human labor in that of

---

conditoris dona, quia perdidi, sed priora ideo sequentibus non exaequabo, quia multipliciter in melius reparata suscepi. extollam beneficia creantis, sed in inmensum praeferam redimentis."

servus and *famulus*.[80] Even though the success and honor of a superior frequently depend upon the service of an inferior, no one would grant the servant undue credit for simply fulfilling an appointed task. So the movements of human will and action are clearly secondary to that of saving grace: "We are not simply equating labor and grace; on the contrary, we give complete preference to grace, without comparison."[81] Because of the secondary and dependent character of human service, both the beginning and the end of even the most arduous labor are owed to the Lord, not to the servant:

> Could you understand the building of the Church as having taken place in any other way than by the labors and offices of the priests, by the ministries and examples of the saints, by the gallant deeds of the apostles and the deaths of the martyrs? Yet for all of these, since a servant is dutybound to strive toward a humble tolerance of all the evils of life, the result of the labor must always be attributed to the Lord. One who presumes to attribute either the beginning or the end of his works to himself, he is the one to whom it is rightly said, "Unless the lord has built the house, they labor in vain who build it."[82]

---

[80]Prol. 4, 3-7.

[81]I. 8. 26, 20-21: ". . . non laborem gratiae coaequamus, sed omnino gratiam sine comparatione praeponimus."

[82]I. 10. 35, 20-29: "numquid aliter aedificatam cognoscis ecclesiam, quam per labores et officia sacerdotum, per ministeria et exempla sanctorum, per apostolorum virtutes et martyrum mortes? sed inter haec cum usque ad omnium malorum tolerantiam vitaeque iacturam laborare debeat famulus, ad dominum tamen semper est referendus laboris effectus. qui vero vel initium operis sibi praesumit adrogare vel finem, ad illum merito dicitur: nisi dominus aedificaverit domum, in vanum laborant, qui aedificant eam." Faustus thus interprets Ps. 126:1 as an injunction against pride and presumption. By contrast, Augustine in *De praed. sanct*. 7, 12 interpreted the verse in a strictly predestinariam sense.

The secondary, derivative character of human labor notwithstanding, Faustus insists throughout the treatise on human labor's necessity in conjunction with divine grace in the pursuit of human salvation. The exhortation to exert oneself is grounded in the notion that human willing and acting is only an appropriate and thankful response to God's gifts. Faustus uses the term *ingratus* to describe those who, though redeemed, have failed to apply themselves diligently and have fallen away.[83] To receive divine grace with the proper disposition is precisely to adjoin to it the service of human cooperation. Faustus uses several terms to describe this connection between the two, among them *iungere, subiungere, sociare, adsociare, subicere,* and *connectere.* The efficacy of grace for salvation, then, depends upon the custodial function exercised by the human agent: those who have been called and redeemed must be zealous for good deeds "in order that we might guard with labor, with enabling help, what we have received without labor."[84] Faustus clearly has in view the affective growth of the Christian, which involves such labor or ascesis, as distinct from the inital movement of divine grace, which does not: "Notice that the stages of vocation and of consummation are kept distinct. He expects faith from children and requires works along with faith from the confirmed, so that the affect of belief

---

[83]I. 6. 21, 21; I. 16. 50, 27; 53, 19. The term *ingratus,* with the special connotation of an enemy of divine grace, had already come to the fore in Prosper's campaign on behalf of Augustine. His poetical work against putative Pelagian excesses was called the *Carmen de ingratis.* So by using so heavily weighted a word, Faustus is perhaps attempting to wrest the banner of grace from predestinarians whom he understands to be advocating an effortless piety.

[84]I. 6. 22, 20-21: ". . . ut quod sine labore accepimus opitulante adiutorio cum labore servemus . . . "

increases in those who progress, and the one who daily helps gives aid to those who labor."[85]

With Augustine, Faustus speaks of the divine impetus to salvation as a process of drawing, using the verbs *trahere* and *adtrahere*, taken from John 6:44: "No one comes to me unless the Father, who sent me, has drawn (*adtraxit*) him." Augustine had meant by such drawing a usurpation of the human will by the divine, such that an elect person was compelled toward salvation.[86] In speaking thus, Augustine was concerned to avoid any notion that the human will could of its own resources merit divine grace; even the beginning of belief must be the special grace of God, if grace is to be gratuitous.[87] For Faustus, however, the drawing or attracting power of grace is not coercive; rather, it comes as an invitation awaiting response: "Hear the Lord drawing, not with harsh bonds but with hands of hope, and inviting with arms of love."[88] An invitation by its nature requires a response, but the human response to God does not rival or vitiate the initiative of divine grace. It has the character of the feeble response of an invalid:

---

[85]I. 6. 22, 23-26: "agnosce distinctos esse gradus vocationis et consummationis. fidem expectat a parvulis, opera etiam cum fide a confirmatis requirit ita tamen, ut credulitatis affectum proficientibus augeat et laborantibus adiutor cotidianus adsistat."

[86]*De corrept. et grat.* 14, 45: ". . . intus egit, corda tenuit, corda movit, eosque voluntatibus eorum, quas ipse in illis operatus est, traxit." Cf. *Contr. duas ep. Pel.* I, 19, 37, *De praed. sanct.* 8, 13.

[87]See, for example, *De dono persev.* XXIV, 66: "Satis docuisse me existimo, vel potius plus quam satis, dona Dei esse, et incipere in Dominum credere et usque in finem in Domino permanere."

[88]I. 16. 52, 15-16: "Audi dominum non duris nexibus, sed spei manibus adtrahentem et dilectionis brachiis invitantem . . ."

He is not, is he, like stupid, senseless matter in being moved about and pulled from place to place? Rather, the servant extends the hand of faith, by which he may be drawn, to the Lord who assists and calls, and he says, "I believe, Lord: help my unbelief." So these two things are joined together: the power of the one who draws and the disposition of the one who obeys, just as if some invalid tried to get up but his strength failed him, and therefore he must ask that a right hand be extended to him. The will cries out, because infirmity by itself, of its own resources, cannot be raised up. In this sense the Lord invites the willing, draws the desiring, raises up the striving.[89]

So the weakened capacities of human will and action, the enduring but diminished constituents of the *prima gratia*, create in their feeble gesture a sufficient disposition to receive the special grace that comes through Christ. Continuing the metaphor of drawing or pulling, Faustus speaks of one being drawn "by a kind of handle of the will"(*per quandam voluntatis ansulam*).[90]

Redemption in Christ extends its scope to all people, yet all manifestly do not enjoy the benefits of redemption. For Faustus, this can be explained only by the fact that some have responded ungratefully to the divine invitation. Coercion, the usurpation of the prerogatives of human choice, is unthinkable, for it would render God less than benevolent and the human

---

[89] I. 16. 52, 2-11: "numquid velut insensibilis et inepta materies de loco ad locum movendus est et trahendus? sed adsistenti et vocanti domino famulus manum fidei, qua adtrahatur, extendit et dicit: credo, domine, adiuva incredulitatem meam. et ita se duo ista coniungunt, adtrahentis virtus et oboedientis affectus, quomodo si aeger aliquis adsurgere conetur et facultas animum non sequatur et propterea sibi porrigi dexteram deprecetur. clamat voluntas, quia sola per se elevari nescit infirmitas. ita dominus invitat voluntatem, adtrahit desiderantem, erigit adnitentem."

[90] I. 16. 53, 5.

being less than human. If divine grace awaits the free human response in order to succeed, it fails only because a person chooses to turn away: "You must recognize here that grace does not fall short, as if it were denied to a person. Rather, the giver's generosity disregards one who has previously spurned grace and held it in contempt."[91]

Is Christ's grace then gratuitous, or is it merited by human initiative, as Faustus's language seems to suggest? The answer is somewhat complicated. Faustus refers to grace, that is, to special grace, as a gift (*donum, munus*)[92] and affirms that the fact of belief is a gift of grace.[93] Certainly the gift of grace does not ultimately depend on human labor or will. Faustus makes this much quite clear in his anti-Pelagian stance. In the time of grace (*tempus gratiae*), God does not seek merits or works but is content with the devotion of faith.[94] Further, as we have already seen, salvation is in the last analysis to be accredited to God, and thus human merit plays no independent role. The gratuity of grace would appear to be well established.

Faustus's language of merit, however, does cast some doubt on this gratuity. He says, for example, that "it is the will which merits aid."[95] Both Koch and Tibiletti, concerned to evaluate Faustus's doctrine of grace in light of Augustine's, have concluded that Faustus's use of *mereor* does not compromise his view of grace as a gift. The "merit" in this connection refers not to earning divine grace, since it is freely offered to all, but to a properly

---

[91]I. 16. 52, 24-25.

[92]I. 10. 34, 3; I. 3. 14.

[93]II. 5. 67, 30: "quod credunt, gratiae largitas est."

[94]I. 6. 21, 11-13.

[95]II. 3. 64, 20: "voluntas est, quae meretur auxilium."

receptive disposition of the will.[96]   This disposition manifests itself as the willingness to obey; labor is simply a servant's duty.   While both Tibiletti and Koch are admittedly anxious to harmonize Faustus with Augustine as much as possible, they are correct in seeing Faustus as a staunch upholder of the gratuity of grace. Any appearance to the contrary stems from Faustus's evaluation of the residual capabilities of the human will. If one regards the ability to choose, to obey, and to orient one's disposition toward God as owing to initial grace, then the will's disposition to receive special grace does not threaten divine initiative. If, on the other hand, one sees that the *prima gratia* has been virtually deleted from the human constitution, the fallen human will can only be a competitor against grace.

Faustus's interpretation of *trahere* and *adtrahere* suggests that he regards redemptive grace as essentially exterior, as compared to Augustine's notion of an inward transformation of the human will. The grace that draws one to salvation is, according to Faustus, primarily found in preaching: "What is it to draw but to preach, to excite with the consolations of the Scriptures, to deter with rebukes, to set forth what must be desired, to draw attention to what must be feared, to threaten judgment, and to promise a reward?"[97]

One must, however, avoid making too facile a distinction here between an "internal" Augustinian operation of grace and an "external" operation in Faustus. The inward latency or potentiality of human faculties, among them reason, will, and faith, is itself a generally given gift. Insofar as

---

[96]Tibiletti, "Libero arbitrio e grazia,"   278-79; Koch, *Der heilige Faustus,* 105.

[97]I. 16. 52, 11-14:   "quid est autem adtrahere nisi praedicare, nisi scripturarum consolationibus excitare, increpationibus deterrere, desideranda proponere, intentare metuenda, iudicium comminari, praemium polliceri?"

these vestiges of creational grace constitute an inward propensity to respond to special grace—a generally granted preparation of the will—one can hardly speak of special grace as being strictly exterior.[98] It remains true, of course, that an internal grace in the Augustinian sense, i.e., as preveniently moving the human will of the elect, would for Faustus compromise human liberty in an unwarranted way.

Would Faustus then understand grace as being prevenient? He certainly does not understand it as such in a predestinarian sense. In Augustine's anti-Pelagian writings grace is intimately connected with predestination, so that the grace of Christ, which inwardly transforms the soul, is granted only to the elect, who are infallibly brought along to salvation. Those who do not possess such grace are simply not the elect, according to God's good pleasure.[99] Thus the prevenience of grace, its origin in God's will prior to any consideration of human merit, shows itself for Augustine principally in the divine decree of predestination.

For Faustus, too, the grace of Christ precedes human merit and initiative, though he does not connect the precedence of grace to predestination. Faustus's general rule is that the divine initiative precedes the human response, whether one refers to origins or to consummation. He cites the example of Abraham: "That he was called came from God's goodness; that he readily followed was of his own will."[100] But while conceding, even insisting upon, the priority of divine grace to human cooperation in the broad

---

[98]The descriptions of grace as exterior by Koch (*Der heilige Faustus*, 97) and by Tibiletti ("Libero arbitrio e grazia," 279), while correct as ways of contrasting Faustus's position with that of Augustine, merit this qualification.

[99]Cf. *De dono persev.* 12, 28.

[100]II. 10. 84, 17-19: "de dei bonitate est, quod vocatur, de propria voluntate, quod promptus obsequitur."

scope of salvation, Faustus asserts that in the narrower matter of one's affective life, one's will sometimes precedes the bestowal of grace:

> I will appear incautious not even in this matter if I should profess that on occasion in our dispositions—not in the origins of our life, but at least in the middle parts—the movement of our will precedes the special graces that come to us from an added generosity, because God has so ordained it. . . . We read in the gospel the Lord saying, "What do you want me to do for you?" and again, "Do you wish to be healed?" You see that he does not grant the gift of salvation unless one is first asked the desire of the will.[101]

So in certain circumstances, without doing violence to the general prevenient character of grace, the human decision precedes special graces. Even in this situation, however, the seeming inversion of the divine-human order takes place by God's arrangement: "deo ita ordinante." And indeed, even the human will that precedes grace is not a bare human property for Faustus, but a gift. The outcome of human willing and acting owes to God: "It seems that in spiritual warfare the conflict has to do with human labor, even as the outcome is credited to God."[102]

---

[101]II. 10. 83, 29-84, 6: "Ne in hoc videbor incautus, si profitear, quod aliquotiens in dispositionibus nostris non quidem in vitae nostrae primordiis, sed dumtaxat in mediis gratias speciales et ex accedenti largitate venientes voluntas nostra deo ita ordinante praecedat . . . legimus in evangelio dicentem dominum: quid tibi vis faciam? et iterum: vis sanus fieri? vides, quia non tribuitur munus salutis, nisi prius interrogetur desiderium voluntatis."

[102]II. 10. 84, 22-24: "in spiritali bello ita ad hominis laborem videtur pertinere conflictus, sicut ad deum refertur eventus."

Faustus has made his own, at least in a broad way, the sensibilities of Augustine as to the prevenience of grace. Augustine had insisted that even the beginning of belief, the *initium fidei*, was a gift of God.[103] Faustus speaks directly to this concern when he writes concerning the occasional precedence of the will: "This does not at all, as I see it, smack of presumption, since I would assert this same thing unceasingly, that I owe the will itself to God, especially since I refer in all its movements, whether the beginning of the beginning or the ends of the end, to the work of grace."[104] Tibiletti has pointed out the two-edged sword of this statement. On the one hand, Faustus aligns himself with Augustine's statement that "a good will is the work of God" (*De civitate Dei* 14, 11). But, on the other hand, for Faustus salvation history begins with the grace given in the order of creation, so the "work of God" is not limited to that of special grace.[105] Thus on the question of the *initium fidei* Faustus accepts Augustine's basic orientation— God alone is the agent of salvation—but insists that the divine agency can manifest itself in, and along with, the movement of the human will.

Faustus has clearly imbibed much of Augustine's teaching, and aligns himself with the bishop of Hippo in affirming the necessity, gratuity, and prevenience of grace versus Pelagianism. Faustus is particularly concerned to demonstrate that taking such a stand need not lead to a decadent,

---

[103]Cf. *Ep.* 217, where, chiding Vitalis, he writes: "initium fidei ubi est etiam initium bonae voluntatis, non vis donum esse Dei, sed ex nobis nos habere contendis ut credere incipiamus."

[104]II. 10. 84, 10-14: "nihil hic, ut opinor, redolet praesumptionis, cum et hoc ipsum incessabiliter asseram, quod deo ipsam debeam voluntatem, praesertim cum in omnibus eius motibus ad opus gratiae referam vel inchoationis initia vel cnsummationis extrema."

[105]"La salvezza umana," 387-88. Tibiletti sees Faustus as anticipating a peculiarly modern theological notion that the creature's prerogatives need not rival those of the creator.

passive, otiose Augustinianism. Nevertheless, his account of the interplay between divine and human initiatives in human salvation shows his ambivalence toward Augustinian thought. While Augustine had insisted on the need for an active Christian life of prayer and ascesis, his theology of grace focused on the special prevenient grace of Christ granted to the elect, which is predominantly a divine action extrinsic to the human being, as the principle of such life. Plainly, Faustus regards this as circumscribing too narrowly the scope of divine activity and as excluding the operation of divine causality in human will and action. Weigel has characterized Faustus's task as battling Augustinianism without appearing to battle Augustine.[106] While this is somewhat overstated, it bears an element of truth: Faustus accepted and made his own many of Augustine's concerns and categories,[107] regarding the latter's absolutizing of sovereign redemptive grace as bearing the seeds of a Christianity that could make of grace a dominion rather than an *auxilium*. And indeed, Faustus saw these seeds as having come near to fruition in Lucidus, the extreme predestinarian. Faustus's own theological formation, rooted in Lerinian monasticism, in a long tradition of monastic writers, in an ethos of moderation, and in the struggle for the life of the Gallic church could hardly countenance such a diminution of human agency in the economy of salvation.

The continuity between creational and redemptive grace in the *De gratia* leads to final consequences that dominate the last two chapters of the treatise: the universality of the redemption brought by Christ and the

---

[106]*Faustus of Riez*, 105.

[107]Arnold is simply wrong when he characterizes Faustus's citing of Augustine as malicious subterfuge or subtle irony; cf. *Caesarius von Arelate und die gallische Kirche seiner Zeit* (Leipzig, 1972), 554. The ironic element in Faustus's treatment does not alter the fact of his generally favorable attitude toward Augustine.

universal distribution of the means for appropriating it. If, as Faustus asserts, the initial grace to humanity includes not only free will and perpetuity, but also faith (II. 8. 76, 23-25), then the psychological and ontological prerequisite for attaining salvation has been granted to all. This position stands in sharp contrast to the predestinarian line of thought, which runs into difficulty at this very point. In Augustine's anti-Pelagian works, for example, his version of the gratuity of grace necessarily excludes its universality; if faith is given solely to the elect, then those who do not believe have simply not been granted the grace of belief.[108] Having taken such a stance, one can maintain the universal scope of Christ's redemptive work only as a purely theoretical notion, for in the actual working out of the plan of salvation, Christ died only for the elect. To be sure, this was a consequence not found in Augustine, but which was the view of those against whom Faustus directs the whole of I. 16.

By contrast, because of his high regard for the continuing vigor of the *prima gratia*, Faustus would extend the reach of salvific grace to all, such that he might invite the accusation of having undervalued the role played by the Church and the sacramental life in the plan of salvation. He does, in fact, give attention to the traditional notion that baptism removes original sin, and explicitly refers to the benefits of regeneration.[109] These are, however, rather minor currents in his thought, for his notion of the distribution of grace extends beyond the temporal confines of the time after the incarnation and beyond the anthropological confines of explicitly Christian peoples. The last part of the treatise, II. 10-12, concerns itself primarily with pagan peoples,

---

[108]Augustine, *De praed. sanct.* 8, 15: "illis datur ut credant, illis non datur"; *De corrept. et grat.* 8, 19: " cur aliis detur, aliis non detur, dignentur ignorare."

[109]I. 14. 46, 18-21, 30-31.

such as the Ninevites, arguing that they possessed the wherewithal to be saved, even though their salvation was somehow to be brought to its completion by redemptive grace: "through grace, I say, in whose time the salvation of the past world was to be consummated."[110]

                              *   *   *

The overarching doctrinal theme of the treatise *De gratia* is the fundamental continuity of God's gifts to humankind, whether in creation as the array of positive capacities and orientations entailed in the *prima gratia* or *imago Dei*, or in redemption as the *auxilium* given in and by Christ to aid and heal the crippled human race. Under either dispensation, divine grace aims at the same end: to bring the human being into the image and likeness of God. Human sin, passed on through concupiscence and given force by habit, has corrupted and weakened the first gifts of God, preventing the unhindered exercise of virtue that would bring human beings to the likeness of God, or adoptive kinship. The grace of Christ, redemptive or special grace, must of necessity have the character of an *auxilium*, an aid to the weakened capacities. At the same time, the grace of Christ has always been the ultimate principle of human salvation, even prior to the incarnation. Thus the effective presence of divine grace shows itself both in the preincarnational saving activity of Christ and in the enduring postincarnational relevance of the *prima gratia* — primarily as free will—in the economy of salvation. Faustus would not, of course, merely equate the two aspects of divine grace; the priority of honor and of efficacy belongs to the grace brought by Christ.

---

[110]II. 12. 90, 25-27:   "per gratiam, inquam, in cuius tempore praeteritorum salus erat consummanda saeculorum . . . "

Precisely Faustus's attempt to strike a note of theological equilibrium places him in a curious position vis-à-vis the anti-Pelagian legacy of St. Augustine. On the one hand, Faustus clearly opposes Pelagian doctrine as he portrays it: the assertion of nature's salvific sufficiency and the denial of original sin and its transmission. In taking this stance he assimilates Augustine's most basic sensibilities and much of his vocabulary. But, on the other hand, many of the Augustinian categories are clearly ill-suited to Faustus's perspective. Whereas Augustine makes a clear demarcation between nature and grace, Faustus knows no nature bereft of grace; while Augustine links the work of Christ's grace to predestination and sees it as specially creating the good will, Faustus makes no such link and sees the possibility of the good will as inherent in all, by grace; while Augustine did not wish to give attention to the grace found in creation in his theology of grace, Faustus saw creation's endowments as fundamental to any discussion of grace. These and other differences make it clear that Faustus's categories simply do not easily match those of Augustine and his disciples, even though Faustus frequently wishes to make his own the Augustinian vocabulary.[111] Such differences notwithstanding, the De gratia does present a doctrine of grace that is in many ways commensurate with that of Augustine, even as it militates against some of the more troubling consequences of Augustinian predestinarianism. The classical Augustinian categories of grace's necessity, gratuity, and prevenience agree with and influence Faustus's conception, if one grants the conceptual difference.

One must also remember the polemical roots of Faustus's treatise; his hesitation to follow the predestinarian line springs neither from hostility

---

[111]Tibiletti's "Libero arbitrio e grazia" has the great merit of drawing attention to the pervasive influence of Augustine upon the De gratia. See above, Introduction.

toward Augustine nor from a compromise with Pelagianism, but from a perception of an incipient indolence among Christians. In sum, the treatise provides us with a deceptively complex interweaving of theological interests. If one wishes to continue using the label "semipelagian" of Faustus, one must immediately recognize how complicated a phenomenon semipelagianism is, even in this single instance. The obligatory anti-Pelagianism of the West after 418, whose champion was Augustine, is combined in the *De gratia* with the monastic ethos of obedience and ascesis, with a more characteristically eastern notion of the *imago Dei* and its indelibility, and with a concern to uphold the strict identity between God the creator and God the redeemer.

CHAPTER FIVE
CONCLUSIONS

Our goal through the whole of this study has been to understand Faustus of Riez's treatise *De gratia* and to locate it theologically by giving careful attention to the text itself. We have pursued this goal first by setting Faustus against the backdrop of his own time, a time of social and political turbulence and of some theological polarization. Second, we have sought to clarify the inner logic and persuasive force of the *De gratia* in order to gain a picture of how Faustus molded the materials of the controversy with Lucidus into a coherently argued exposition. Third, we have attempted to illumine the contours of Faustus's own theological culture by identifying the most likely sources of his thought. Fourth, we have illustrated the main doctrinal affirmations of the treatise, which emerge from the crucible of the author's historical and theological milieu, his rhetorical purpose, and his own theological formation. Now, at the end of our inquiry, we may begin to answer the broader question of Faustus's place in the history of Christian thought: Ought one to label him as Pelagian, Augustinian, semipelagian, or something else?

The Question of Pelagianism

Our study has shown conclusively, if indeed it required demonstration, that the oldest charge—Pelagianism—alleged against Faustus by John Maxentius and those who depended upon him is without foundation. The first two chapters of the *De gratia* show that Faustus knew, from Augustine, Pelagius's denial of original sin and consequently of the need for divine grace. So on the most central matter of contention between Augustine and Pelagius, Faustus adopts a firmly anti-Pelagian position. This position is underscored by the fact that Faustus did not use Pelagius as a source of his own theology. The accusation of clever and deceptive Pelagian teaching is, at least in the narrowest sense, simply untenable.[1]

The question of Pelagianism, however, cannot be limited to asking whether or not Faustus was consciously sympathetic to Pelagius or made use of his writings. To be sure, Faustus rejected Pelagius's doctrine as understood from Augustine's portrayal, namely, as a denial of the need for divine grace. Modern scholarship on Pelagius has, however, shown that such an understanding of his doctrine is really a caricature. In particular, the studies of Torgny Bohlin and Robert Evans have demonstrated that Pelagius did not so much deny grace as define it differently from Augustine.[2] Bohlin has exposed the anti-Arian and especially anti-Manichean context of Pelagius's writings; in his battle against dualistic determinism, Pelagius was anxious to affirm the human free will as a divine gift, a grace that is also constitutive of human nature. Other divine gifts are also grace for Pelagius:

---

[1]Thus the judgments of Erasmus, Driedo, Tapper, Sirmond, Stilting, Koch, Wörter, Weigel, Simonetti, and Tibiletti (see above, Introduction) find confirmation.

[2]Bohlin, *Die Theologie des Pelagius und ihre Genesis;* Robert F. Evans, *Pelagius: Inquiries and Reappraisals.*

revelation, both through the law and through Christ, and the remission of sins effected by Christ and applied in baptism.[3] So in the struggle against Manichean determinism, Pelagius's intention was never to give a precise account of either the *initium fidei* or the relation between divine and human action. Evans has expanded Bohlin's account and given it more detail.[4] So if one turns from the stylized and extreme Pelagius of classical "Pelagianism" to the—to borrow a term—historical Pelagius, one finds a figure whose thought has some affinities with that of Faustus: the notion of the perduring efficacy of the human power of choice, the idea of an innate goodness that is never completely deleted, a conception of sin as external and reinforced by habit, and the ability of some (Abel, Noah) to live righteously according to the natural law.[5]

Thus while Faustus owes nothing to Pelagius in the formal sense of having depended on his thought, he does share at several points Pelagius's way of speaking about sin and grace. This is due, it would seem, to their partaking of a common stream of Christian anthropological thought that stresses the human capacity for obedience and choice. Our study has shown that Faustus inherits such thought from Cassian, Origen-Rufinus, and perhaps Hilary of Poitiers. Bohlin and Evans have found among Pelagius's sources the early Augustine, Ambrosiaster, Origen-Rufinus, and the *Sentences* of Sextus.[6]

---

[3]Bohlin, *Die Theologie des Pelagius*, 15-29. Bohlin uses the terms *Schöpfungsgnade, Offenbarungsgnade,* and *Vergebungsgnade.*

[4]*Pelagius: Inquiries and Reappraisals*, 90-121.

[5]Ibid., 95-101.

[6]Ibid., 43-65; Bohlin, *Die Theologie des Pelagius*, 46-103.

Inasmuch as Faustus and Pelagius shared a common polemical opponent—a species of determinism—and certain anthropological emphases, one can speak of some measure of congruence between their theologies. Faustus was certainly not Pelagian in the sense intended by his long line of detractors; he unambiguously allied himself with Augustine in affirming the utter necessity of divine grace and the incapacity of unaided human nature. Nor was he Pelagian in the more historically exact sense of being in full accord with the actual thought of Pelagius. But the charge of crypto-Pelagianism that has attached itself to Faustus's reputation becomes understandable when one realizes that at least a part of his thought draws upon the same monastic and Origenian traditions that nurtured Pelagius.

The Question of Augustinianism

This study and the recent work of Carlo Tibiletti have uncovered several instances of Faustus's dependence upon Augustine. The frequent positive use to which Augustine's thought is put comes as something of a surprise if one is accustomed to regarding Faustus as part of the resistance to Augustinianism. Few have in fact held that Faustus was essentially an Augustinian; one thinks of Erasmus and Stilting.[7] In light of our inquiry, however, the question demands at least to be reconsidered: To what extent can Faustus of Riez be seen as an Augustinian?

The question itself is immediately problematic, for we must first have agreed on a definition of "Augustinian." On one side, we cannot simply define as Augustinian anyone who drew upon Augustine as a theological source; to do so one would have to include Pelagius, to name only the most

---

[7]Erasmus, *Praefatio*, 3-3A; Stilting, "De Fausto Regiensi," 683-84.

notorious example. To move to the other extreme, we cannot restrict the term to those who accepted in its most radical form the predestinarian logic of Augustine's later anti-Pelagian works; to do so would be to include Lucidus, Fulgentius, and Gottschalk, but to exclude the Fathers of Orange and Trent.

The most sensible option, it seems, would be to define as Augustinians those who (1) drew upon Augustine as their primary theological source, (2) consciously regarded themselves as theological allies of Augustine, and (3) shared Augustine's concerns for the absolute necessity, gratuity, and prevenience of the grace of Christ in human salvation. Such a definition is specific enough to describe a discernable school of thought, yet broad enough to allow for variations within that school.

In many ways Faustus could be seen as meeting the requisite criteria. We have shown not only that Augustine was the sole nonbiblical source explicitly cited in the *De gratia*, but also that his thought is frequently Faustus's point of reference. The most notable example lies in Faustus's discussions of original sin and concupiscence; we have drawn attention to several other areas. One could argue that apart from Holy Scripture, Augustine is Faustus's most recognizable source.

In addition, Faustus assuredly regarded himself, or at least portrayed himself, as an ally of Augustine. We recall that he drew what we have called his "hermeneutic of equilibrium" from his understanding of Augustine. We have further suggested that a central motif of Faustus's treatment—that of treading the centrist path between Pelagian and Manichean extremes—echoes Augustine's language. And, of course, Faustus certainly took aim against Pelagius from the Augustinian point of view. While many of Faustus's critics in the history of doctrine have tended to depict his Augustinian, anti-Pelagian sentiments as a pose, we have shown them to be integral parts of his theology. In light of our study it is virtually impossible to argue that Faustus did not imbibe Augustine's thought at several points.

The most substantial and difficult question is whether Faustus shared Augustine's view of divine grace. Tibiletti has argued that Faustus upheld the necessity, prevenience, and gratuity of divine grace,[8] and our study has tended to confirm this. Throughout the treatise, but with exceptional force in the anti-Pelagian chapters I. 1-2, Faustus clearly affirms the necessity of divine grace for salvation. He is more circumpsect in considering the prevenience of grace. One recalls the cautious, almost apologetic, tone of Faustus's assertion in I. 10 that occasionally the movement of one's own will precedes the advent of special grace: "I shall seem incautious not even in this matter if I profess that often in our dispositions—not in the origins of our life but at least in the middle parts—the movement of our will precedes the special graces that come to us from an added generosity, because God ordains it so."[9] His framing of the statement in this way, that is, fearful that he might be seen as denying prevenient grace and stressing the divine ordination, shows that he shared Augustine's concern that divine grace must precede any human effort toward salvation.[10] Because his argument is directed against the danger of an otiose Christianity and urges the zealous application of the will, the question of prevenient grace does not arise as a discrete theme, but is nevertheless reflected in the language of the treatise.

Grace for Faustus is gratuitous. Regardless of the human effort involved in the life of a Christian, one ultimately must confess that the credit for salvation belongs wholly to God, who is the source even of the capacity

---

[8]"La salvezza umana," 384ff.

[9]I. 10. 84, 17-19.

[10]Cf. my discussion of this passage above, chapter 4.

to obey.[11] But this God-given capacity, weakened by sin, can still in its weakness bring about a certain disposition to receive the further gift of assistance brought by Christ.[12] Faustus employs on occasion the language of merit to describe the disposition to receive the grace of Christ; but "merit" certainly cannot mean, in the broader context of Faustus's thought, that bare human efforts "earn" salvific grace. Rather, it describes the proper use made of the human will so as to receive the divine gifts.

But while Faustus, appropriating the sensibilities of Augustine in affirmations about original sin and grace, was demonstrably familiar with the corpus of anti-Pelagian works, one still hesitates to place Faustus's doctrine of grace squarely within the limits of Augustinianism. Faustus's distance from Augustine's position lay at a level more fundamental than that of categories like necessity, prevenience, and gratuity. Because Faustus's theological anthropology had many deep roots in non-Augustinian (which is not to say anti-Augustinian) sources, he inherited a conceptual framework that was not easily commensurable with that of Augustine's last works. Stated in its broadest terms, this conceptual difference had to do with the extent to which one may regard as grace, that is, as salvifically significant, the gifts of God that constitute human nature. Faustus certainly argued for the perduring force of what Bohlin has called *Schöpfungsgnade*, the grace given in creation.[13] While Augustine occasionally used the term *gratia* to refer to created human capacities, he did not regard postlapsarian human nature as bearing significance in the economy of salvation. The grace that could bring one to salvation was specifically the grace of Christ, inwardly working

---

[11]Cf. II. 10. 84, 10-14.

[12]Cf. I. 16. 52, 2-11; 53, 5.

[13]*Die Theologie des Pelagius*, 15ff.

to free the human will and recreate the capacities of human nature. For Faustus, the image and likeness of God, rather than vitiated human nature, continue to be controlling anthropological categories, and the primal grace embodied in them is completed, but not made irrelevant, by the restorative grace of Christ.

One sees that Faustus's theological culture, formed by the monastery of Lérins, conditioned by the difficult times in which the Gallic church lived, and nourished by Origen and Cassian, shaped the manner of his reception of Augustine's thought. In Faustus's world of thought, the human constitution, with its realm of freedom and choice, stood aligned with divine aid against the external pull of sin and necessity. The counterposition between grace and sin is fundamental, while that between grace and nature does not fit easily.[14] The values of obedience to commandments, of ascetical effort, and of a life of prayer for divine assistance were prominent in Faustus's theological formation; he was therefore inclined to reject interpretations of Augustine's thought that threatened these values. The predestinarian Lucidus provides an example of an excessive and potentially damaging use of Augustine. Faustus, by contrast, receives those aspects of Augustine's anti-Pelagian thought that best accord with his notion of the theological mainstream while respectfully ignoring tendencies of thought—dual predestination, the utter incapacity of human nature—that could prove harmful to Christian life and piety.

On the whole, the evaluation of Faustus's Augustinianism largely depends on one's perspective. Certainly two extreme views can be ruled out, namely, that Faustus was fundamentally anti-Augustinian and that he was

---

[14]These two problematics in the history of the doctrine of grace are helpfully discussed in E. M. Burke, "Grace," *New Catholic Encyclopedia* 6: 658ff.

thoroughly Augustinian. Between these two extremes, the question remains whether Faustus should be seen primarily as an example of resistance to Augustine's thought or of an attempt to accommodate it. Most treatments of Faustus, even the sympathetic studies by Koch and Weigel, have located him among those Gallic writers like Cassian and Vincent of Lérins who opposed Augustine's doctrine of grace.[15] Yet if one considers that Faustus's native theological culture was in large measure non-Augustinian, as it surely was, the more surprising and noteworthy feature of the *De gratia* is the extent to which a sympathy for Augustine's concerns shows itself. That a monastic writer from the south of Gaul should be cautious, even suspicious, in his reception of Augustine's doctrine of grace is unremarkable; that he should attempt to align himself with Augustine in more than a purely cosmetic manner deserves our attention. Whether or not one wishes to label Faustus of Riez an Augustinian, the *De gratia* should probably be seen at least as representing an attempt to receive a palatable interpretation of Augustine's doctrine of grace into the theological mainstream of fifth-century Gaul.

The Question of Semipelagianism

While few, apart from polemicists in the line of John Maxentius, have taken Faustus to be a Pelagian, and even fewer have regarded him as an Augustinian, the assertion that Faustus was a semipelagian has held nearly universal sway from the seventeenth century to the present. To be sure, the term itself is late and tendentious, but its referent is clear enough: *semipelagianism* refers specifically to the thought of the monks centered in Marseilles who constituted the second movement of resistance to Augustine's

---

[15]Koch, *Der heilige Faustus*, passim; Weigel, *Faustus of Riez*, 104ff.

anti-Pelagian teaching on grace.[16] Prosper of Aquitaine and his associate
Hilary wrote to Augustine of these monks in 427,[17] and Augustine addressed
their concerns in the two treatises *De dono perseverantiae* and *De
praedestinatione sanctorum.* Cassian, who as founder of the monastic
community at Marseilles was the especial target of Prosper's pro-Augustinian
campaign, is generally regarded as the father of semipelagianism, and Vincent
of Lérins as one of its chief apologists.[18] Faustus of Riez, on the strength
of the *De gratia*, has come to be seen by many as having given the
semipelagian position its clearest exposition.[19] Our study of the *De gratia*,
however, has yielded several reasons for qualifying, though not completely rejecting, the characterization of Faustus as a semipelagian.

One must admit at the outset that in many ways such an evaluation
is appropriate. Faustus, like Cassian, Vincent of Lérins, and Hilary of Arles,
was a product of the monastic environs of southern Gaul whence came the
opposition to Augustine's teaching mentioned by Prosper in 427. We have
shown the likelihood that Faustus knew Cassian's *Conlationes* and have
suggested that he shared Vincent's centrist ideal and characteristic Lerinian
moderation. Further, the charges brought by Faustus in the *De gratia* against
predestinarian teaching often echo those reported by Prosper among the
Massilians: absolute predestination deprives the fallen of a motive for

---

[16]Arguably the term could also be applied to the monks at Hadrumetum
in North Africa, to whose queries Augustine addressed the treatise *De correptione
et gratia* in 427. Amann, "Semipélagiens," 1798f. uses the term in this way.

[17]*Ep.* 225, 226 (CSEL 57: 454-83).

[18]Amann, "Semipélagiens," 1802ff.

[19]So Koch, *Der heilige Faustus*, 204-5. Amann, in "Semipélagiens,"
1833, styles Faustus: "l'homme qui allait être le plus authentique représentant de
l'antiaugustinisme, le vrai fondateur de la doctrine que nous appelons aujourd'hui le
semi-pélagianisme."

improvement, undermines effort and virtue, and makes the creator appear arbitrary.[20] Also, much of the positive doctrine of these semipelagians finds expression in the *De gratia*: redemption in Christ is offered to all, not merely to the elect; foreknowledge and predestination do not impinge upon human freedom; the grace of the creator renders one capable of observing the commandments.[21] Without question, then, Faustus shared the hesitancy of Augustine's semipelagian opposition with regard to the most extreme consequences of Augustine's anti-Pelagian teaching.

Yet some features of the *De gratia* make one hesitate to assign it to a corpus of semipelagian writings. The first and simplest of these is the work's date. Augustine's treatises against his Gallic opposition and Prosper's campaign on Augustine's behalf occupied the years 427-31, culminating in the letter of Pope Celestine I to the bishops of Gaul in 431, which settled the matter in Prosper's favor.[22] Faustus's *De gratia* was written in 474, nearly two generations after these events. During the intervening period, Augustinian sensibilities about grace and free will had established themselves to such an extent that Faustus had to explicate his doctrinal position in light of them. To return to an example already cited, one need only point out that in speaking somewhat haltingly of a movement of the human will prior to grace, Faustus carefully guards the priority of divine grace. So one must at least speak of some differences among semipelagians owing to chronology.

A second and related problem has to do with the historiography of semipelagianism. E. Amann has spoken of two "paroxysms" of the semipelagian controversy, one around the time of Augustine's death (430),

---

[20]*Ep.* 225, 3 (CSEL 57: 457-58).

[21]Ibid.

[22]Cf. my discussion in chapter 1.

the other in the late fifth and early sixth centuries, ending with the second Council of Orange in 529.[23] Chronologically Faustus's work falls squarely between these two episodes of controversy. He took no part in the first, and there is no conclusive warrant for supposing that the second Council of Orange made any reference to the *De gratia*. Had Gennadius's evaluation of Faustus as a teacher of the priority of grace been allowed to stand, without the later polemics of Maxentius and the Scythians, one could easily imagine Faustus being celebrated as an Augustinian. So even as we concede the theological affinities between Faustus and the semipelagians, we must admit that the propensity to align Faustus with anti-Augustinian elements has arisen from a partisan, and frequently prejudiced, brand of historiography. Viewed with more balance, Faustus's doctrine may appear as much Augustinian as semipelagian.

To identify Faustus as semipelagian can, further, lead to a misrepresentation of the doctrinal configuration of Faustus's own time. Quite apart from the matter of the late and polemical origin of the term *semipelagian*, its use in an inquiry which seeks historical clarity is inappropriate, for it describes a set of categories foreign to the fifth century. As Simonetti has pointed out, the ancients did not employ an Augustinian-Pelagian polarity, but saw *Pelagiani* and *praedestinati* as occupying two opposite, extreme points of view, between which lay the virtuous middle path of orthodoxy.[24] If our account of the circumstances of the treatise's writing withstands scrutiny, Faustus was certainly not the mouthpiece of a faction or party, but was giving voice to the consensus of the Gallic church as it sought to exclude both poles of error.

---

[23]"Semipélagiens," 1797.

[24]"Il *De gratia*," 125.

In short, the designation semipelagian does not seem to be entirely helpful in understanding the *De gratia* of Faustus of Riez. To be sure, it locates the work in one vitally important context: the monastic milieu of southern Gaul. But the label fails to do justice to other aspects of Faustus's work, especially the clear extent of his absorption of Augustine's anti-Pelagian thought. If the term is to be retained, it demands the qualifications suggested above.

Locating the De gratia

Interpretations of the *De gratia* that would portray it as Pelagian, Augustinian, or semipelagian all bear elements of truth. This is so precisely because it is a work which attempts a synthesis. The bipolarity and antithesis which dominate Faustus's rhetoric are not simply ornaments; they reflect his attempt to find a point of equilibrium among theological concerns which competed against one another even as they converged in the western Church of the fifth century. Manlio Simonetti is exactly right in seeing the concern for harmony and equilibrium as paramount in the treatise.[25]

Equilibrium and synthesis do not necessarily reflect a spirit of compromise and lack passion and fervor; the centrist path pursued by Faustus is not one of mere expediency. Rather, his middle course, to use his own analogy from the *De gratia*, is that of the helmsman who must, at great peril, steer between the dangers of Scylla and Charybdis, avoiding both the evident and the submerged obstacles.[26] To Faustus, whose theological culture comprehended not only the moderate, tradition-conscious Lerinian ascetic

---

[25]Ibid., 143-44.

[26]I. 1. 7, 19-8,2.

ethos, but also Augustine's language of moderation and a bishop's concern for unity, the quest for a proper path in the "royal mean" was a matter of the essence of theology.

The *De gratia* was the product of a clash between theological cultures. On the one side stood those whose theology and experience simply could not comprehend a human nature so vitiated by sin as to be oriented toward evil;[27] such was the stance of those to whom Faustus owed his most basic theological formation. On the other side stood the anti-Pelagian argument of Augustine, which was quickly becoming the coin of the realm in the western Church; in its most extreme interpretation it militated against Faustus's sensibilities. Faustus's treatise, in its attempt to balance and synthesize the deepest concerns of both orientations, should not be seen as an example of resistance to Augustine's thought so much as a moment in the ongoing reception of Augustinianism into the mainstream of the western Church. J. J. O'Donnell has remarked that "nothing is so striking about Western monasticism . . . as that, while it came out of a theological environment which drew on eastern sources, it quite soon rejected their suppositions in favor of a native, Augustinian theology."[28] One may disagree with O'Donnell's use of *native* here, but his point is important. The monks of southern Gaul resisted Augustine's predestinarian teaching in the 420s and 430s, but within a century Caesarius of Arles, himself a product of Lérins and a leader of the Church in Gaul, was a zealous Augustinian. The *De gratia* represents a point on the continuum of this century-long process of

---

[27]An excellent, illuminating discussion of the different, and often incompatible, language used to describe the human will by Gregory of Nyssa and Augustine is Mühlenberg, "Synergism in Gregory of Nyssa," 93-122. Mühlenberg suggests that such a conceptual problem may have lain at the root of the controversy between Augustine and Pelagius.

[28]"Liberius the Patrician," 54.

absorbing Augustinian sensibilities about grace and free will. It is not Pelagian, though it shares certain anthropological ground with Pelagius. It is not Augustinian, though it makes extensive use of Augustine. If it is semipelagian, it expresses a semipelagianism of the second or third generation, which has begun to understand and to incorporate Augustinianism.

Faustus's attempt at synthesis is not entirely successful. Perhaps the chief example of its lack of success is its failure to express with sufficient clarity the distinction between the grace given to all in creation and that of Christ given in baptism.[29] Systematic consistency was not Faustus's strength; indeed, one might well ask whether he grasped Augustine's thought in its depth. But while he was not of the speculative caliber of Augustine, or even of Claudianus Mamaertus, he was an eloquent spokesman for the concerns of Christian piety. His enemy was no metaphysical construct, but *otium*, the indolent approach to Christian life which he feared would result from an extreme, one-sided version of Augustinianism; indeed, Augustine had expressed the same concern.[30] Faustus was determined, it would seem, that the reception of Augustinianism in fifth-century Gaul, of which he himself was an agent, would not mean the death of prayer and ascesis.

Much work remains to be done toward understanding the history of theology between the death of Augustine and the second Council of Orange. The necessary first step in this task is to reach behind the labels applied— sometimes misleadingly—by later dogmatic theology. When one has done so and has attempted to read the texts of the period on their own terms, the rigidity of certain accepted categories may give way to a rather more fluid

---

[29]This is a weakness identified by Simonetti, "Il *De gratia*," 143-44, and Koch, *Der heilige Faustus*, 99-100.

[30]*Ep*. 215, 7-8 (CSEL 57: 393-95).

portrayal. The *De gratia* of Faustus of Riez, for example, might not be seen simply as an exemplary species of the genus semipelagianism, but as one part of a broad and variegated reception of Augustinianism in the fifth century.

BIBLIOGRAPHY

I. Texts

Ado. *Chronicon.* PL 123: 139-436.

Augustine. *Confessiones libri* XIII. CCL 27.

————. *Contra duas epistulas Pelagianorum.* CSEL 60, v: 423-70.

————. *De anima et eius origine.* PL 44: 475-548.

————. *De civitate Dei.* CCL 47, 48.

————. *De correptione et gratia.* PL 44: 915-46.

————. *De diversis quaestionibus ad Simplicianum.* CCL 44. PL 40: 101-48.

————. *De diversis quaestionibus LXXXIII.* CCL 44A: 11-249.

————. *De doctrina christiana.* CCL 32: 1-167.

————. *De dono perseverantiae.* PL 45: 1665ff.

————. *De gestis Pelagii.* CSEL 42, ii.

————. *De gratia Christi et de peccato originali.* CSEL 42, iii: 125-206.

————. *De gratia et libero arbitrio.* PL 44: 881-912.

————. *De natura et gratia.* CSEL 60, iii: 233-99.

————. *De nuptiis et concupiscentia.* CSEL 42, iv: 14-319.

————. *De peccatorum meritis et remissione et de baptismo parvulorum ad Marcellinum.* PL 44: 109-200. CSEL 60: 3-151.

————. *De perfectione iustitiae hominis.* PL 44: 291-318.

————. *De praedestinatione sanctorum*. PL 44: 959-92.

————. *De spiritu et littera*. PL 44: 199-246.

————. *De Trinitate libri* XV. CCL 50-50A.

————. *Enchiridion ad Laurentium [De fide, spe, et caritate]*. PL 40: 231-90.

————. *Epistulae*. CSEL 34, i, ii; 44; 57; 58.

————. *Expositio quarundam propositionum ex epistula ad Romanos*. PL 35: 2063-84.

Avitus, Alcimus, of Vienne. *Epistola IV, ad Gundobadum regem*. PL 59: 219-24.

Cassian, John. *Conlationes*. SC 42, 54, 64.

————. *De incarnatione Domini contra Nestorium*. PL 50: 9-270. CSEL 17: 235-391.

Celestine I. *Epistola ad episcopos provinciae Viennensis et Narbonensis*, Ep. IV. PL 50: 429-36.

Claudianus Mamaertus. *De statu animae libri tres*. CSEL 11.

Collectio Gallicana. See Eusebius "Gallicanus."

Epistula scytharum monachorum ad episcopos VIII. CCL 85A. [See Peter the Deacon.]

Eucherius of Lyons. *De contemptu mundi*.

————. *De laude eremi*. CSEL 31, iv: 177-94.

————. *Instructiones ad Salonium*. CSEL 31, ii.

————. *Passio Acaunensium martyrum, S. Mauricii et sociorum eius*. PL 50: 827-32.

Eusebius "Gallicanus." *Collectio Gallicana*. Eusebius "Gallicanus" collectio homiliarum. CCL 101-101B.

Faustus of Riez. *De gratia Dei et libero arbitrio libri duo*. PL 58: 783-836.

————. *Epistula Fausti Reiensis tertia.* Ed. A. G. Elg. Uppsala: Almquist and Wiksell, 1946.

————. *Fausti aliorumque epistulae ad Ruricium aliosque.* Ed. Bruno Krusch. MGH, AA VIII. Berlin, 1887.

————. *Fausti episcopi de Gratia Dei, et humanae mentis arbitrio.* With preface by Erasmus. Basel, 1528.

————. *Fausti Reiensis praeter sermones pseudo-Eusebianos opera.* CSEL 21. Ed. A. Engelbrecht. Vienna, 1891.

————. *Sermo de S. Maximo episcopo et abbate.* Ed. S. Gennaro. Catania: Centro di Studi sull'antico cristianesimo, 1966.

Fulgentius of Ruspe. *De veritate praedestinationis et gratiae Dei.* PL 65: 603ff.

————. *Epistula* XVII. CCL 91A: 563-615.

Gaudemet, Jean. *Conciles Gaulois du IVe siècle.* Text, trans., notes. SC 241. Paris: Éditions du Cerf, 1977.

Gennadius of Marseilles. *Gennadius liber de viris illustribus.* Ed. E. C. Richardson. Texte und Untersuchungen XIV/1. Leipzig: J. C. Hinrichs, 1896.

Gottschalk of Orbais. *Gotteschalci Orbac. monachi confessio prolixior.* PL 121.

Hilary of Arles. *Sermo de vita Honorati.* PL 50, 1249ff.

Hilary [disciple of Augustine]. *Epistola ad Augustinum (Ep. Aug. 226).* CSEL 57: 468-81.

Hormisdas. *Epistulae papae Hormisdae.* CCL 85A.

Isidore of Seville. *De viris illustribus.* PL 83.

Lucidus. *Epistula II (Libellus subiectionis).* CSEL 21: 165-8.

Lupus, Servatus, of Ferrière. *Servati Lupi epistulae.* Ed. Peter K. Marshall. Leipzig: Teubner, 1984.

Maxentius, John. *Responsio adversus epistulam Hormisdae.* CCL 85A: 123-53.

Orientius. *Commonitorium.* CSEL 16: 205-53.

Origen-Rufinus. *De principiis.* GCS 22.

Paulinus of Nola. *Epistulae.* PL 61.

Pelagius. *Pelagius' Expositions of Thirteen Epistles of St. Paul.* Ed. Alexander Souter. Cambridge: Cambridge University Press, 1922-31. Reprint ed. Nedeln/Lichtenstein: Kraus Reprint, 1967.

Peter the Deacon. *Epistula* XVI. CCL 91A: 551-62. [= *Ep. scytharum monachorum ad episcopos VIII.* CCL 85A.]

Possessor. *Epistola ad Hormisdam.* PL 63: 489.

Prosper, Tiro, of Aquitaine. *Carmen de ingratis S. Prosperi Aquitani.* Trans. Charles T. Huegelmeyer. Washington: Catholic University of America Press, 1962.

————. *De gratia Dei et libero arbitrio liber contra Collatorem.* PL 51: 213-76.

————. *De vocatione omnium gentium libri duo.* PL 51: 647-722.

————. *Epistula ad Rufinum.* PL 51: 77-79, 1793-1802.

————. *Pro Augustino responsiones ad capitula objectionum Gallorum calumniantium.* PL 51: 155-76; PL 45: 1833-44.

————. *Pro Augustino responsiones ad capitula objectionum Vincentianarum.* PL 51: 177-86; PL 45: 1843-50.

Prudentius. *Psychomachia.* CSEL 61: 167-211.

Regula quattuor patrum. Règles des Saints Pères. Ed. Adalbert de Vogüé. SC 297 (vol. I) and 298 (vol. II). Paris: Éditions du Cerf, 1982.

Salvian of Marseilles. *De gubernatione Dei.* CSEL 8: 1-200.

Statuta patrum. [See *Regula quattuor patrum.*]

Vincent of Lérins. *Commonitorium.* PL 50: 630-86.

Vita Fulgentii. PL 65.

II. Studies

Abel, M. "Le 'Praedestinatus' et le pélagianisme." *Recherches de théologie ancienne et médiévale* 35 (1968): 5-25.

Amann, É. "Semipélagiens." *Dictionnaire de théologie catholique* 14: 1796-1850.

Arnold, Carl F. *Caesarius von Arelate und die gallische Kirche seiner Zeit.* Leipzig: Zentralantiquariat der Dt. Demokrat. Republik, 1972.

Bardy, G. "Gélase (Decret de)." *Dictionnaire de la Bible*, Supplement 3 (1938): 279-90.

Barnard, L.W. "Pelagius and Early Syriac Christianity." *Recherches de théologie ancienne et médiévale* 35 (1968): 193-96.

Baronius, Caesar. *Annales ecclesiastici.* Rome, 1603.

Basange, Jacques. *Animadversiones criticae de S. Fausto Rhegiensi.* In PL 58: 777-84.

Bellarmine, Robert. *De scriptoribus ecclesiasticis.* Rome, 1613. In PL 49: 477-1321.

Bergmann, Wilhelm. *Studien zu einer kritischen Sichtung der südgallischen Predigtliteratur des fünften und sechsten Jahrhunderts.* Part 1: *Der handschriftlich bezeugte Nachlass des Faustus von Reji.* Leipzig: Dieterlich, 1898.

Bohlin, Torgny. *Die Theologie des Pelagius und ihre Genesis.* Uppsala: Lundequistska, 1957.

Bonner, Gerald. *Augustine and Modern Research on Pelagianism.* Villanova: Villanova University Press, 1972.

―――. "How Pelagian was Pelagius? An Examination of the Contentions of Torgny Bohlin." *Studia Patristica* IX. Texte und Untersuchungen 94, 350-58. Berlin: Akademie-Verlag, 1966.

Brown, Peter. *Augustine of Hippo.* Berkeley: University of California Press, 1967.

————. *Religion and Society in the Age of St. Augustine*. London: Faber and Faber, 1972.

————. *Society and the Holy in Late Antiquity*. Berkeley: University of California Press, 1982.

————. *The World of Late Antiquity*. London: Thames and Hudson, 1971.

Buchem, L.A. van. *L'homélie pseudo-eusébienne de Pentecôte: L'origine de la confirmation en Gaule méridionale et l'interpretation de ce rite par Fauste de Riez*. Nijmengen: Janssen, 1967.

Burns, J. Patout. "Augustine's Role in the Imperial Actions against Pelagius." *Journal of Theological Studies* 30 (1979): 67-83.

————. *The Development of Augustine's Doctrine of Operative Grace*. Paris: Études Augustiniennes, 1980.

————. "The Economy of Salvation: Two Patristic Traditions." *Theological Studies* 37 (1976): 598-619.

Cabrol, F. "Le 'Liber Testimoniorum' de St. Augustin et deux traités de Fauste de Riez." *Revue des questions historiques* 47/1 (1890): 232ff.

Cappuyns, M. "Fragments-tests de Fauste de Riez et de Lactance dans un manuscrit d'Averbode." *Revue Bénédictine* 74 (1964): 36-43.

Carle, P.L. "L'homélie de Pâques Magnitudo (in CCSL t.101, p. 192-208) de Saint Fauste de Riez (ou de Lérins) (fin de Ve siècle). Aux sources patristiques lointaines de la transsubstantiation." *Divinitas* 27 (1983): 123-154.

Chadwick, Nora K. *Poetry and Letters in Early Christian Gaul*. London, 1955.

Chadwick, Owen. *John Cassian*. 2d ed. Cambridge: University Press, 1968.

Chéné, J. "Le semipélagianisme du midi de la Gaule d'après les lettres de Prosper d'Aquitaine et d'Hilaire à saint Augustine." *Recherches de science réligieuse* 43 (1955): 321-41.

————. "Les origines de la controversie sémi-pélagienne." *Année Théologique Augustinienne* 13 (1953): 56-109.

————. "Que signifiaient *initium fidei* et *affectus credulitatis* pour les Semipélagiens?" *Recherches de Science Réligieuse* 35 (1948): 566-88.

Chisolm, John Edward. *The Pseudo-Augustinian Hypomnesticon against the Pelagians and Caelestinians.* 2 vols. Fribourg: The University Press, 1967-80.

Collins, Roger J. H. "Faustus von Reji." *Theologische Realencyclopädie* 11: 63- 67.

Cooper-Marsdin, A. *The History of the Islands of the Lérins.* Cambridge, 1913.

Courcelle, Pierre. *Late Latin Writers and Their Greek Sources.* Trans. Harry E. Wedeck. Cambridge: Harvard Univ. Press, 1969.

————. "Nouveaux aspects de la culture lérinienne." *Révue des Études Latines* 46 (1968): 379-409.

Dill, S. *Roman Society in the Last Century of the Roman Empire.* 2d ed. New York: Meridian, 1958.

Dobschütz, E. von. *Das decretum Gelasianum de libris recipiendis et non recipiendis.* Texte und Untersuchungen, 3d series, 38/4. Leipzig, 1912.

Doignon, J. "Hilarius ecclesiarum magister (Cassien, Contra Nestorium 7, 24)." *Bulletins de la Société des Antiquaires de l'Ouest* [BSAO] 15 (1979): 251-62.

Driedonis, Ioannis. *De Captivitate et redemptione humani generis.* Louvain, 1571.

————. *De concordia liberi arbitrii et praedestinationis divinae.* Louvain, 1566.

Duval, Yves-Marie. *Le livre de Jonas dans la littérature chrétienne greque et latine.* 2 vols. Paris: Études Augustiniennes, 1973.

Elg, A. G. "De usu dativi comparationis apud Faustum Reiensem." *Eranos* (1947): 78-80.

————. *In epistulam Fausti Reiensis tertiam adnotationes.* Lund: Ohlsson, 1945.

————. "In Faustum Reiensem adversaria." *Eranos* (1944): 24-46.

————. *In Faustum Reiensem studia.* Diss. Uppsala. Almquist & Wiksell, 1938.

Engelbrecht, August. "Beiträge zur Kritik und Erklärung der Briefe des Apollinaris Sidonius, Faustus und Riricius." *Zeitschrift für österreichischen Gymnasien* 32 (1890): 677ff.

————. "Kritische Untersuchungen über wirkliche und angebliche Schriften des Faustus Reiensis." *Zeitschrift für österreichischen Gymnasien* (Vienna), 32 (1890): 290ff.

————. *Studien über die Schriften des Bishofes von Reii Faustus.* Vienna, 1889.

Erasmus, Desiderius, of Rotterdam. Preface to *Fausti episcopi de gratia Dei, et humanae mentis arbitrio.* Basel, 1528.

Evans, Robert F. *Pelagius: Inquiries and Reappraisals.* New York: Seabury, 1968.

Fliche, A., and V. Martin. *Histoire de l'église depuis les origines jusqu'à nos jours.* Paris: Bloud & Gay, 1944.

Fontaine, J., and C. Pietri, eds. *Le monde antique latin et la Bible.* Bible de Tous les Temps, 2. Paris: Beauchesne, 1985.

Frend, W. H. C. "Paulinus of Nola and the last Century of the Western Empire." *Journal of Roman Studies* 59 (1969): 1-11.

————. "The Divjak Letters: New Light on St. Augustine's Problems." *Journal of Ecclesiastical History* 34, 4 (1983): 497-512.

Gaiffier, B. de. "Sermons latins en l'honneur de S. Vincent antérieurs au Xe siècle." *Analecta Bollandiana* 67 (1949): 267-86.

Geyer, B. *Die patristische und scholastische Philosophie.* In *Ueberwegs Grundriss der Geschichte der Philosophie,* ed. F. Ueberweg, vol. 2. 11th ed. Berlin, 1928.

Godet, P. "Fauste de Riez." *Dictionnaire de théologie catholique* 5/2: 2101-5.

Gouilloud, A. *Saint Eucher, Lérins et l'église de Lyon au Ve siècle.* Lyons, 1881.

Griffe, Élie. *La Gaule Chrétienne à l'époque romaine.* 3 vols. Vol. 2, *L'église des Gaules au Ve siècle.* Paris: Letouzy et Ané, 1964.

————. "Nouveau plaidoyer pour Fauste de Riez." *Bulletin de littérature ecclésiastique* 74 (1973): 187-92.

————. "La pratique réligieuse en Gaule au Ve siècle, *saeculares* et *sancti.*" *Bulletin de littérature ecclésiastique* 63 (1962): 241-67.

————. "Les Sermons de Fauste de Riez. La Collectio Gallicana du Pseudo-Eusèbe." *Bulletin de littérature ecclésiastique* 61 (1960): 27-38.

Haarhoff, T. *Schools of Gaul: A Study of Pagan and Christian Education in the Last Century of the Western Empire.* 2d ed. Johannesburg: Witwatersrand University Press, 1958.

Hagendahl, H. *La Correspondance de Ruricius.* Göteborg, 1952.

Hanson, R. P. C. "The Reaction of the Church to the Collapse of the Western Roman Empire in the Fifth Century." *Vigiliae Christianae* 26 (1972): 272-87.

Hårleman, Einar. "La litterature gallo-romaine vers la fin de l'empire d'Occident." *Eranos* 76 (1978): 157-69.

Harnack, Adolf von. *History of Dogma.* Trans. from the 3d German edition by N. Buchanan. New York, Dover Publications, 1961.

————. *Lehrbuch der Dogmengeschichte.* Vol. 3. Halle, 1893.

Heinzelmann, Martin. *Bischofsherrschaft in Gallien. Zur Kontinuität römischer Führungsschichten vom 4. bis zum 7. Jahrhundert. Soziale, prosopographische und bildungsgeschichtliche Aspekte.* Zürich und München: Artemis Verlag, 1976.

————. "L'aristocratie et les évêchés entre Loire et Rhin du 4ème au 7ème siècle." *Revue d'Histoire de l'Église de France* 62 (1976): 75-90.

Holmes, T. Scott. *The Christian Church in Gaul.* London: Macmillan, 1911.

Huhn, J. *"De ratione fidei* als ein Werk des Faustus von Reji." *Theologische Quartalschrift* 30 (1950): 176-83.

Jacquin, M. "A quelle date apparaît le term 'semipélagien'?" *Revue des sciences philosophiques et théologiques* I (1907): 506-8.

————. "La question de la prédestination aux Ve et VIe siècles." *Revue d'histoire ecclésiastique* 7 (1906): 269-300.

Jiménez, J. "Un texto de Fausto de Riez y el vocabulario eucarístico medieval." In *Estudios patristicos*. Santiago: Pontif. Universidad catól de Chile, 1982.

Koch, Anton. "Der anthropologische Lehrbegriff des Bischofs Faustus von Riez." *Theologische Quartalschrift* 71 (1889): 287-317, 578-648.

————. *Der heilige Faustus, Bischof von Riez. Eine dogmengeschichtliche Monographie*. Stuttgart: Jos. Roth'sche Verlagshandlung, 1895.

Koch, Hugo. *Vincenz von Lérin und Gennadius: ein Beitrag zur Literaturgeschichte des Semipelagianisimus*. Leipzig: J. C. Hinrichs, 1907.

Kuhn, Johannes Ev. von. *Katholische Dogmatik*. Tübingen, 1859.

Latouche, Robert. "De la Gaule romaine à la Gaule franque: aspects sociaux et économiques de l'évolution." In *Il passagio dall'antichità al Medioevo in Occidente*, Settimane di studio del Centro italiano di studi sull'Alto Medioevo, 9. Spoleto, 1962.

Leeming, B. "The False Decretals, Faustus of Riez and the Pseudo-Eusebius." In *Studia Patristica: Papers Presented to the Second International Conference on Patristic Studies, Held at Christ Church Oxford, 1955*, ed. K. Aland and F. L. Cross, 2: 122-40. Berlin: Akademie-Verlag, 1957.

Leroy, J. & Glorie, F. "Eusèbe d'Alexandrie source d'Eusèbe de Gaule." *Sacris Erudiri* 19 (1969-70): 33-70.

MacQueen, D. J. "John Cassian on Grace and Free Will. With Particular Reference to *Institutio* XII and *Collatio* XII." *Recherches de théologie ancienne et médiévale* 44 (1977): 5-28.

Madoz, J. "Un caso de materialismo en España en el siglo VI." *Revista Española de teologia* 8 (1948): 203-30.

Mâle, Emile. *La fin du paganisme en Gaul. Et les plus anciennes basiliques chrétiennes.* Paris: Flamarrion, 1950.

Mansi, Giovanni Domenico. *Sacrorum Conciliarum Nova et Amplissima Collectio.* 31 vols. 1759-78. Reprint ed. Arnhem, Paris, and Leipzig: H. Welters, 1901-1927.

Markus, R. A. *Christianity in the Roman World.* New York: Scribner's, 1974.

Marrou, H.I. *Saint Augustin et l'augustinisme.* Avec la collaboration de A.-M. La Bonnardière. Paris: Éditions du Seuil, 1959.

Mauguin, Gilbert. *Veterum auctorum qui IX saeculo de praedestinatione et gratia scripserunt.* 1650.

Mohrmann, Christine. "*Credere in Deum.* Sur l'interprétation théologique d'un fait de langue." *Mélanges J. de Ghellinck* 1: 277-85. Gembloux: Duculot, 1951.

Morin, G. "La collection gallicane dite d'Eusèbe d'Emèse et les problèmes qui s'y rattachent." *Zeitschrift für die neutestamentliche Wissenschaft* 34 (1935): 92-115.

————. "Hiérarchie et liturgie dans l'église gallicane au Ve siècle." *Revue Bénédictine* 8 (1891): 97ff.

Mühlenberg, Ekkehard. "Synergism in Gregory of Nyssa." *Zietschrift für die neutestamentliche Wissenschaft* 68 (1977): 93-122.

Nodes, Daniel J. "Avitus of Vienne's Spiritual History and the Semipelagian Controversy. The Doctrinal Implications of Books I-III." *Vigiliae Christianae* 38 (1984): 185-95.

————. "Avitus of Vienne's *Spiritual History*: Its Theme and Doctrinal Implications." Diss. Toronto, 1981.

Noris, Henri de. *Historia Pelagiana et Dissertatio de Synodo Oecumenica.* Petavii, 1708.

O'Donnell, James J. "Liberius the Patrician." *Traditio* 37 (1981): 31-72.

Peñamaria, A. "Libertad, mérito y gracia en la soteriologia de Hilario de Poitiers. ¿Precurso de Pelagio o Agustin? *Revue des études Augustiniennes* 20 (1974): 234-50.

Plinval, Georges de. *Essai sur le style et la langue de Pélage; suivi du traité inédit De induratione cordis Pharaonis.* Texte communiqué par dom G. Morin. Fribourg en Suisse: Librairie de l'Université, 1947.

──────. *Pélage; ses écrits, sa vie, et sa reforme.* Lausanne, 1943.

──────. "Prosper d'Aquitaine, interprète de saint Augustin." *Récherches Augustiniennes* 1 (1958).

Pricoco, Salvatore. *L'isola dei santi. Il cenobio di Lerino e le origini del monachesimo gallico.* Rome: Ateneo & Bizzarri, 1978.

──────. "Studi su Sidonio Apollinare." *Nuovo Didaskaleion* 15 (1965): 69-150.

Randers-Pehrson, J.D. *Barbarians and Romans. The Birth Struggle of Europe, A.D. 400-700.* Norman: Univ. of Oklahoma Press, 1983.

Riché, Pierre. *Les Écoles et l'enseignement dans l'Occident chrétien de la fin du Ve siècle au milieu du XIe siècle.* Paris: Aubier Montaigne, 1979.

──────. *Education and Culture in the Barbarian West. Sixth through Eighth Centuries.* Trans. from the 3d French edition by John J. Contreni. Columbia: University of South Carolina Press, 1976.

Rippinger, J. "The Concept of Obedience in the Monastic Writings of Basil and Cassian." *Studia Monastica* 19 (1977): 7-18.

Roger, M. *L'enseignement des lettres classiques d'Ausone à Alcuin.* Paris: A. Picard, 1905.

Rousseau, Philip. *Ascetics, Authority, and the Church in the Age of Jerome and Cassian.* Oxford: University Press, 1978.

──────. "Cassian, Contemplation, and the Coenobitic Life." *Journal of Ecclesiastical History* 26 (1975): 113-26.

──────. "The Spiritual Authority of the 'Monk-Bishop': Eastern Elements in Some Western Hagiography of the Fourth and Fifth Centuries." *Journal of Theological Studies* 22 (1971): 380-419.

Serry, H., O. P. *Opera Omnia.* Lyons, 1770.

Simon, E. *Étude sur sainte Fauste, abbé de Lérins, évêque de Riez*. Toulon, 1879.

Simonetti, Manlio. "Il *De gratia* di Fausto di Riez." *Studi Storico-Religiosi* 1/1 (1977): 125-45.

———. "Fausto di Riez e i Macedoniani." *Augustinianum* 17 (1977): 333-54.

Sirago, Vito Antonio. *Galla Placidia e La Trasformazione Politica dell' Occidente*. Louvain, 1961.

Sirmond, Jacques. *Jacobi Sirmondi historia praedestinatiana*. In PL 53: 682ff.

Smith, A. J. "The Latin Sources of the Commentary of Pelagius in the Epistle of St. Paul to the Romans." *Journal of Theological Studies* 19 (1918): 162-230; 20 (1919): 55-65; 127-77.

Souter, Alexander. *The Earliest Latin Commentaries on the Epistles of St. Paul*. Oxford: Clarendon, 1927.

———. "Observations on the pseudo-Eusebian Collection of Sermons." *Journal of Theological Studies* 41 (1940): 47-57.

Stilting, Johann. "De S. Fausto Regiensi." In *Acta Sanctorum Septembris* VII. Antwerp, 1760.

Suarez, Francisco. *Operis de divina gratia tripartiti*. Lyons, 1620.

Tibiletti, C. "Fausto di Riez nei giudizi della critica." *Augustinianum* 21 (1981): 567-87.

———. "Libero arbitrio e grazia in Fausto di Riez." *Augustinianum* 19 (1979): 259-85.

———. "Polemiche in Africa contro i teologi provenzali." *Augustinianum* 26 (1986): 499-517.

———. "La salvezza umana in Fausto di Riez." *Orpheus* 1 (1980): 371-90.

Tillemont, L.S. Le Nain de. *Mémoires pour servir à l'histoire ecclésiastique des six premiers siècles*. Brussels: Fricx, 1694-1709.

Tixeront, J. *Histoire des dogmes*. Vol. 3. 3d ed. Paris, 1912.

Turner, H. E. W. *The Pattern of Christian Truth*. London: Mowbray, 1954.

Van Andel, G. K. "Sulpicius Severus and Origenism." *Vigiliae Christianae* 34 (1980): 278-87.

Viard, Paul. "Fauste de Riez." *Dictionnaire de Spiritualité* 5 (Paris: Beauchesne, 1964): 113-18.

Vogüé, A. de. "Sur une série d'emprunts de saint Colomban à Fauste de Riez." *Studia Monastica* 10 (1968): 119-23.

Weigel, Gustave. "El Concepto de la fe, según los semipelagianos. Un analisis de la doctrina de Fausto de Riez." *Revista Universitaria* 25 (1940): 35-53.

―――. *Faustus of Riez: An Historical Introduction*. Philadelphia: Dolphin Press, 1938.

Wermelinger, Otto. *Rom und Pelagius: Die theologische Position der romischen Bischöfe im pelagianische Streit in den Jahren 411-432*. Stuttgart: A. Hiersemann, 1975.

Weyman, C. "Zu Herondas V, 14." *Philologus* 54 (1895).

Wörter, Friedrich. *Zur Dogmengeschichte des Semipelagianismus*. Kirchengeschichtliche Studien, 2. Münster, 1899.

AUTHOR, WORKS, AND SUBJECT INDEX

Weigel, Gustave, 17, 55 n.
    89, 157 n. 1, 171 n.
    21, 211, 219, 226

Wermelinger, O., 40 n. 48

Weyman, Carl, 145

Will, 166ff

Wörter, Friedrich, 16, 219

Zosimus, 40

SCRIPTURE INDEX